*frontier politics on the
eve of the civil war*

FRONTIER POLITICS
on the
EVE OF THE CIVIL WAR

By ROBERT W. JOHANNSEN

University of Washington Press

SEATTLE AND LONDON

Originally published as *Frontier Politics and the Sectional
Conflict: The Pacific Northwest on the Eve of the Civil War*

to **LOIS**

preface

AMERICAN HISTORIOGRAPHY OF the last half century has been characterized by a preoccupation with the American frontier. Ever since the publication of Frederick Jackson Turner's provocative essay in 1893, American historians have studied the frontier in an effort to explain American social and political behavior. In spite of this preoccupation, however, relatively little historical scholarship has been directed toward a study of American frontier politics and their relation to the national politics of the United States. Frontier political life did not operate in a vacuum but was closely linked at all times with national politics. The dynamic political energy of the nineteenth-century frontiersman was in large part responsible for this identification, but the formal connection between local frontier politics and national politics was furnished by the national political organizations. Like the very life of the frontiersman himself, the principles of the national political parties were often altered or modified to meet unique frontier conditions. The expression of frontier political activity through the national party organizations often resulted in an odd and contradictory mixture of national and local issues. The experience of the Pacific Northwest frontier on the eve of the Civil War graphically illustrates not only the significance and character of national politics on the level of frontier politics but also the strong connecting tie that existed between the frontiersmen of the Pacific Northwest and the national government during one of the most crucial periods of American history.

The increasing interest on the part of professional historians in the Civil War period has also been of great importance to American historiography during the last fifty years. Although a great wealth of scholarly historical work has been done on the Civil War, the story of the reaction of the frontier to this national cataclysm has remained untold. In the Pacific Northwest, the issues that precipitated the national upheaval of the sixties lacked the vital potency that characterized these same issues in other areas of the nation. The great distance which separated the Pacific Northwest frontier from the center of political activity, as well as the slow and difficult means of transportation and communication with the East, made the burning issues of the sectional controversy seem remote. In spite of this apparent detachment, the small and scattered population of Oregon and Washington Territory expressed a strong interest in national affairs and a vital concern over the sectional crises that finally culminated in the Civil War. The frontier heritage of these pioneers, as well as their agrarian Midwestern backgrounds, gave the Pacific Northwest the characteristics of a transplanted "border state." In their attitudes toward the sectional issues of slavery and secession, the settlers on the Pacific Northwest frontier expressed a nationalism and conservatism that was reminiscent of the states in the Ohio and Mississippi valleys.

The purpose of this study is twofold: to describe the penetration of national issues to a relatively undeveloped and politically immature frontier area at a time when the national fabric was suffering the greatest strain, and to explore the reaction of this frontier region to the explosive issues of the sectional controversy.

For their continued guidance in the preparation of this study, I am indebted to Charles M. Gates and Thomas J. Pressly of the University of Washington, who gave generously of their time and rendered valuable assistance in matters of research and composition. W. Stull Holt of the University of Washington made many valuable suggestions and offered encouragement when it was most appreciated. Acknowledgments are also due to Ronald Todd of the University of Washington Library; Miss Priscilla Knuth of the Oregon

Historical Society; Martin Schmitt of the University of Oregon Library; George P. Hammond and his staff of the Bancroft Library, University of California, Berkeley; and to Miss Dorothy W. Bridg-water of the Yale University Library, all of whom lightened the often arduous task of research by generously offering assistance in the loca-tion and use of manuscript materials. Finally, I am deeply grateful to my wife, Lois Adele Johannsen, for her constant encouragement and valuable assistance.

ROBERT W. JOHANNSEN

University of Kansas
May, 1955

contents

illustrations

frontier politics on the
eve of the civil war

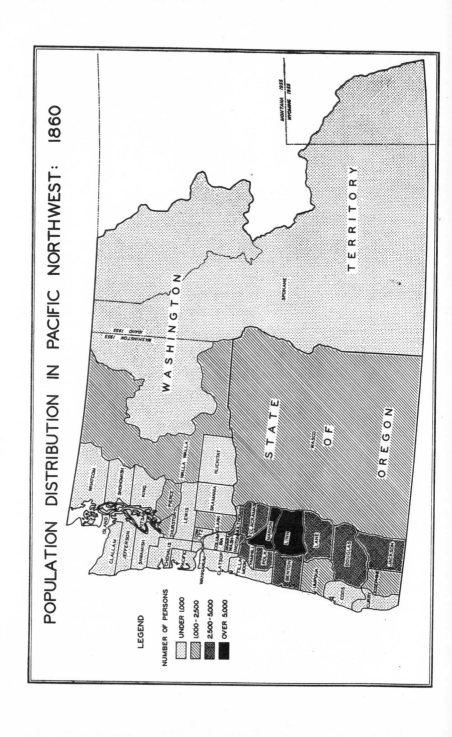

POPULATION DISTRIBUTION IN PACIFIC NORTHWEST: 1860

> *the land and*
> *the people*

THE PACIFIC NORTHWEST IN 1860 embraced over 285,000 square miles, almost one-tenth the entire area of continental United States.[1] Extending from the Pacific Ocean to the crest of the Rocky Mountains and from the northern boundary of California to the international boundary with Great Britain, this vast area included rugged seacoasts, fertile valleys, an island-studded inland sea, jagged and formidable mountain ranges, and a high waterless plateau, giving credence to the pioneers' boast that the Pacific Northwest had "everything."[2] Known for many years as the Oregon Country, this region was divided into two major political units: Oregon, which had been admitted to statehood in 1859, and Washington Territory, created in 1853 and including, in addition to the present state of Washington, all of what is now Idaho and parts of western Montana and Wyoming. Washington Territory itself was almost three times the size of New England.

The Pacific Northwest became a part of the United States in 1846, after years of negotiation between British and American diplomats.

[1] U.S. Bureau of the Census, *Historical Statistics of the United States, 1789-1945* (Washington, 1949), p. 25.

[2] John Burkhart to David E. Blair, December 5, 1849, Robert W. Johannsen, ed. "John Burkhart and Oregon Territory, 1849," *Oregon Historical Quarterly*, LIII (Sept., 1952), 196-203.

Two years later it was organized as the Territory of Oregon. The first census, taken in 1849 under the direction of the newly appointed territorial governor, numbered slightly over nine thousand persons living on this far-flung frontier.[3] Nearly all had reached the Pacific Northwest by the long and often arduous trek overland from the frontier settlements of the Mississippi Valley. Although there were a few people living in the region from very early times, the migrations from the East did not begin in earnest until 1843, when several hundred men, women, and children crossed the plains in what has become known as the "Great Migration." Each succeeding year witnessed an increasing number of immigrants.

The migration of settlers to the Pacific Northwest was almost exclusively a movement of agrarian people, and many different motives, ranging from the quest for more healthful living conditions to patriotism, operated to bring them westward. The most important, however, was a desire for economic betterment, a feeling made more acute by the "hard times" in the Mississippi Valley following the panic of 1837. The discontent and restlessness that accompanied the depression, combined with the expansionist fervor of the times, resulted in the movement of frontier farmers to new lands in the Far West.[4] Once begun, the movement gained momentum, persisting, in varying degrees, through the next two decades. Seen in a larger perspective, the migration to the Pacific Northwest was but one incident in the march of the American people westward.

Once in the Northwest, the settlers occupied the fertile valleys of western Oregon. Seeking areas similar to those they had left, the migrating farmers staked out their claims in the Willamette Valley and the smaller "cross valleys" to the south. The new environment was well suited to the type of humid-land agriculture they had practiced in the East; in addition, the natural grasslands favored stock raising, and the abundant forests provided wood for fences and homes.[5] The mild climate and the fertility of the soil fulfilled their greatest expectations. "I don't believe that there are ten acres of

[3] Summary of Census Returns of the Territory of Oregon for the year 1849 . . ., MS in the Oregon Historical Society Library, Portland.
[4] Jesse Applegate, Views of Oregon History, MS in the Bancroft Library, University of California, Berkeley (microfilm in the University of Washington Library, Seattle), p. 31; Melvin C. Jacobs, *Winning Oregon, a Study of an Expansionist Movement* (Caldwell, Ida., 1938), pp. 34-65.
[5] Ralph H. Brown, *Historical Geography of the United States* (New York, 1948), p. 470.

poor land, and unfit for agricultural purposes, in the whole valley,"
wrote one enthusiastic settler.[6] Following the settlement of the international boundary dispute, immigrants crossed the Columbia River
into the valley of the Cowlitz and the area surrounding Puget Sound.
The soil around the sound, however, was "gravelly" and less suited
to the production of wheat;[7] consequently, the growth of the area
north of the Columbia was slower and less agrarian in character than
that to the south of the river.

Towns were few and far between in the Pacific Northwest when
the area was organized as a territory. Oregon City, located at the
falls of the Willamette River some fifteen miles above its junction
with the Columbia, was the metropolis of the Oregon Country in
1848, boasting a population of between six and seven hundred persons. Because of its location at the falls, some thought the town was
destined to be "one of the greatest manufacturing cities in the
Western world."[8] Already it counted two "large and valuable" flour
mills and two sawmills. Portland, soon to become Oregon City's
chief rival, was only a "small and beautiful village," numbering
about one hundred inhabitants.[9]

The favorable agricultural conditions in early Oregon were not
matched by adequate outlets for its produce. The discovery of gold
in California early in 1848, however, provided a market for Oregon's
farmers, inaugurating an era of gold mining that became highly
significant in its effect on the economy of the Pacific Northwest.[10]
The California discovery was followed by a rapid succession of gold
strikes in southern Oregon, eastern Washington Territory, and

[6] Thomas S. Kendall to Smith, January 25, 1852, J. Orin Oliphant, ed. "Thomas
S. Kendall's Letter on Oregon Agriculture, 1852," *Agricultural History*, IX (Oct.,
1935), 195; Ezra Fisher to Benjamin H. Hill, February 27, 1846, Sarah Fisher
Henderson, Nellie Edith Latourette, and Kenneth Scott Latourette, eds. "Correspondence of the Reverend Ezra Fisher, Pioneer Missionary of the American
Baptist Home Mission Society in Indiana, Illinois, Iowa and Oregon," *OHQ*, XVI
(Sept., 1915), 285.
[7] Burkhart to Blair, December 5, 1849, Johannsen, ed. "John Burkhart and
Oregon Territory, 1849," p. 199.
[8] A. N. Armstrong, *Oregon: Comprising a Brief History and Full Description
of the Territories of Oregon and Washington* (Chicago, 1857), p. 11.
[9] J. Quinn Thornton, *Oregon and California in 1848* (2 vols.; New York, 1849),
I, 329. Even as early as 1848, Portland had an "air of neatness, thrift, and
industry."
[10] James Henry Gilbert, *Trade and Currency in Early Oregon, a Study in the
Commercial and Monetary History of the Pacific Northwest* (New York, 1907);
Elaine Tanner, "A Study of the Underlying Causes of the Depression of 1854,"
Reed College Bulletin, XXV (April, 1947), 35-65.

southern British Columbia. The first effect of the gold excitement was a rapid depopulation of the Northwest. Crops were left unharvested, businesses were abandoned, families were left behind as nearly every able-bodied male departed for the mines.[11] Ultimately, however, the gold discoveries proved a great boon to the economy of the Pacific Northwest. Most of those who left eventually returned with large amounts of gold dust. Agriculture was stimulated, an infant lumber industry was encouraged, and small country villages grew into marketing and commercial centers. After the first excitement had passed, the population enjoyed a steady increase. By 1860, there were over sixty-four thousand people living on this far frontier. Agriculture remained the economic base of the region. As the migrations of the Middle Western agrarian population continued throughout the fifties, the area under cultivation was rapidly expanded, particularly in those valleys that lay closest to the mines.[12] In 1860, Oregon ranked twenty-second, out of thirty-three states in the nation, in wheat production.[13] Portland, by that date, had become the largest town in the Pacific Northwest, with a population exceeding twenty-eight hundred. Salem and Eugene City each had populations surpassing one thousand. Jacksonville, in the heart of the southern Oregon mining region, and Corvallis, on the trade route to the mines, had populations of over seven hundred. East of the Cascade Mountains, The Dalles and Walla Walla, each serving an extensive mining area, had become centers of population.[14]

The Middle Western states were "the crucible in which the population of the Pacific Northwest was molded."[15] According to the census of 1860, roughly 39 per cent of the population in the Pacific Northwest was born in the seven states of Missouri, Kentucky, Tennessee, Illinois, Indiana, Iowa, and Ohio. Missouri alone contributed almost

[11] George H. Atkinson to Josiah Little, February 17, 1849, George H. Atkinson Papers, Henry E. Huntington Library (microfilm in the University of Washington Library) ; William Strong, History of Oregon, MS in the Bancroft Library (microfilm in the University of Washington Library), p. 15; G. A. Barnes, Oregon and California in 1849, MS in the Bancroft Library (microfilm in the University of Washington Library), p. 8.

[12] Jesse Applegate to Thomas Ewbank, December 28, 1851, "Umpqua Agriculture, 1851," *OHQ*, XXXII (June, 1931), 143.

[13] Eighth Census, *Agriculture of the United States in 1860* (Washington, 1864), p. xxix.

[14] Eighth Census, *Population of the United States in 1860* (Washington, 1864), pp. 400-405, 580-585.

[15] Jesse S. Douglas, "Origins of the Population of Oregon in 1850," *Pacific Northwest Quarterly*, XLI (April, 1950), 108.

10 per cent of the population, more than any other single state. But the Midwestern influence cannot be measured by nativity alone. Many of the settlers born in the Eastern states were conditioned by years spent on the Middle Western frontier before they embarked for the Northwest. Broken down according to section, the census figures indicate 21 per cent of the population from the slaveholding states of the South, almost 22 per cent from the Old Northwest, 8 per cent from the Middle Atlantic states, and a little over 4 per cent from New England.[16]

Although their number was small, the population from the New England states left a lasting impression on this frontier. Settled principally along the water courses, in the towns, and on Puget Sound, the New Englanders provided the merchants and businessmen in this young country. At Portland, which had more New England people than any other locality, they made a more or less conscious effort to transfer the New England way of life to the banks of the Willamette.[17] The lumber industry in the Pacific Northwest owed its beginnings to the energy of New Englanders during these early years. Late in 1853, one Oregon newspaper reported, "The active and enterprising Yankee—whose habitation is every where—is among us, and is making *his mark* in the great progress of affairs. Here he (the live Yankee) finds full scope for the exercise of his prolific genius. . . . We learn that some 12 saw-mills have been erected on the [Puget] sound by the Bostonians alone within the past 18 months."[18] The presence of a small group of New Englanders on a frontier settled primarily by Middle Western farmers did not always result in domestic harmony.[19] Antagonism between the two groups often erupted into open resentment during the Civil War years.

The heterogeneity of the population on the Pacific Northwest frontier is significant in explaining the early political and social attitudes of the region. Most of the older frontiers had been settled

[16] Eighth Census, *Population of the United States in 1860,* pp. 400-405, 580-585. The remaining 45 per cent included a small number of foreign born and those born in the Far West, most of whom were minors in 1860.

[17] Matthew P. Deady, History and Progress of Oregon after 1845, MS in the Bancroft Library (microfilm in the University of Washington Library), pp. 39-40; Marie Lazenby, "Down-Easters Out West," *Reed College Bulletin,* XXV (April, 1947), 1-33.

[18] Oregon City *Oregon Spectator,* December 31, 1853; Edwin T. Coman, Jr., and Helen M. Gibbs, *Time, Tide and Timber: A Century of Pope & Talbot* (Stanford, 1949).

[19] George H. Atkinson to Josiah Hale, August 8, 1851, Atkinson Papers.

from a contiguous eastern area. The Pacific Northwest was an exception to this pattern. To reach Oregon, the pioneers were compelled to cross a vast expanse of prairie, desert, and mountain ranges. The population was drawn from all the areas of the East and Middle West, lacking the homogeneity that had characterized many previous frontiers.

In making the journey from the old to the new frontier, the settlers of the Pacific Northwest carried with them their democratic beliefs. As in the older frontier areas during the first half of the nineteenth century, politics played an important role in their daily lives; the population of Oregon early established a reputation for dynamic political energy. A California newspaper once remarked that in Oregon there were but two occupations, "agriculture and politics."[20] The preoccupation with politics was reflected in the newspapers that flourished in the Northwest during the early years of the territory. They devoted their columns so completely to political invective and virulence (there were no libel laws) that for years this type of journalism was known as the "Oregon Style."[21]

A strong element in the political thought of this frontier was a feeling of independence from external authority, an almost religious devotion to the principle of popular self-government. The settlers of the Pacific Northwest identified their beliefs with the agrarian democracy of Thomas Jefferson, bolstered by the Jacksonianism of the trans-Allegheny frontier.[22] One early pioneer assured a Fourth of July audience, "You were created to govern, not to be governed."[23] The editor of the first newspaper to be published west of the Rocky Mountains, the *Oregon Spectator,* announced in his first issue, "We are now, as we always have been, and ever shall be, a democrat of the Jeffersonian school."[24] In 1856, a settler, annoyed by the infrequent meeting of the district courts, wrote: "Western people do not hear the declaration of Independence read every fourth of July for nothing. They remember very well that if government . . . becomes 'destructive of the ends for which it was instituted, the people

---

[20] Quoted in James Rood Robertson, "The Social Evolution of Oregon," *OHQ,* III (March, 1902), 32.

[21] George S. Turnbull, *History of Oregon Newspapers* (Portland, 1939).

[22] Dorothy O. Johansen, "A Tentative Appraisal of Territorial Government in Oregon," *Pacific Historical Review,* XVIII (Nov., 1949), 497-498.

[23] Address of William Green T'Vault, July 4, 1846, Oregon City *Oregon Spectator,* July 23, 1846.

[24] Oregon City *Oregon Spectator,* February 5, 1846.

have a right to alter or abolish the same.' "[25] Delazon Smith, destined to become one of Oregon's first United States Senators and a prominent local politician throughout the fifties, published his political credo in 1857. Believing that "the world is too much governed," Smith favored only a few, simple, practical laws. He believed in small legislative bodies, the election of all legislative, executive, and judicial officers by a direct vote of the people, and the limitation of terms of office, and was unalterably opposed to banks and lotteries.[26] In 1855, the Democratic party of Washington Territory resolved, "The best government is that which governs least."[27]

The Jeffersonianism of the Pacific Northwest frontier also had economic and social manifestations. One early farmer expressed the sentiments of a great many of Oregon's settlers when he wrote that "the substantial wealth and permanent prosperity of a country depends upon the productive powers of its soils."[28] One of Oregon's leading jurists declared, "We have an agricultural community, and the domestic virtues incident to an agricultural people; and there is where you look for the true and solid wealth and happiness of a people."[29] Shortly before, he had written to a friend:

> We will render independent and attractive agricultural pursuits and thus induce the bulk of our population to continue tillers of the soil, instead of swarming into over grown cities to strive to live by their wits,—becoming in some instances purse proud millionaires, but more frequently sharpers, thieves, rowdys, bullies and vagabonds.[30]

The strong faith in human capacity and in the institutions of democracy was accompanied by a firm belief in "manifest destiny." Just a few months after the acquisition of Oregon by the United States, one of Oregon's pioneer newspaper editors recounted the material progress of the United States, finally asking, "Do not all these seem given by Heaven for the extension of our country, and the ex-

[25] G. W. Lawson to the Editor, November 30, 1856, Salem *Oregon Statesman,* December 16, 1856.

[26] Delazon Smith to Asahel Bush, May 12, 20, 1857, Salem *Oregon Statesman,* May 19, 26, 1857.

[27] Olympia *Pioneer and Democrat,* May 12, 1855.

[28] Wesley Shannon to the Editor, [n. d.], Oregon City *Oregon Statesman,* April 4, 1851.

[29] Charles H. Carey, ed. *The Oregon Constitution and Proceedings and Debates of the Constitutional Convention of 1857* (Salem, 1926), p. 249.

[30] Matthew P. Deady to Benjamin Simpson, July 29, 1857, Matthew P. Deady Papers, Oregon Historical Society Library. The original spelling in this and all following quotations has been retained.

pansion of republicanism?—to work out the redemption of the
human race?—to re-image man in his god-like lineaments?"[31]   A
year later, the same individual expressed the sentiments of a large
part of Oregon's population: "We believed that in settling in this far
off region we were extending and enlarging the 'area of freedom,'
and by planting civilization, liberty, and Christianity upon the
shores of the great Pacific, we should render a lasting benefit to
mankind."[32]   Joseph Lane, whose name for many years was synonymous with Oregon politics, gave voice to this enthusiasm:

> We are now upon the far west; we can go no further. Many would regret that
> the coast did not extend two thousand miles further, that our institutions
> might be extended over them. They will be extended to the islands, and ulti-
> mately, I trust, they will be extended over the whole world. Democracy is
> progressive, our republican institutions are progressive, and they must prevail,
> for they are adapted to the happiness of man.[33]

The frontier belief in man's capacity for self-government was reflected in many ways, not the least important of which was the formation of a provisional government in the Oregon Country in the early
forties. The small but growing population in the Willamette Valley
had repeatedly sent petitions to the United States government asking
that the national authority be extended over the region. These petitions were ignored, largely because the title to the Oregon Country
was still in dispute. The attitude of the Willamette Valley settlers,
upon the refusal of their petitions, was expressed by Peter H. Burnett, one of Oregon's early politicians and first state governor of
California: "The population of this country are no doubt desirous
to live under the government of the United States, but if she will
never do anything for us, we must and will do it for ourselves."[34]
By gradual stages, beginning in 1841, a provisional government was
established, deriving its sovereignty wholly from the people in the
area and exercising all the powers of an independent government.
This "grassroots" government flourished until March, 1849, when

[31] George L. Curry, Oregon City *Oregon Spectator,* October 29, 1846.

[32] The Petition of the Free Citizens of the United States Resident in Oregon . . .
to the Senate and House of Representatives of the United States of America . . .,
Territorial Papers of the United States Senate, 1824-1871, National Archives
(microfilm in the University of Washington Library) .

[33] Report of Lane's speech at the banquet of the Jackson Democratic Association in Washington, D.C., January 8, 1852, Oregon City *Oregon Statesman,* March
30, 1852.

[34] Letter of Peter H. Burnett, "Documentary,"*OHQ,* XXIV (March, 1923) , 107.

it was superseded by the territorial government. During the inter-
vening years it confirmed the people in their conviction that they
possessed a capacity for self-government.[35]

This experiment in self-government had a great influence in the
years that followed. Hardly a year had passed after the organization
of the territorial government in Oregon before the people began to
resent and regret their reduction from self-rule to territorial status.
The territorial system of the United States, with its close congressional control and its onerous policy of "foreign" appointments, was
considered a rebuke against the right and ability of the frontiersman
to govern himself. Having once tasted the fruits of self-government,
settlers did not easily submit to the rather arbitrary and haphazard
"carpetbag" government provided by Congress for the territories.
To add insult to injury, the territorial appointees were, with few
exceptions, mediocre individuals, interested only in attaining public
office and reaping the greatest rewards possible. One old pioneer
compared Oregon to a kind of Botany Bay to which the president
"banishes all the worthless needy and recreant of his party."[36]

This situation inspired an agitation for a return to self-government. The agitation took the form, first of all, of a rather nebulous
movement for statehood. As early as July, 1849, only four months
after the arrival of the territorial officers in Oregon, a bill was presented to the territorial legislature providing for an "expression of
the people, for and against the formation of a State government."[37]
One editor commented that a state government was the only remedy
for the situation that then existed, adding, "And we are strongly
inclined to the opinion that if all our officers were dependent on the
voice of the people for their official tenure, our business would be
attended to more promptly."[38] The movement toward statehood
gained momentum in succeeding years. One young legislator, a native Kentuckian, stoutly maintained:

> Since all Territorial systems of government are repugnant to the true spirit of
> our Constitution, never was it intended to govern men able to govern them-

[35] For the history of the Oregon provisional government see Marie M. Bradley,
"Political Beginnings in Oregon—The Period of the Provisional Government,
1839-1849," *OHQ,* IX (March, 1908), 42-72; Charles H. Carey, *A General History
of Oregon, Prior to 1861* (2 vols.; Portland, 1935-36), I, 317-360.
[36] Jesse Applegate to Joseph Lane, November 1, 1851, Jesse Applegate Papers,
Oregon Historical Society Library.
[37] Territory of Oregon, *House Journal,* 1849 (Oregon City, 1850), p. 13.
[38] Oregon City *Oregon Spectator,* March 7, 1850.

selves, and never can such a system be imposed long on Americans, who have
the spirit of freedom established by their fathers.[39]

Many strong objections, however, were raised against statehood, particularly the burden of taxation that would be imposed upon the
scattered frontier settlements to support a state government. Nevertheless, sentiment increased during the decade until in 1857 the
proposal to organize a state government received overwhelming approval from the people in Oregon.

The statehood movement during the early years of the territory,
however, was at best only secondary to a larger and more popular
scheme for the attainment of self-government. This was embodied
in an attempt to secure a revision of the territorial system itself. In
the winter of 1851, Jesse Applegate, an important figure in local
Pacific Northwest politics, wrote a series of letters to one of the newspapers, outlining the basic provisions of this revision. Reminding
the readers that "our Territories are governed on almost the precise
plan of the British Colonial system resisted by our ancestors," Applegate wrote, "Let us ask of our country again to restore us our birthright—the privilege of making our own laws, and electing our own
judges and rulers, and to be freed from charlatans and strangers that
are neither with us nor of us."[40] The principal point in the proposed program was the restoration to the people of the Pacific Northwest of their political rights, "by allowing them to adopt their own
form of Government—to choose their own officers—as a body politic,
to have their voice in the councils of the nation, and to vote in the
election of President and Vice President of the United States."[41]
All this was to be achieved, according to Applegate, while still retaining territorial status. The territorial legislature drew up a long
and elaborate memorial, purportedly written by Matthew P. Deady,
a prominent lawyer and jurist, in which these demands were expressed. The first part of the document included a review of the
grievances which Oregon's settlers felt they had suffered as a result
of the territorial system. The provisional government was cited as
proof that Oregonians were capable of self-government. Finally, the
memorial asked that Congress permit the people of the territory to

[39] John A. Anderson, Portland *Oregon Weekly Times,* December 20, 1851.
[40] Jesse Applegate, "An Old Oregonian," to the Editor, Oregon City *Oregon
Statesman,* December 2, 1851.
[41] *Ibid.,* December 16, 1851.

elect their governor, secretary, and judges.[42] The memorial was for-
warded to Congress and was referred to the House Committee on
Territories, where it seems to have died. The settlers of the Pacific
Northwest became more persuaded than ever that Congress was indifferent to their situation.[43]

Territorial government in Oregon meant the extension of the
principles and policies of the national political parties over the
Pacific Northwest. During the period of the provisional government,
political organization did not express itself along national party
lines. The issues and candidates of the elections held during this
early period were based on local interests, classified according to the
three distinct elements in the population: those connected with the
Hudson's Bay Company, the American settlers, and the Methodist
Mission group. With the organization of Oregon Territory, the people in the Pacific Northwest were bound to the currents of national
partisan politics. Their administrative and judicial officers were
appointees of a partisan government. As citizens of a territory, they
were allowed to elect a delegate to Congress who would be expected
to work through partisan channels. Gradually, the pioneers returned
to their old party affiliations and attempted to adapt them to their
new environment. They lost much of their isolation and became
more closely integrated with the national government.[44]

The Democratic party was the first to organize in Oregon Territory and throughout the territorial period maintained a tight mono-
poly over local politics. The territory had been established under
the tutelage of a Democratic administration, and all of the first territorial appointments were Democratic. As in any territory, the federal
officeholders furnished a major impetus toward a close political relationship with the nation and often encouraged the identification of
local parties with national issues as means to their own political
ends. However, the political background of the individual pioneer
is probably the most important factor in the determination of party
affiliation on the frontier. Having emigrated for the most part from

[42] Territory of Oregon, *House Journal,* 1851-1852 (Salem, 1852), Appendix,
pp. 1-6.
[43] The movement for self-government during the early years of the territory
has been treated in Robert W. Johannsen, A Study of the Movement for Self-
Government in the Territory of Oregon, 1848-1853, unpublished B.A. thesis, Reed
College, 1948.
[44] Allen Johnson, "The Nationalizing Influence of Party," *Yale Review,* XV
(Nov., 1906), 285, 287.

the Mississippi Valley, the settlers of the Pacific Northwest were steeped in the Jeffersonian-Jacksonian tradition. Those from the slaveholding states of the upper and deep South may not have brought their slaves with them, but they did bring the principles of the Democratic party. The strong belief in self-government and the conviction of social and political equality that the frontier generated favored the transplanting of Democratic party principles to the Pacific Northwest. The supremacy of the Democratic party in local politics was never seriously threatened until events far removed from the Pacific Coast brought about the disruption of the national organization. The Whigs in early Oregon differed but little from the Democrats. Often referring to themselves as "Clay national" Whigs,[45] they achieved, at best, only a cursory organization during the early years. Strongly opposed to party organization at first, they remained in a hopeless minority.[46] The first germs of the Republican party took shape both north and south of the Columbia River in 1855, but it was not until four years later that the party achieved a complete organization and became a force in Pacific Northwest politics. The Whig party, on the other hand, persisted long after its national counterpart had disappeared from the scene.

During the decade of the fifties, this scattered, heterogeneous, politically conscious population on the Pacific Northwest frontier attempted to meet the challenges of the mounting sectional struggle over slavery. While the settlers felt a detachment from the center of the struggle, they nevertheless had a strong interest in it. They first became aware of the pervasiveness of this explosive issue when Congress debated the organization of a territorial government for the far Northwest.

[45] In 1853, John R. Hardin, a member of the Oregon territorial legislature, commented that with the death of Clay and Webster "all that was national—all that was glorious—all that was good of the Whig party" had died (Oregon City *Oregon Statesman,* January 8, 1853).

[46] David Logan, an enterprising young lawyer from Illinois, lamented to his sister in 1851, "This is no place for a Whig" (January 3, 1851, Harry E. Pratt, ed. "22 Letters of David Logan, Pioneer Oregon Lawyer," *OHQ,* XLIV [Sept., 1943], 260).

*the settlers
and slavery*

THE ACQUISITION OF A VAST AND
relatively unsettled western area by the United States following the
Mexican War marked the recrudescence of the slavery issue. The
question of the expansion of slavery into the West had been settled
by the Missouri Compromise in 1820, when an arbitrary geographical
line designed to separate free from slave territory was drawn across
the Louisiana Purchase. With the acquisition of new western territory, the slavery problem again demanded attention. Many proposals
and formulae were offered in an attempt to compromise the difference of opinion between the North and the South. Fundamental to
these proposals were several basic attitudes. The principle of the
Wilmot Proviso, calling for the exclusion of slavery from the new
territories of the West, represented a large block of Northern opinion
and eventually became the creed of the Republican Party. Opposed
to this view was the demand of many Southerners that Congress
refrain from interfering with slavery in the West, one way or another.
A third attitude, held generally in the West itself, embodied the concept of popular sovereignty as developed by Stephen A. Douglas,
maintaining that slavery was dependent upon local law and consequently the responsibility of the people in the territories acting
through their elected legislatures. Still a fourth attitude was the

suggestion that the Missouri Compromise be extended to the Pacific Ocean. The Pacific Northwest became an unwilling participant in the conflict over these points of view.

The area first became a part of the mainstream of American politics when James Knox Polk was elected president of the United States in 1844 on a frankly expansionistic platform. In his campaign, Polk had pledged himself and his party to the acquisition of the Oregon Country and the annexation of one of Mexico's rebellious provinces, Texas. The former was accomplished peaceably, after much negotiation, by treaty with Great Britain in the summer of 1846. The latter, although a *fait accompli* soon after Polk's inauguration, led indirectly to war with Mexico.

A few weeks after the Oregon treaty had been signed and shortly before Congress was to adjourn, David Wilmot, a young Democratic representative from Pennsylvania, offered his famous proviso. Written in the language of the Ordinance of 1787, presumably to give it a Jeffersonian ring, the proviso stipulated that slavery should not exist in any territory acquired from Mexico as the result of the war then in progress. It failed to pass, but the resolution was later revived, occupying the attention of Congress for four years. The reaction of the nation to the proviso was immediate. Many Northerners were enthusiastic, and a few Northern states passed resolutions endorsing the proviso. Southerners, on the other hand, were denunciatory in their criticism of the principle, regarding it as a threat to their rights and privileges as members of the Union. The agitation, instead of subsiding in later years, increased until it almost completely dominated the deliberations of Congress.

The organization of Oregon Territory was accomplished in the midst of this bitter controversy. The efforts of Congress to provide a territorial government for this region, a routine matter at any other time, became inseparably linked with the sectional conflict over the expansion of slavery. From December, 1846, until the summer of 1848, Congress argued and debated a bill to organize a territorial government for Oregon, but failed to come to any agreement. The controversy raged particularly over the question whether slavery should be specifically prohibited in the Oregon bill. To many Northerners the organization of Oregon Territory with such a specific prohibition was essential as a precedent for future Western legislation. David Wilmot, for example, argued, "Extend slavery to the

Pacific Ocean, and it insures the ultimate subjugation of the whole southern half of this Continent to its dominion."[1] To the South, also, a great principle was at stake. Few Southerners advocated the extension of slavery into Oregon itself, but the passage of a bill embodying an explicit slavery prohibition would establish a dangerous precedent for other Western areas which presumably were more congenial to the Southern institution. To both the North and the South, the destiny of the vast area won from Mexico depended upon the final outcome of the struggle over Oregon. Many of the arguments in Congress were concerned with the efficacy of introducing slavery into the Pacific Northwest, although few members of Congress actually believed that slavery could thrive there.[2]

In the meantime, the settlers in the Pacific Northwest became increasingly impatient for an organized territorial government. An Indian uprising, occasioned by the Whitman massacre (in which a small missionary station in eastern Oregon Territory had been wiped out), made the need for a United States administration in the area all the more acute. When news of the embroilment of the Oregon bill in the slavery controversy reached the Pacific, the settlers became disappointed and disheartened.[3] Thomas Hart Benton assured them, however, that they would "not be outlawed for not admitting slavery." "A home agitation, for the election and disunion purposes, is all that is intended by thrusting this fire brand question into your bill!" he wrote.[4] Oregon's frontier newspaper complained of the "long, cold and unnatural neglect which the people of Oregon have received at the hands of the mother country."[5]

In August, 1848, a bill for the organization of Oregon Territory, with a section extending the provisions of the Ordinance of 1787 to the area and thus implicitly barring slavery, passed the House of Representatives. After considerable debate, the Senate concurred by

[1] *Congressional Globe*, 30 Congress, 1 Session, Appendix, p. 1078.

[2] See for example the argument of Senator John A. Dix of New York, in *ibid.*, p. 866.

[3] Oregon City *Oregon Spectator*, August 5, 1847. In the course of the debate over the Oregon bill in the Senate, one Southern Senator, Arthur P. Bagby of Alabama, declared, "If this principle of abolition or exclusion . . . touches or taints this bill at all, so far as I am concerned, the people of Oregon will go without a government to the day of judgement" (*Cong. Globe*, 30 Cong., 1 Sess., Appendix, p. 691).

[4] Thomas Hart Benton to the People of Oregon, March, 1847, Oregon City *Oregon Spectator*, September 17, 1847.

[5] Oregon City *Oregon Spectator*, December 28, 1848.

a close vote.[6] Thus an organized territorial government for the scattered settlements of the Pacific Northwest became a reality. The passage of the bill, however, brought forth an ominous warning from the South. Senator Butler of South Carolina warned the Senate that

> his advice to his constituents would be, to go to these new Territories with arms in their hands; to go as armed communities, and take possession of the lands which they had helped to acquire, and see who would attempt to dispossess them. Would the military force of the United States shoot down the ploughman at his plough? So help him God, he would so advise his constituents, to take them with their property there, and settle at all hazards.

The bill to organize Oregon Territory, he said, was a "masked battery, from behind which the institutions of the South were to be assailed with a firm determination to subdue them."[7] Many wondered if in the achievement of a territorial government for the far Northwest irreparable damage had not been done to the Union itself.

The passage of the Oregon bill did not end Oregon's connection with the sectional controversy. As a part of the United States, the Oregon Country was drawn into the discussion over slavery expansion. One Senator declared the bill actually solved nothing, that it would merely shift the agitation "to the Pacific to stir up dissension among the first settlers."[8]

On the Western frontier, slavery assumed a political importance out of all proportion to its economic value. The number of actual slaves in the Western territories was negligible. The question of the expansion of slavery, however, played a dominant role in frontier politics. The institution had not reached its natural limits of expansion in the years prior to 1850. Slavery, it has been said, "could show profits only as long as it could find plenty of rich land to cultivate and the world would take the product of its crude labor at a good price."[9] Many areas in the Far West offered just these conditions, although some Westerners claimed that environmental conditions would prevent the spread of slavery into the West. Southerners, on the other hand, emphatically declared that the premise "that there exists *no territory* into which the Southern people can go with slave

---

[6] *Cong. Globe,* 30 Cong., 1 Sess., pp. 1007, 1031, 1043, 1048, 1074-1080.

[7] *Ibid.,* pp. 1060-1061.

[8] *Ibid.,* Appendix, p. 1182. The statement was made by Senator Dix of New York.

[9] Charles W. Ramsdell, "The Natural Limits of Slavery Expansion," *Mississippi Valley Historical Review,* XVI (Sept., 1929), 151-171.

property" was false, and they insisted that Southerners could profitably expand into all the areas of the West.[10]

In the Pacific Northwest, the issue of slavery expansion was discussed almost exclusively in connection with the achievement of statehood. Although some territories had taken action on slavery in the past, it was generally considered to be outside their jurisdiction. Following the passage of the Kansas-Nebraska Act in 1854, providing for the local determination of slavery in those two territories, many frontiersmen hoped that slavery would soon become the exclusive responsibility of the territories concerned. This hope, however, became entangled in a web of conflicting partisan interpretations. The slavery question was of practical importance in Pacific Northwest frontier politics only when the people of Oregon Territory began to move in the direction of a state government.

The sectional origins of the population in the Pacific Northwest furnish clues to an explanation of the attitude of the region toward the slavery question. Because of the heterogeneity of the population, with settlers drawn from both free and slave areas, the region followed a conservative, middle road in the national controversy.[11] Both extremes, the Northern abolitionist and the Southern "fire-eater," were rejected by the frontier population. The pioneers who had migrated from the border areas of the upper South and the Old Northwest helped to transplant the "border state" attitude toward slavery and the Negro to the Pacific Northwest frontier. One of Oregon's early judges expressed the sentiments of many pioneers when he wrote that the "true policy of Oregon [was] to keep as clear as possible of negroes, and all the exciting questions of negro servitude."[12] It did not prove possible, however, for the frontier population to remain completely isolated from the problem of slavery expansion.

The greatest impetus to the migration to the Far West of Southern slaveholders with their slaves was the California gold rush. Although the exact number is not known, slaves were brought to California to work with their owners in the mines.[13] After the original rush had

[10] *Charleston Mercury,* February 28, 1860, quoted in Dwight L. Dumond, ed. *Southern Editorials on Secession* (New York, 1931) , p. 41.

[11] See Robert W. Johannsen, "Spectators of Disunion: The Pacific Northwest and the Civil War," *PNQ,* XLIV (July, 1953) , 106-114.

[12] Salem *Oregon Statesman,* July 28, 1857.

[13] *Memoirs of Cornelius Cole* (New York, 1908) , p. 92.

subsided, many of the Negroes remained in California in a condition of slavery, in some instances not receiving their freedom until after emancipation had become national.[14] Since California was technically a free state, the presence of slaves gave rise to many constitutional and judicial problems.[15] Slavery existed in California chiefly because of the white settlers' lack of interest in enforcing the slavery prohibition in their state constitution and because of the docile character of the Negro population, most of whom were unaware that they could claim their freedom.

The situation in Oregon during the first years of territorial experience was in some ways parallel to that of California. Slaves were brought over the plains to the Pacific Northwest, and some remained in a condition of slavery. The settlers, however, recognized the nature of their problem early. Their initial efforts to define the status of slavery in the Pacific Northwest were made before the area became a part of the United States.[16]

The first organic act of the provisional government of Oregon, adopted by the settlers of the Willamette Valley in 1843, employed the language of the Ordinance of 1787 to prohibit slavery.[17] Although this provision was challenged from time to time, it remained a part of the frame of government. The law was modified in 1844 to prohibit free Negroes and mulattoes from settling in the Oregon Country. Slaveowners were given three years in which to remove their slaves, after which time the slaves became free. All free Negroes or mulattoes were required to leave the Pacific Northwest under penalty of periodic floggings.[18] This action resulted partly from a number of disturbances involving free Negroes, one of whom threat-

---

[14] Clyde A. Duniway, "Slavery in California after 1848," *Annual Report of the American Historical Association,* 1905 (Washington, 1906), I, 244.

[15] *Ibid.,* pp. 245-247; Helen Tunnicliff Catterall, ed. *Judicial Cases Concerning American Slavery and the Negro* (5 vols.; Washington, 1926-37), V, 331-334; Frederick W. Howay, "Negro Immigration into Vancouver Island in 1858," *British Columbia Historical Quarterly,* III (April, 1939), 101-114.

[16] Sherman Savage, "The Negro in the History of the Pacific Northwest," *Journal of Negro History,* XIII (July, 1938), 225-264; D. G. Hill, "The Negro as a Political and Social Issue in the Oregon Country," *Journal of Negro History,* XXXIII (April, 1948), 130-145.

[17] LaFayette Grover, comp. *The Oregon Archives, Including the Journals, Governors' Messages and Public Papers of Oregon* (Salem, 1853), p. 29; Jesse Applegate, Views of Oregon History, MS in the Bancroft Library, University of California, Berkeley (microfilm in the University of Washington Library, Seattle), pp. 39-40.

[18] Peter H. Burnett, Recollections of the Past, 2 vols., MS in the Bancroft Library, I, 237-250.

ened to arouse the Indians against the white settlers.[19] The anti-Negro bias of these frontier settlements persisted into the territorial period. The law excluding free Negroes was re-enacted by the territorial legislature and in 1851 was upheld as constitutional by the territorial supreme court in a decision which was, according to one of the local newspapers, but the "re-affirmation of a well-settled doctrine."[20]

The exact number of slaves in the Pacific Northwest during the decade of the fifties is not known. The number, however, was negligible; it is probable that most of the slaves that had been brought to Oregon were free by the middle fifties. According to available evidence, the slaves were employed primarily as domestics or farm hands.[21]

During the decade, several situations involving Negro slaves arose which were of more than local significance. Perhaps the most famous slaves in the Pacific Northwest belonged to Nathaniel Ford, an emigrant from Missouri. These slaves were granted their freedom by the Oregon territorial supreme court in 1853 in one of the few cases of its kind in the Far West. Ford had brought a small party of slaves, including a married couple with several children, with him from Missouri when he crossed the plains in 1844. After the return of one of the slaves from California, where he had panned gold with one of Ford's sons, the adults sued for their freedom on the ground that slavery was prohibited in Oregon.[22] In Ford's own words, "the abolitionists interfered—and the country is full of them—the interference was so great that I had to let them go." Ford, however, kept the children. He was advised to take the entire family back to Missouri where they could be sold, but he refused. Ford finally wrote to his former home in Missouri asking that the sheriff place an execution

19 Marie M. Bradley, "Political Beginnings in Oregon—The Period of the Provisional Government, 1839-1849," *OHQ*, IX (March, 1908), 58; *Senate Executive Document*, 28 Cong., 2 Sess., I, no. 1 (#431), 503-504; *House Executive Document*, 29 Cong., 1 Sess., I, no. 2 (#480), 629.
20 Territory of Oregon, *House Journal*, 1849, p. 56; Territory of Oregon, *Council Journal*, 1849, pp. 89, 94; Oregon City *Oregon Statesman*, September 2, 1851.
21 Instances of slaves residing in the Pacific Northwest are recorded by Fred Lockley, "Some Documentary Records of Slavery in Oregon," *OHQ*, XVII (June, 1916), 107-115; see also "The Case of Robin Holmes vs. Nathaniel Ford," *OHQ*, XXIII (June, 1922), 111-137; John Minto, "Antecedents of the Oregon Pioneers and the Light These Throw on Their Motives," *OHQ*, V (March, 1904), 38-63.
22 Reuben P. Boise to T. W. Davenport, June 4, 1906, in T. W. Davenport, "The Slavery Question in Oregon," *OHQ*, IX (Sept., 1908), 196; Lockley, "Case of Robin Holmes vs. Nathaniel Ford," pp. 117-118.

on the Negroes so that they could be returned there under the Fugitive Slave Law.[23]

The territorial supreme court had declined to hear the case prior to the appointment of George H. Williams to the chief justiceship. Williams, a free-soil Democrat from Iowa, placed the case at the head of his docket, scheduling it for the spring of 1853. In his decision, Williams maintained that, without some positive local legislative enactment establishing slavery in Oregon, slavery could not exist in Oregon. As soon as the laws of Oregon touched the parties concerned, the relation of master and slave was dissolved. The Negroes were given their freedom, and Ford was assessed to the amount of the court costs.[24] The decision in the case was not based on the slavery restriction in Oregon's organic act but rather on the lack of local legislation respecting slavery.

The Pacific Northwest witnessed one other incident regarding slavery that was of more than local importance. In the fall of 1860, a young slave boy held by James Tilton, Washington Territory's surveyor general, escaped to Victoria where he was aided by the British authorities. Tilton protested to the Secretary of State in Washington, D.C., but no action was taken on his behalf. The chief justice of the British colony granted the slave his freedom on the ground that a person aboard a foreign vessel in a British port was subject to the laws of Great Britain.[25] One Puget Sound newspaper concluded, "Our proximity to the British Possessions on this Coast afford the same facilities to an underground railroad that the Canadas do on the Atlantic."[26]

The real importance of the slavery issue to the Pacific Northwest, however, was on the level of political discussion. Two events during the fifties stimulated this discussion: the passage of the Kansas-Nebraska Act by Congress in 1854, and the approval of statehood by the voters of Oregon Territory in 1857.

[23] Nathaniel Ford to James A. Shirley, June 22, 1852, in Frederic A. Culmer, ed. "Emigrant Missourians in Mexico and Oregon," *Missouri Historical Review*, XXV (Jan., 1931) , 287.

[24] George H. Williams, "Political History of Oregon from 1853 to 1865," *OHQ*, II (March, 1901) , 5-6; Salem *Oregon Statesman*, July 26, 1853.

[25] James Tilton to Henry M. McGill, September 30, 1860, Letters and Documents Relating to the Offices of Governor and Secretary of Washington Territory, 1860-1864, University of Washington Library. The incident is described in detail in Robie L. Reid, "How One Slave Became Free," *British Columbia Historical Quarterly*, VI (Oct., 1942) , 251-256.

[26] Steilacoom *Puget Sound Herald*, October 5, 1860.

Before the passage of the Kansas-Nebraska Act, the interest in the slavery question in the Pacific Northwest was sporadic and of minor importance. The issue had ostensibly been settled for all time by the compromise measures of 1850, and there was no desire, locally or nationally, to revive it. One editor regarded slavery as a "fruitful theme for polemical declamation and useless excitement" and was astonished that the issue could ever arouse the "national mind."[27] When it was reported that a Baltimore newspaper had maintained that Washington Territory was open to slavery because Congress had neglected to extend the Ordinance of 1787 or the Wilmot Proviso over the area, Asahel Bush, editor of the *Oregon Statesman,* replied:

> We shall not enter upon the discussion of the question whether citizens of slave States can enter organized territories of the United States with their slaves, and hold them as such, in the absence of any law authorizing or prohibiting the same. We do not think the subject involves any such question.[28]

The territorial legislature during these early years continued in its efforts to establish an all-white society in Oregon. In 1854, a bill was introduced into the legislature to prevent Negroes and mulattoes from coming to and settling in Oregon.[29] A similar bill was debated the following year. One member of the territorial house of representatives declared that

> niggers . . . should never be allowed to mingle with the whites. They would amalgamate and raise a most miserable race of human beings. . . . If niggers are allowed to come among us and mingle with the whites, it will cause a perfect state of pollution. Niggers always retrograde, until they get back to the state of barbarity from whence they originated. . . . I don't see that we should equalize ourselves with them by letting them come among us.[30]

Opposition to such Negro exclusion acts came not only from those who believed that Oregon was so isolated that few Negroes would make the long journey but also from those elements that wished to see slavery firmly planted in the Pacific Northwest.[31]

[27] Oregon City *Oregon Spectator,* April 4, 1850.

[28] Salem *Oregon Statesman,* August 2, 1853. References to the problem of the expansion of slavery during these early years may be found in the Oregon City *Oregon Statesman,* June 13, 1851, and the Oregon City *Oregon Spectator,* September 9, 1851.

[29] Territory of Oregon, *House Journal,* 1854 (Salem, 1855), pp. 42-43; Salem *Oregon Statesman,* December 19, 26, 1854.

[30] Portland *Weekly Oregonian,* January 6, 1855.

[31] A proslavery member of the territorial legislature from southern Oregon attempted to amend these bills on several occasions in such a way as not to

These legislative bills were designed to exclude all Negroes, free and slave alike. Oregon's attitude in this regard was not unique. During the debates in Congress over the creation of Oregon Territory, one Northern Senator held that it was Congress' sacred duty to consecrate the West for the multiplication of the white race. A representative from Massachusetts argued against the introduction of slavery into the Pacific Northwest on the ground that a free Negro population would inevitably follow slavery—by keeping out slavery, an all-white free population would be guaranteed.[32] It was not the expansion of slavery that was feared as much as the thought of free Negroes living in a white society. Some states in the Midwest expressed this fear by excluding both free Negroes and mulattoes from their borders.[33] The free Negro issue was thus linked in Oregon to the slavery question; the anti-Negro bias of these frontier settlements was manifested in the debates over the future status of slavery in the Pacific Northwest.

The passage of the Kansas-Nebraska Act in 1854 brought an end to this initial period of calm speculation regarding slavery in the West. Reaction to the act in Oregon was expressed more by a quickening of the statehood movement and a realization of increased territorial responsibility than by a fear that slavery was about to be extended to the area. In the Pacific Northwest, the act was considered as part of a broader movement for increased self-government in the territories, a movement that had already gained considerable strength in the region. Many of the settlers fervently hoped that the terms of the Kansas-Nebraska Act would be broadened and eventually extended over all the territories of the United States.[34] Slavery assumed a

"affect persons bringing in or holding negroes or mulattoes as slaves in this Territory" (Salem *Oregon Statesman,* December 19, 26, 1854; Portland *Weekly Oregonian,* January 6, 1855).

[32] *Cong. Globe,* 30 Cong., 1 Sess., Appendix, pp. 866, 792.

[33] Almost every Northern state had by 1860 passed discriminatory laws against the free Negroes. Ohio, Indiana, and Illinois barred the entry of Negroes into the state, forbade them to vote, refused to permit them to serve on juries, and denied their children access to white public schools (Harvey Wish, *Society and Thought in Early America* [New York, 1950], p. 425).

[34] Oregon's territorial governor, George L. Curry, declared, "The noble principle enunciated in the Kansas-Nebraska act is a step in the advance, and may be regarded as an evidence of the encouragement that is in the future in this respect" (Territory of Oregon, *House Journal,* 1856-57 [Salem, 1857], Appendix, p. 7). This point of view has been developed in detail in Robert W. Johannsen, "The Kansas-Nebraska Act and the Pacific Northwest Frontier," *Pacific Historical Review,* XXII (May, 1953), 129-141.

secondary role in their interpretation of the act. The frontier population in the Pacific Northwest saw the Kansas-Nebraska Act as its
author, Stephen A. Douglas, had intended it to be seen. "The great
principle involved in the bill," according to Douglas, was popular
sovereignty, or territorial self-government. The repeal of the Missouri Compromise strengthened popular sovereignty by removing
from it a possible source of ambiguity.[35]

As a step in the direction of greater territorial self-government,
the Kansas-Nebraska Act stimulated the discussion of slavery in the
Pacific Northwest. Oregonians expressed approval that this disruptive issue had finally been removed from the jurisdiction of the
national Congress. The editor of the *Oregon Statesman* was convinced that the act would bring an end to the agitation of the slavery
question on the national level.

> It will place the question [he wrote] where it properly belongs—with those
> whose interest it affects. It is a democratic step forward, enlarging the rights of
> American citizens in the Territories, admitting them to be, at once, competent
> and equal to self-government in this respect.

Later, he argued that the bill actually was a measure for "African
freedom." With the removal of the slavery question from national
politics, abolitionism would lose much of its driving force. With the
abolitionists quiet, the editor reasoned, genuine slavery reform could
begin in the South.[36] Some opposition was expressed in the territory
to the repeal of the Missouri Compromise and the reopening of the
slavery question, but it remained nebulous and ill defined.[37]

The Kansas-Nebraska Act was discussed in the Oregon territorial
legislature during the winter of 1854-55. In December, 1854, Delazon
Smith, representing Linn County, introduced a series of resolutions
endorsing the Kansas-Nebraska Act. In his resolutions, Smith contended that the act was, in essence, a recognition by the national
government of the territorial right to self-government. The fourth

[35] Matthew P. Deady to Asahel Bush, May 12, 1854, Asahel Bush Papers (Photostats), University of Oregon Library, Eugene. Cf. Walter C. Woodward, *The Rise
and Early History of Political Parties in Oregon, 1843-1868* (Portland, 1913), p. 89.

[36] Salem *Oregon Statesman,* April 4, August 22, 1854.

[37] In a circular to the voters of two Oregon counties, one candidate for the
territorial council made the accusation that the Democratic party had opened
"afresh the agitation of the slavery question, so happily and justly settled by Clay,
Webster, Fillmore, Foote, and others;—and [had] again convulsed our nation and
driven it to the very verge of a bloody revolution" (Portland *Weekly Oregonian,*
November 18, 1854).

resolution read in part, "We claim for ourselves what we freely con-
cede to our brethren in the States, the *right* to decide for *ourselves*
what we will adopt, and what we will *not* adopt, in the government
of our local affairs." He went on to argue that the slavery prohibition
in Oregon Territory's organic act had been superseded by the principles of the Kansas-Nebraska Act. Smith, however, did not expect
to see slavery extended to the Pacific Northwest. His fifth resolution
embodied his point of view in this and all future discussions of the
slavery issue:

> That notwithstanding the perfect *constitutional right* of the people of the
> Territories to establish or adopt the institution of domestic slavery, yet in our
> opinion the laws of nature, climate, soil, production, immigration, interest, and
> the convictions and will of a large majority of the people of this Territory, and
> of all the other organized Territories of the Union, are *against* such an estab-
> lishment, and will conspire to prevent its adoption.[38]

Smith argued that the Kansas-Nebraska Act recognized the right and
capacity of the territories to govern themselves. However, he maintained that slavery could not be governed by statutory laws, that
legal enactments never could restrict slavery. Only those principles
which are contained in climate, soil, production, the wants of com-
merce, and the interest of man, Smith argued, could ever successfully
restrict the spread of the South's "peculiar institution."[39]

R. J. Ladd, a Democratic proslavery member of the legislature,
proposed that Smith's resolutions be amended in order that they
"might not operate against slaveholders coming to Oregon with their
property, if they saw fit."[40] In the debate that followed, Smith declared that "he would vote against slavery being introduced into
Oregon, if the question was up tomorrow." Ladd's motion lost, but
only by a narrow margin.

Smith's resolutions endorsing the Kansas-Nebraska Act were
countered by Anson G. Henry, a Whig representative from Yamhill
County and a former resident of Illinois, who introduced a series of
resolutions intended to present the view of the opposition. Henry,
however, was careful to endorse the principle of popular sovereignty,
concentrating his attacks on the repeal of the Missouri Compromise.
Congress, according to Henry, held the power to determine whether

[38] Salem *Oregon Statesman,* December 26, 1854.
[39] *Ibid.,* January 16, 1855.
[40] *Ibid.,* January 23, 1855.

or not slavery should exist in the territories; this implied that popular sovereignty, in its practical application, was limited in its scope. When a state or territory had voluntarily yielded up a portion of its sovereignty in the interest of sectional harmony, as in the Missouri Compromise, it was bound to honor that agreement.[41] In his arguments on the floor of the house, Henry objected to mixing the repeal of the Missouri Compromise with the question of territorial self-government. Taking a strong position against the spread of slavery, Henry nevertheless expressed a conservative view, declaring:

> I shall oppose with all the power the God of nature has given me any and everything that shall have a tendency, directly or indirectly, to fix the bonds of slavery on any human being now free; or that shall extend the boundaries of slavery. I will stand by the right; stand by the abolitionist in restoring the compromise line of 1820; and I will stand by the slaveholder in maintaining and enforcing the fugitive slave law, and the compromise measures of 1850 in letter and spirit.

Henry objected to Smith's contention that slavery could not exist in Oregon simply by force of nature, maintaining that "the history of slavery in this country shows it to be true, that in the settlement of all the territories of this Union, *slavery had gone where there was no law to prevent it,* without regard to soil, climate or production."[42]

Henry's point of view was not a popular one among his fellow Whigs. David Logan, an influential Whig leader and also a member of the legislature, refused to endorse Henry's resolutions because they were "too ultra, and tinctured with abolitionism, to pledge the Whig party of Oregon to." Henry himself admitted that his fellow Whigs had warned him that his course was impolitic and could only lead to disaster for the Whig party.[43] Delazon Smith's resolutions endorsing the Kansas-Nebraska Act were approved by the territorial legislature. There is no record of Henry's resolutions having been brought to a vote.[44]

The debate over the Kansas-Nebraska resolutions in the territorial legislature evoked an immediate response from one of Oregon's oldest and most respected citizens, Jesse Applegate. A member of the "Great Migration" of 1843, Applegate had spent his early life in

[41] Territory of Oregon, *House Journal,* 1854, pp. 53-55.
[42] Portland *Weekly Oregonian,* February 17, 1855.
[43] Salem *Oregon Statesman,* January 23, 1855; Portland *Weekly Oregonian,* February 17, 1855.
[44] Territory of Oregon, *House Journal,* 1854, pp. 73-74.

Missouri, where he clerked in Edward Bates's law office and practiced surveying. Familiarly known as the "Sage of Yoncalla," Applegate was, in politics, "a cross between the old-fashioned, honest notions of Hamilton and Jefferson." While he remained aloof from an active political life, he identified himself most often with the Whig-Republican group. Throughout his life he held a deep resentment against slavery, a feeling that originated in his early Missouri days.[45] In a letter to one other early Oregon settler, Applegate condemned those Whigs who seemed to favor the Kansas-Nebraska Act. The Whigs in his own county, he charged, had supported the act "not upon the flimsy and lying pretense of 'squatter sovereignty' but upon its real meaning as a pro-slavery measure and from a desire to have slaves in Oregon." He pledged himself to oppose "with all my powers to the last" the extension of slavery to the free territories of the West, declaring, "Whoever is against the *extension of slavery* is of my party; whoever is for it is against me. My platform has but this single plank." Applegate described his opposition to slavery:

> You and I made our livings by honest labor. We both expect to leave our children in Oregon. One of the worst features of slavery is to degrade labor. If slavery is introduced into Oregon our children must blush for themselves or their fathers; if forced to labor they will be degraded from social equality, and blush for themselves; if rich and slave owners, they will blush to confess that their father toiled by the "sweat of his face."[46]

To Applegate, the Whig party, with which he had been nominally associated since his arrival in Oregon, no longer spoke his language. The time was ripe for a new organization.

The first organization in the Pacific Northwest of a political party devoted exclusively to halting the extension of slavery took place north of the Columbia River, in Washington Territory. In August, 1854, a handful of men met at Olympia to nominate candidates for county offices. Drawing their inspiration from the national Free-Soil party, which had been organized in 1848 with the nomination of Martin Van Buren for president, the members of the "convention" endorsed the Pittsburgh Free-Soil platform of 1852. All men,

[45] James W. Nesmith, "The Occasional Address," *Transactions of the Oregon Pioneer Association*, 1875, p. 62; Joseph Schafer, "Jesse Applegate: Pioneer, Statesman and Philosopher," *Washington Historical Quarterly*, I (July, 1907), 217-233; Charlotte Odgers, "Jesse Applegate, Study of a Pioneer Politician," *Reed College Bulletin*, XXIII (Jan., 1945), 7-20.

[46] Jesse Applegate to Medorem Crawford, February 4, 1855, Medorem Crawford Papers, University of Oregon Library.

irrespective of party, who agreed "in promoting the cause of liberty and justice, and resisting the encroachments and extension of slavery by all practicable and constitutional means," were invited to co-operate with these Free-Soilers.[47] The chairman of the meeting, however, took an abolitionist position in a letter explaining the party to the voters. He demanded the extinction of slavery wherever it might exist, at the same time opposing the amalgamation of the white and black races as degrading to the "superior" whites.[48] Motivated by "principles and not party preferences," the Free-Soilers did not make any independent nominations but rather endorsed candidates from both the Whig and Democratic parties who, they thought, were sympathetic to their views. By the spring of 1855, this small group had received sufficient strength to warrant an independent nomination. In May, fifteen to twenty delegates, almost exclusively from Thurston County, met and nominated a candidate for territorial delegate. Resolutions were drafted attacking the institution of slavery as a "sin against God, and a crime against man" and calling for "no more slave states, no slave territory." The Fugitive Slave Act was declared "obviously unconstitutional," and its amendment or repeal was recommended.[49] In the election, the Free-Soil nominee received only forty-one votes in the entire territory, thirty-one of these from Thurston County.[50]

The organization of Free-Soilers south of the Columbia River followed soon afterward. Heretofore, abolition sentiment had been expressed only by a few churchmen in Oregon Territory. In September, 1854, the Oregon Association of Congregational and Presbyterian Churches went on record as favoring the abolition of slavery "in the way most conducive to the welfare of the slave and his master."[51] The move to organize free-soil sentiment in Oregon Territory was also inspired by churchmen. In June, 1855, thirty-nine men met together at Albany "to take under consideration the proper

[47] Olympia *Pioneer and Democrat*, August 26, 1854.

[48] Samuel James to the Editor, August 21, 1854, Olympia *Pioneer and Democrat*, September 2, 1854.

[49] Olympia *Pioneer and Democrat*, June 8, 1855.

[50] Election Returns, 1855, Washington Territory, Washington State Archives, Olympia (microfilm in the University of Washington Library) ; Olympia *Pioneer and Democrat*, September 7, 1855.

[51] Salem *Oregon Statesman*, November 14, 1854. It is significant, however, that even within this church group the resolutions attacking slavery were the only ones that did not pass unanimously.

course to be pursued by those in Oregon, who are opposed to the extension of slavery." The resolutions were written by two ministers, Rev. Wilson Blain and Rev. W. Carey Johnson. The question of slavery was described as "the great agitating element in the politics of our country, which can never be compromised or settled but by the overthrow of an institution so utterly opposed to every principle of political as well as of all moral and religious right." All the friends of free soil in Oregon were urged to direct public attention to the evils of slavery and to support only those candidates who were pledged against the spread of slavery.[52] A future meeting was scheduled but was never held. The movement languished and passed rapidly from public notice. The opposition of both the Democratic and Whig parties and the presence of several Know-Nothings at the meeting discredited the organization publicly. Delazon Smith ridiculed the idea that Oregon was threatened by slavery. In his opinion, slavery had as much chance of spreading to the moon as of being extended to Oregon. He conjectured that nineteen-twentieths of the people in Oregon were opposed to the institution. If slavery should be introduced into Oregon, he argued that "the acts, declarations, denunciations, misrepresentations and *defiant tones* of these '*Liberty men*' will *bring it* here!" The *Oregon Statesman* concluded, "If anything could make the people of Oregon desire slavery, it would be the agitation of the subject by such fanatics as these."[53]

In December, 1855, a new element was injected into the discussion of slavery. Rev. Wilson Blain, one of the organizers of the incipient free-soil movement, urged William L. Adams, editor of the newly founded *Oregon Argus,* to present the antislavery argument to the people of the territory. Adams, often dubbed the "Parson Brownlow of the West," was a Campbellite preacher who had migrated to Oregon from Illinois in 1848. In 1855, he purchased the printing plant of the defunct *Oregon Spectator* and began publication of the *Oregon Argus,* principally to promote the organization of the Republican party in Oregon. Blain felt that it was important for the people of the territory to think about slavery before they adopted a

[52] Portland *Weekly Oregonian,* July 7, 1855; Oregon City *Oregon Argus,* July 7, 1855.

[53] Delazon Smith to Asahel Bush, July 16, 1855, Corvallis *Oregon Statesman,* July 21, 1855; Corvallis *Oregon Statesman,* July 14, 1855.

state constitution. Slavery, he thought, was the greatest political issue then before the American people; "why shall not the people of Oregon keep up with the spirit of the times, and labor to have intelligent views of this, the leading question of the age in which we live?" he asked. According to Blain's estimate, one-third of Oregon's population favored the introduction of slavery.[54] Adams continued to present vigorous antislavery arguments throughout the decade.

The discussion of slavery in connection with the Kansas-Nebraska Act was usually subordinated to what was considered by most of the settlers in the Pacific Northwest to be the greater principle of the act, popular sovereignty or territorial self-government. The attempts on the part of both the free-soilers and the abolitionists to organize a crusade against slavery met with failure. The movement for statehood in Oregon, however, gave the discussion a new impetus.

The first territory-wide election to determine the sentiment regarding statehood was held in June, 1854, not long after the passage of the Kansas-Nebraska Act. Subsequent elections were held in 1855 and 1856. Finally, in 1857, Oregonians voted overwhelmingly to organize a state government. The prospect of statehood immediately raised the significant question: Shall Oregon be a free or a slave state? Not only was this question important from a local point of view, but many also considered it vital nationally. The chances for Oregon's admission might depend solely on her decision of the slavery problem. The Kansas-Nebraska Act, by providing for territorial responsibility over the slavery issue, stimulated the feeling that an intelligent decision would be prerequisite to admission into the Union. It was in relation to the statehood movement, the "democratic dogma of statehood" as it became known in territorial politics, that the slavery issue was discussed and debated to its fullest extent.

The statehood issue was strongly supported by the Democratic party during the early fifties. The Whigs, through the medium of the *Oregonian,* opposed statehood, partly because the Democratic majority in the territory would mean a Democratic state. During the year 1856, however, a decisive change in sentiment regarding the expediency of statehood occurred. The election of Buchanan, events in Kansas, and an increasing fear that slavery might be forced into Oregon Territory were responsible for this shift.

---

[54] Wilson Blain to William L. Adams, [n. d.], Oregon City *Oregon Argus,* December 1, 1855.

In May, 1856, the Republican party held its first national convention in Philadelphia and nominated John C. Fremont for president on a platform pledged to the restriction of slavery. The status of slavery in the territories became the principal issue of the election campaign. Enthusiasm for the Fremont ticket in the East was so unexpected that some in the Pacific Northwest thought his election was assured.[55] Stimulated by this enthusiasm, another attempt was made to organize free-soil sentiment in the Pacific Northwest. In August, a meeting of "friends of the Republican cause" was held at Albany. Those present at the meeting decided that "it is expedient *now* to organize a republican party in the territory." Resolutions were passed opposing the extension of slavery and approving the national platform.[56] A series of county Republican conventions followed. In Yamhill County, the Republican slogan was considerably expanded: "We are for free territories and free states, for free farms and free labor, free society and free schools, free thought and free discussion, free speech and free press, free religion and free votes— for *freemen, Fremont,* and *freedom.*" In order to remove from the meeting any abolitionist taint, a resolution was passed opposing interference with slavery in the states where it existed.[57] This attempt to organize free-soil sentiment in Oregon Territory was no more successful than the earlier ones. The Whigs still clung to their old party organization. For example, Thomas J. Dryer, the editor of the *Oregonian,* continued to support the Whig party organization. During the presidential campaign he raised the names of the Whig–Know-Nothing candidates, Fillmore and Donelson, to the masthead of his paper.[58]

The election of James Buchanan, the Democratic candidate, had

[55] Asahel Bush to Matthew P. Deady, November 2, 1856, Florence Walls, ed. The Letters of Asahel Bush to Matthew P. Deady, 1851-1863, unpublished B.A. thesis, Reed College, 1941, p. 140; William H. Farrar to Deady, November 16, 1856, Matthew P. Deady Papers, Oregon Historical Society Library.

[56] Salem *Oregon Statesman,* September 9, 1856; Portland *Weekly Oregonian,* September 13, 1856; Oregon City *Oregon Argus,* September 6, 1856.

[57] Portland *Weekly Oregonian,* November 22, 1856.

[58] Dryer was particularly annoyed at a resolution of the Republicans calling for the establishment of a Republican press in the territory. He commented: "There are some who appear to think there has heretofore been no republicans in this country. . . . We have always supposed we were a republican, and think so still. We have ever advocated republican doctrines, we intend to do so if there should be a thousand republican presses established in our midst. If our republicanism don't suit you, gentlemen, your republicanism won't suit us, and we shall not indorse it" (Portland *Weekly Oregonian,* November 8, 1856).

a considerable effect on the statehood question in Oregon. The prospect of four more years of Democratic rule on a platform that allowed the extension of slavery to the territories convinced the doubters that the time for action was at hand. The conversion of Dryer and the *Oregonian* was complete as soon as the election was over. Dryer became alarmed at the situation in Kansas and the endorsement by the Democratic administration of what he called "border ruffianism." In an editorial, he expressed a desire for a state government, incidentally employing the arguments of the Kansas-Nebraska Act:

> Let us have a state government and make the issue at once. If we are to have slavery forced upon us, let it be by the people here and not by the slavery propagandists at Washington City. If the majority of the people in Oregon, fairly expressed, desire slavery, we are too much of a democrat to future oppose introduction, reserving to ourselves the right to go hence or remain, as we may deem best. If they do not want it, and so express themselves fairly, then we take it the majority should and must rule, and the question is at once settled.[59]

The feeling grew that if Oregon were to enter the Union as a free state it must be at once. Jesse Applegate, two years earlier, had favored statehood for that very reason, explaining to a friend, "I voted . . . and used my little influence to call a convention to form a Constitution while there was yet sufficient of the old spirit of 1845 among us to secure to our children the blessings of a free State."[60] The decision of the Supreme Court in the Dred Scott Case further augmented the ranks of those who favored statehood. The Democrats in the territorial legislature rejoiced at the change of sentiment on the part of the opponents of statehood and welcomed the opposition into the ranks of those who stood for popular sovereignty.[61] When the question of statehood was submitted to the electorate in June, 1857, it was carried by a vote of 7,617 to 1,679, a majority of almost 6,000 votes.

With the approval of statehood, the question of slavery became the absorbing issue in local politics. Linked with the question of free Negroes, it disturbed the deliberations of the territorial legislature. In the course of debate on a free Negro exclusion bill, many argu-

[59] Portland *Weekly Oregonian*, November 1, 8, 1856.
[60] Applegate to Crawford, February 4, 1856, Crawford Papers.
[61] Salem *Oregon Statesman*, December 23, 1856.

ments regarding the future status of the Negro in Oregon were expressed. Asa Lawrence Lovejoy, a native of Massachusetts, declared that the Kansas-Nebraska Act and a recent opinion of Attorney General Cushing[62] had destroyed the antislavery clause in Oregon's territorial act and that masters might bring their slaves to Oregon with perfect legality. As to the future status of slavery, however, Lovejoy remarked, "With me it is a matter of dollars and cents." If slavery should promote prosperity he would not oppose its introduction. Since Lovejoy thought slavery would not and could not be useful in Oregon, he opposed it on economic grounds. LaFayette Grover, another New Englander, maintained that the United States was a government of white men; the Declaration of Independence applied only to the white race. He expressed the view that if the Negro were excluded entirely from Oregon the area would not be plagued by the questions that were distracting the rest of the country.[63] All agreed that the people themselves should decide both the slavery and the free Negro questions. The proslavery and antislavery forces immediately began to marshal their arguments in an effort to sway the populace. During the greater part of the year 1857, these issues monopolized the public journals and much of the private correspondence.

The opening gun in the controversy was fired by the *Oregon Statesman*. Asahel Bush, the Massachusetts-born editor who had migrated to Oregon in 1850, set the tone for the discussion. The slavery restriction in the organic act of the territory, he thought, would have little influence in the final determination of the institution. Slavery, he pointed out, should be argued entirely on its own merits. Few in Oregon would be motivated in their decision by the morality or immorality of the institution. According to the paper, the real consideration should be whether or not slavery would prove a profitable institution in Oregon. Slavery was, he thought, regulated by nature, climate, and soil, which alone could introduce it in one place or abolish it in another. Sentiment in favor of slavery in

[62] The decision referred to by Lovejoy was rendered in October, 1855, by Attorney General Caleb Cushing. According to Cushing the provisions of the Northwest Ordinance had been extinguished by the Constitution; if a case had ever come before a court, it would have had to rule the antislavery provision of the ordinance null and void (*Official Opinions of the Attorneys General of the United States*, VII [Washington, 1856], 571).

[63] Salem *Oregon Statesman*, January 13, 20, 1857.

Oregon, the editor observed, was much greater than it had been in the past. He attributed this increase to the "insane agitation" of a few fanatics who regarded slavery as a moral issue and to the attempts of some Northern states to "subjugate" Kansas through emigrant aid societies. Persistence in this agitation might conceivably drive Oregon into the ranks of the slaveholding states. Summarizing the attitude of the Pacific Northwest toward this national issue, the editor assured his readers that "the people of Oregon are eminently National in their sentiments and attachments, and whether she enters the Union slave or free, she will be a conservative National State, and in every emergency will stand by the Union and the constitution as they are, with the compromises upon which they were formed and upon which they rest."[64] As the tension between the North and the South steadily mounted, the settlers on this frontier expressed this attitude of nationalism and conservatism with renewed conviction.

The *Statesman* opened its columns to the slavery debate. Many of those who sent in letters repeated Bush's arguments. One correspondent maintained that the climate was too cold in Oregon for Negro labor and that no staples could be grown there which Negroes could work with profit. He emphasized the fact that Oregon would be exposed on all sides to the operation of the underground railroad; if abolitionists in the East could "steal, without remorse" thousands of slaves annually, what could they not accomplish in Oregon?[65] Another contributor felt that slavery in Oregon would prove both unprofitable and ruinous; surrounded by free territory, Oregon's slaveowners would be unable to hold their slaves with any degree of security.[66] Both men believed that all Negroes, free and slave alike, should be kept out of Oregon. An "intelligent Tennessean," who favored slavery in the abstract, opposed it in Oregon because he thought its introduction might soon abolitionize the state; as a free state, Oregon would be able to exert a far greater influence on behalf of Southern rights than if she were a slave state.[67]

The Republican *Argus* also gave some attention to the question of

[64] *Ibid.*, March 31, 1857.

[65] B. Robinson, "State Constitution," Salem *Oregon Statesman*, July 21, 1857. Robinson's estimate of the number of fugitive slaves each year was grossly exaggerated. See Allan Nevins, *The Emergence of Lincoln* (2 vols.; New York, 1950), II, 489.

[66] Thomas Norris to the Editor, July 20, 1857, Salem *Oregon Statesman*, August 4, 1857.

[67] Salem *Oregon Statesman*, October 6, 1857.

slavery. One settler, writing to the editor, argued that slaves were by nature lazy, and that "the great object of a slave's being is to pass away the time." Because of Oregon's winter rains, slaves could not work more than half a year. Their presence in Oregon would discourage migration from the Northern states, and the local population would soon lose its "habits of industry" and its "thrift."[68]

The most publicized statement of this point of view was expressed by Oregon's territorial chief justice, George H. Williams, in what became known as his "Free State Letter." Writing to the *Statesman*, Williams urged that Oregon reject slavery. At the same time, he made it clear that he had no objections to local slavery and held a great respect for the Southern slaveowners. Williams' first argument was that slavery would not be profitable in the Pacific Northwest. Negroes, being naturally lazy, would require constant attention, and no farmer could afford an overseer. Accustomed to the "blazing sun of Africa," the Negroes would be out of place chopping wood or splitting rails "in the cool drenching rains of an Oregon winter." Next, Williams emphasized Oregon's isolation from the other slave states. The slaveholder would hesitate before migrating with his slaves to an area where his property would not be secure.[69] Finally, Williams took a strong anti-Negro position. Since Negroes were an ignorant and degraded class of beings, they would, if brought in any numbers to this frontier, inevitably pull the white man down to their level. The migration of whites to Oregon would be discouraged by the presence of Negro slave laborers. Disclaiming sympathy with "abolition agitators," Williams asked if it was not "the true policy of Oregon to keep as clear as possible of negroes, and all the exciting questions of negro servitude."[70] Williams expressed the conservative attitude of the settlers in the Pacific Northwest toward the problem of slavery. By avoiding the Negro altogether, he thought, they could

[68] O. Dickinson to Adams, March 9, 1857, Oregon City *Oregon Argus,* March 21, 1857.

[69] One Oregon pioneer wrote, "Missouri will have a worse time of it in trying to force her laws upon oregonians then she did in kansas there is no country more favurably for slaves to make their escape from their masters than oregon and there is plenty of us that is not to good to assist them in getting away if they should make it a slave state" (Wilson M. Tigard to James and Nancy Winn, June 28, 1857, Dorsey D. Jones, ed. "Two Letters by a Pioneer from Arkansas," *OHQ,* XLV [Sept., 1944], 235).

[70] George H. Williams to the Editor, Salem *Oregon Statesman,* July 28, 1857. The letter has been reprinted in "The 'Free State Letter' of Judge George H. Williams," *OHQ,* IX (Sept., 1908), 254-273.

avert the vexing problems of Negro slavery. Although not opposed to slavery elsewhere, Williams opposed it in Oregon on social and economic grounds. Like his neighboring frontiersmen, he denied sympathy with those who viewed slavery as a moral question. The appearance of Williams' letter caused free state men in the territory to be jubilant and, since it emanated from an influential Democrat, cast no little gloom in the proslavery camp.[71]

To assist in the fight for a free state, the Republicans again attempted to organize in the early spring of 1857. Calling themselves the "Free State Republicans," the group met at Albany and passed resolutions deploring the extension of slavery over any area that was then free. A committee was appointed to draft an address to the people of Oregon reviewing the history of the slavery question from the 1780's to the present in order to prove that the founding fathers were at heart opposed to slavery.[72] A month later a similar group gathered at Eugene, resolving to confine its activities "to the sole and single object of making Oregon a free state, as the best and only means of securing it to the white race."[73] The editor of the *Oregonian* again scoffed at these efforts, apparently unwilling to admit that the Whig party was dead. Dryer remarked, "The gentlemen who composed the convention seemed to have imagined themselves the first *advanced guard* who have ever had the courage to assault the citadel of the Salem dynasty, or who dare strike for freedom."[74]

As the time for the meeting of the constitutional convention approached, the *Statesman* reiterated its stand in favor of a free state. In a statement that undoubtedly expressed the sentiments of many Oregonians, the editor wrote:

> In arriving at this conclusion we are not influenced by hostility to the institution of African slavery, *per se*. We are of the opinion that in the sugar and cotton growing States it is a necessary, if not indispensable system of labor. We believe, also, that the African, whatever his *nominal* condition, is destined to be the servant and subordinate of the superior white race, and that it is best for both races that that servitude and subordination should be regulated by law. And we believe, also, that the wisdom of man has not yet devised a system

[71] James M. Pyle to Matthew P. Deady, August 4, 1857, Deady Papers. Pyle asked Deady, also a territorial justice, "to demolish the alpine mountain of *highflanuten* and *poppycock* which your honourable associate has oiled up to frighten the little fishes with."

[72] Oregon City *Oregon Argus*, February 21, April 11, 1857.

[73] Portland *Weekly Oregonian*, April 11, 1857.

[74] *Ibid.*, February 21, 1857.

under which the negro is as well off as he is under that of American slavery. Still, we think that our climate, soil, situation, population, &c., render it, to any *useful* extent, an *impossible* institution for Oregon.[75]

In the meantime the proslavery advocates had not been idle. Many of the immigrants to Oregon from the border slave states were generally favorable to slavery. Most of them followed agricultural pursuits and thought that slaves would be feasible in Oregon as farm hands and household servants. Some took a national point of view, being anxious to preserve a political equilibrium between the slave states and the free states. "Those who favored slavery talked loud and made a good deal of noise," wrote George H. Williams, which gave their group the illusion of greater strength than it actually had.[76]

The proslavery forces took full advantage of the *Statesman's* offer to print signed articles and letters concerning the slavery question. Their arguments, like those of their opponents, were based entirely on considerations of utility. One of the strongest arguments concerned the shortage of farm labor in Oregon. The mining rushes had reduced the labor supply of the Pacific Northwest; at the same time, the existence of the mines created a ready market for agricultural produce. This situation prevailed during the California gold rush and during the later rush to southern Oregon.[77] After 1855, the northern mining areas were opened up, and for the next decade mining dominated the economic life of the Northwest. White labor, it was noted, went to the mines immediately upon its arrival in the Pacific Northwest. Thus, although the demand for agricultural produce was greater than before, the available supply of labor to work the farms had dwindled. Many farmers concluded that the answer lay in the introduction of slave labor. One Yamhill County settler maintained that without slave labor Oregon could not advance to "that high destiny which labor would bring her in a few short years." Most of the settlers, he noted, had 640 acres of land; the high price of labor had caused the value of these farms to decrease. This farmer was convinced that slavery was the only means

[75] Salem *Oregon Statesman*, August 4, 1857.
[76] George H. Williams to George H. Himes, August 26, 1907, in Charles H. Carey, "The Creation of Oregon as a State," *OHQ*, XXVII (March, 1926), 9.
[77] George H. Atkinson to Josiah Little, October 20, 1851; May 9, 1856, George H. Atkinson Papers, Henry E. Huntington Library (microfilm in the University of Washington Library).

for obtaining an adequate supply of labor.[78] One other settler argued that, "if labor does pay, would not slave labor, which is always at hand subject to your call, be better than labor hired, (when you can get it) at a high price, and liable to 'stampede,' no matter what may be the emergency, at the first appearance of the gold fever?"[79]

Other arguments were advanced by the proslavery men. The productivity of Oregon and the mildness of climate would considerably improve the condition of slaves that might be brought to this region. The work would also be lighter than in the Southern slave states. "One plowing in the summer season," one of them wrote, "will make an average yield of from thirty to forty bushels of grain per acre; so the negro would only have to do one half of the labor in Oregon that he would in any of the States east of the mountains, which would materially lighten his burden." As soon as slave labor was no longer profitable, the slaves might be emancipated by state action.[80] In answer to those who claimed that the climate of Oregon was not suitable to slavery, it was demonstrated that Oregon's climate was similar to that of Missouri, Kentucky, or Virginia. Negroes, according to the argument, were almost "amphibious" in their native country, "exposed to rain in winter, and spending a large portion of their time in water in summer. Rain and sun alike appear to have no terrors to the negro. The heat and drought of our summers are just what they like, while during our winters they would be in their almost native element."[81]

The proslavery faction enjoyed the support of several prominent political leaders in the territory. Joseph Lane, the leader and idol of the Oregon Democracy, was reported to have campaigned at several locations in Oregon in favor of slavery.[82] Stephen F. Chadwick, a native of Connecticut and a local Democratic politician from southern Oregon, advocated the introduction of slavery into Oregon, "contrary to his instincts."[83] Perhaps the most prominent proslavery advocate in the territory was Matthew P. Deady, an associate justice of the territorial supreme court. Maryland-born and Ohio-bred,

[78] F. B. Martin to Asahel Bush, July 12, 1857, Salem *Oregon Statesman,* August 4, 1857.
[79] J. W. Mack, "State Constitution," Salem *Oregon Statesman,* August 18, 1857.
[80] Martin to Bush, July 12, 1857, Salem *Oregon Statesman,* August 4, 1857.
[81] Mack, "State Constitution," Salem *Oregon Statesman,* August 18, 1857.
[82] Deady to Bush, July 14, 1857, Bush Papers.
[83] Addison C. Gibbs to Deady, February 3, 1857, Addison C. Gibbs Papers, Oregon Historical Society Library.

Deady was outspoken in his support of slavery. Deady's arguments revealed his legalistic turn of mind. Negroes, he maintained, were recognized as property by law, as much as horses or cattle or land; it was the duty of the government to protect its citizens in the possession of their property, not to teach or compel them to own this or that kind of property.

> If a Citizen of Virginia [Deady wrote] can lawfully own a Negro (of which there is no doubt) then I a citizen of Oregon can lawfully obtain the same right of property in this Negro, by either purchase or inheritance, and am as much entitled to the protection of Government in Oregon as Virginia.

He believed that a discussion of the profitability of Negro slavery in Oregon was begging the question and had no connection with the right of every individual in Oregon to own slaves. Slavery, he thought, could be made profitable; "yet if it would not pay a shirt and a pair of shoes to the hand per annum, it would not affect the question of the individual right pro or con, because the question of profit and loss is for each man to determine for himself." Deady phrased his proslavery arguments in Jeffersonian terms. By the introduction of slavery into Oregon, he wrote, agricultural pursuits would be made more attractive, the bulk of the population would remain tillers of the soil, and the drift to the cities would be checked. "All that is necessary to carry the question," he concluded, "is to have it properly understood."[84]

Benjamin Simpson, a close friend of Deady and several times a member of the territorial legislature, expressed a strong preference for slavery in Oregon. In a letter to Deady, he summarized the arguments in favor of slavery:

> . . . in the first place when we become a State we must take our place in the Union of States either with the North or South. Then in that case we wish to be Identified with the Southern Liberalist, and not with the Northern Fenatics. and again I am of the opinion that the perpetuity of our Glorious Union greatly depends upon the position we take in Oregon upon that vexed question, as the South has not nor never will interfere with the institutions of the North while the North would crush the South if they had the power. then let us come up and do Battle on the Side of Justice, and again as in all probability under a free constitution we cannot prevent free negroes comeing to Oregon let us have them Slaves and we can control them
>
> and as it regards Slave labour paying in oregon I am of the opinion that a

[84] Deady to Benjamin Simpson, July 28, 1857, Deady Papers.

reasonable number would pay a fair per cent as it would enable the Farmer to work on a much surer bases he would then be able to raise wheat for fifty cents per Bushel while he can not now afford to raise it for one dollar this is oweing to our being as it were almost surrounded by an extensive Mining Country. . . . and there is an other matter that Strikes me very sensible and that is that the white Females of oregon are very weakly and those of them that have charge of Families are greater Slaves if possible than the affricans in the South as it is the next thing to an impossibility to hire girls to assist them . . . now this is oweing to the scarcety of girls which will always be the case, where they Marry as young as they do in oregon and this is oweing to some extent to there being Such a great disproportion in numbers of the two sexes.[85]

At least one person in Oregon threatened to vote for a slave state merely because he feared the Republican leadership a free state might bring.[86]

As the leading proslavery advocate in Oregon Territory, Matthew P. Deady received several appeals from his political friends. Simpson warned him that the friends of slavery should be "up and doing" if they expected to carry their measure in the constitutional convention and expressed confidence in Deady's ability to present the slavery question "to the entire satisfaction of all unprejudiced minds."[87] The appearance of Judge Williams' "Free State Letter" caused further anxiety in the proslavery camp. Although one of Deady's friends considered Williams' argument as having little force with the "honest yeomanry," he nevertheless expected Deady to become the champion of the "noble, Union loving, law abiding south . . . in defiance of all opposition" and to "hurl back these living lies into the teeth and eyes of those who would give them vitality; and to vindicate the justice and righteousness of her time honored and Heaven favored institutions." His friends promised to stand by him "with a real 'Border Ruffian' fidelity."[88]

All the proslavery advocates in Oregon Territory, at least those who were vocal, were members of the Democratic party. Several of them were important cogs in the local Democratic machine. Not all Democrats, however, favored slavery; as a matter of fact, the majority

[85] Benjamin Simpson to Deady, June 22, 1857, Deady Papers.

[86] Wilson M. Tigard to James and Nancy Winn, June 28, 1857, Jones, ed. "Two Letters by a Pioneer from Arkansas," p. 235.

[87] Simpson to Deady, June 22, 1857, Deady Papers. It is interesting that both Simpson and Deady became Republicans and strong supporters of the Union during the Civil War.

[88] James M. Pyle to Deady, August 4, 1857, Deady Papers.

of them opposed slavery in Oregon.[89] In spite of this free-soil element, the party found itself struggling against the popular notion that it was a proslavery party, an idea that was played up with considerable force by members of the opposition. This association was based partly on some utterances of the Democrats themselves. Joseph Lane, for example, maintained in a speech at Winchester, Oregon, that it was doubtful whether a man could be a good Democrat and vote against slavery. Other Democratic politicians remained silent on the subject for fear their chances for official position in a state government would be injured by taking sides. Even some members of the rank and file felt that a free state Democrat was but an abolitionist under a different name.[90]

The territorial Democratic party attempted to dispel this notion. Free state Democrats particularly objected to the association of their party with the proslavery agitation. At the same time, they were very careful to avoid an endorsement of the Republican position on the slavery question. One Democrat wrote that nothing in either the Kansas-Nebraska Act or the Cincinnati platform of the national Democratic party could be interpreted, "without doing violence to language," as favoring slavery over freedom. He went on to note that "a man can favor slavery, and be a good Democrat, or he can oppose slavery, that is, *in a proper manner,* and be a good democrat." The difference between a Democrat and a Free-Soiler was apparently one of degree; "for a man to oppose the introduction of slavery into Oregon . . . by no means makes him a free-soiler, but if he opposed its introduction into any and all new Territory, he would undoubtedly be a free-soiler."[91]

This problem of guilt by association became so serious that official pronouncements by the Democratic organizations in the territory

[89] Prominent among those Democrats who opposed slavery was Addison C. Gibbs, an attorney and member of the territorial legislature from Umpqua County. He opposed slavery both on principle and because he could never be elected to office if he favored it. One of his principal arguments against slavery seems to have been that Daniel Webster had said, "God had decided it could not flourish" (Gibbs to Deady, February 3, June 23, 1857, Gibbs Papers; Gibbs, Notes on the History of Oregon, MS in the Bancroft Library [microfilm in the University of Washington Library], pp. 16-17) .

[90] Deady to Bush, July 14, 1857, Bush Papers; Williams to Himes, August 26, 1907, Carey, "Creation of Oregon as a State," p. 9; Jackson Cooley to the Editor, October 2, 1857, Salem *Oregon Statesman,* October 13, 1857.

[91] "W. J.," Lane County, to the Editor, Salem *Oregon Statesman,* March 31, 1857. Italics mine.

were deemed necessary. The Lane County Democratic convention, meeting at Eugene City in April, 1857, declared that the Democratic party was not a proslavery party, but contended "that slave-holders have equal rights in the Territories with their northern brethren." The convention recognized that many Democrats might wish to see Oregon a free state; it warned them, however, that in voting for their favorite measure "they guard against affiliating with, or in any way countenancing that contention-loving, union-hating party called the Black Republican party." Similar resolutions were approved by the Polk County Democrats. Democrats meeting in Marion County declared that the Democratic party, being a national party, allowed its members

> to hold such opinion as [they] think proper, as to the advantages of slavery, in the localities where they respectively reside, and therefore no Democrat['s] views as to the practicability or expediency of negro servitude in the future State of Oregon, can, or ought to be made a test question of his Democracy.

The final word came from the territorial Democratic convention, which resolved that

> each member of the Democratic party in Oregon may freely speak and act according to his individual convictions of right and policy upon the question of slavery in Oregon, without in any manner impairing his standing in the Democratic party on that account, Provided, That nothing in these resolutions shall be construed in toleration of Black Republicanism, Abolitionism, or any other faction or organization arrayed in opposition to the Democratic party.[92]

This problem and the Democratic attempts to solve it evoked ridicule from the antislavery Republican camp. "O what wondrous liberty that a democrat may freely speake act and think upon the slavery question without impairing his standing as a Democrat," wrote one Republican.[93]

Interest in Oregon's forthcoming decision on slavery was felt beyond the boundaries of the Pacific Northwest. As the time for the meeting of the constitutional convention approached, several Eastern newspapers expressed genuine concern over Oregon's future status. Horace Greeley, apparently influenced by the arguments of Oregon's proslavery element, was convinced that Oregon would legalize slavery. The triumph of Buchanan in 1856, Greeley thought, was

[92] Salem *Oregon Statesman*, April 14, 21, 1857.
[93] Tigard to James and Nancy Winn, June 28, 1857, Jones, ed. "Two Letters by a Pioneer from Arkansas," p. 233.

the victory of slavery extension. Since many of Oregon's residents had migrated from slave states, he was certain a proslavery constitution would be adopted. Many who opposed slavery, he thought, would vote for it merely to spite the Republicans. Greeley considered the importation of Negroes into Oregon impractical and unprofitable but thought that Oregonians might soon reduce the Indian population to slavery. The antislavery forces had lost Kansas by force, he concluded; now they were losing Oregon by stealth.[94] The editor of the New York *Commercial Advertiser* saw a larger significance in the action Oregon was about to take. He wrote:

> If Oregon, where there is not the least necessity for slave labor, and where in fact the African slave can never be profitably employed, elects to become a slave State, where is the security that other territories, now deemed ineligible for slave labor and forever devoted to free labor, will not follow her example? Or that states now free may not so amend their constitutions as to open themselves to slavery? The moral effect upon the cause of freedom of Oregon becoming a slave State would be disastrous in the extreme, for the unavoidable inference would be that however loud the professions of attachment to freedom may be, no inconsiderable number of those who make such professions, belie them when sheltered by the secrecy of the ballot-box.[95]

The Pacific correspondent of the Washington *Era* discussed at length the problem of slavery in the Pacific Northwest. Oregon, he wrote, was the scene of a "long and undisturbed plot of Missouri Democracy" in favor of a proslavery constitution. He went on:

> A large proportion of the inhabitants of Oregon are emigrants from Western Missouri. The hatred of these people for the dark races, mixed with the hope of plunder and prospect of speculation, have led to those infamous aggressions on the rights of the weaker, denominated Indian wars.

He concluded with a suggestion that must have startled even the antislavery people in the Pacific Northwest; he urged the formation of emigrant aid societies to keep slavery out of Oregon.[96]

On August 17, 1857, the constitutional convention assembled at Salem. Freedom and slavery were the only questions which excited the least interest among the members.[97] Matthew P. Deady, the only

---

[94] *New York Tribune*, [n. d.], quoted in Salem *Oregon Statesman*, June 9, 1857.
[95] New York *Commercial Advertiser*, [n. d.], quoted in Salem *Oregon Statesman*, June 9, 1857.
[96] "E. B. K." to the Editor, Washington *Era*, [n. d.], quoted in Salem *Oregon Statesman*, June 9, 1857.
[97] Thomas J. Dryer to the *Oregonian*, August 17, 1857, Portland *Weekly Oregonian*, August 22, 1857.

member who had campaigned for election on a proslavery platform, was elected president of the convention. The majority of the members were Democrats, and by means of a party caucus they succeeded in naming most of the officers of the convention as well as the committee heads. Although an attempt was made to write a slavery prohibition into the constitution,[98] most of the members were reluctant to be responsible for a decision of the issue. Consequently it was agreed almost from the first that the question of slavery would be submitted to the electorate as a separate schedule. Jesse Applegate, a member of the convention, made an unsuccessful attempt to declare all discussion of the slavery question out of order. Both parties agreed that the slavery question was the most important question then agitating the public mind and that nothing would be gained by stifling a discussion of it.[99] The question of allowing free Negroes to settle in Oregon was closely linked in the discussions with that of slavery, and it was finally decided to refer this issue to the voters also as a separate schedule.

The failure of the convention to assume responsibility over these issues inspired the proslavery group to renew its activity. In Corvallis, the *Occidental Messenger,* a newspaper published by one of the early Willamette Valley settlers, Joseph C. Avery, was dedicated to the introduction of slavery into Oregon. According to the paper, slavery in Oregon would be followed by unlimited prosperity. Only the barrier of free state Republicanism, "that enemy to human advancement, that destroyer of the peace of the Union," stood in the way of this prosperity. The production of wheat, hemp, flax, and Chinese sugar cane would attract many small slaveholders from the Southern states; their slaves would insure a permanent labor supply in the Northwest. The high price of labor and its scarcity were detrimental to the development of Oregon agriculture. This was, according to the paper, the "strong argument in favor of slavery."[100] J. W. Mack, a proslavery member of the territorial legislature, strongly urged the adoption of slavery in Oregon. Armed with a Biblical justification of slavery, he maintained that white labor

[98] Charles H. Carey, ed. *The Oregon Constitution and Proceedings and Debates of the Constitutional Convention of 1857* (Salem, 1926), p. 328; John R. McBride, "The Oregon Constitutional Convention, 1857," *Proceedings of the Oregon Historical Society, 1902-1905* (Salem, 1906), p. 33.

[99] Carey, ed. *The Oregon Constitution . . .*, pp. 79, 81-82.

[100] Corvallis *Occidental Messenger,* September 26, 1857.

would be treated with dignity and respect only if slavery were introduced.[101] A future governor of Oregon, John Whiteaker, expressed the fear that a free constitution would "abolitionize" the Pacific Northwest.[102] The newspaper supported the view that a Democrat could not favor a free state and still remain a Democrat; that a free state Democrat and a "Black Republican" were but two names for the same thing.[103]

As the election approached, the proslavery forces took an extreme position. Charles E. Pickett, one of the more vocal of proslavery men, urged that a convention be called whether slavery was accepted or rejected in order to effect a separate organization "that will insure to this party the balance of power in Oregon." Pickett called on those who favored slavery to stick together and to vote only for those who favored their creed, even if by so doing they were to insure the election of a "Black Republican."[104]

In early November, 1857, the voters of Oregon approved the proposed state constitution by a decisive margin. At the same time slavery was excluded, 7,727 to 2,645, and free Negroes were prohibited from settling in Oregon, 8,640 to 1,081.[105] The proslavery vote, compared to the amount of agitation that had emanated from the proslavery camp, made the whole affair seem like a tempest in a teapot. The electorate wanted none of the Negro race; free Negroes were barred from Oregon by an even greater majority than slavery. Although the small proslavery vote may have come as a surprise to some, it was rather accurately predicted by members of the free state wing of the Democratic party.[106]

[101] J. W. Mack, "Slavery in Oregon," Corvallis *Occidental Messenger,* October 17, 1857.

[102] John Whiteaker to the Editor, *Occidental Messenger,* quoted in Salem *Oregon Statesman,* October 27, 1857. Bush answered Whiteaker's fears by assuring him that abolitionism would burn out from its own excesses long before it could reach Oregon. The only way Oregon could be abolitionized, Bush declared, "would be by her voting for slavery by such a small majority as would not settle the question, leaving a large minority to agitate the amendment of the constitution."

[103] Salem *Oregon Statesman,* August 25, 1857.

[104] Letters from Charles E. Pickett to the *Occidental Messenger,* quoted in Salem *Oregon Statesman,* November 10, 1857.

[105] The complete returns are reprinted in Woodward, *Rise and Early History of Political Parties in Oregon, 1843-1868,* Appendix I.

[106] Ralph Wilcox to Deady, November 20, 1857, Deady Papers; Bush to Deady, November 8, 1857, Walls, ed. *Letters of Asahel Bush to Matthew P. Deady,* p. 147. Bush warned against misinterpreting the results of the vote, declaring that a majority of the voters were sound, constitutional men—"let not black republican-

The election results reflected the underlying anti-Negro bias in the Pacific Northwest. The people in Oregon had no desire to furnish a refuge for the Negro in any condition, intending to build up their state on a white basis. One of the members of the constitutional convention, John R. McBride, justified this feeling: "We were building a new state on virgin ground; its people believed it should encourage only the best elements to come to us, and discourage others." The presence in Oregon of many "poor whites" was also a determining factor. Hating slavery, this class hated the free Negro even more; their sentiment could be expressed in the statement, "If we must have negroes among us let them be slaves."[107] Many Northern newspapers denounced this decision of the Oregon voters as "inhuman and oppressive." The *Statesman* came to the defense by pointing out that the wisdom of the course "is abundantly vindicated by the experience of those States where free negroes are tolerated."[108]

Oregon's decision on the slavery question was considered a triumph of the principles of the Kansas-Nebraska Act. Oregonians were particularly proud that they had been able to solve the question by means of popular sovereignty without resorting to the bloodshed that characterized Kansas' struggle for statehood.[109] They expressed confidence in the speedy admission of the territory into the Union as a state.

This confidence proved unjustified, for Oregon's admission was anything but speedy. Oregon found itself involved once again in the national struggle over slavery. In Congress, Oregon's statehood bill was linked for a time with that of Kansas. The Republicans viewed the struggle as a political contest with Kansas and Oregon as the stakes, and announced their intention to oppose Oregon's statehood bill until the Democrats should relent in their stand on Kansas. Certain parts of the Oregon constitution, notably the restriction on free Negroes, aroused controversy in Congress. The

ism lay the flattering unction to its soul that we are free soilish here" (Salem *Oregon Statesman*, November 17, 1857).

[107] John R. McBride, "Annual Address," *Transactions of the Oregon Pioneer Association*, 1897, p. 42; LaFayette Grover, Notable Things in a Public Life in Oregon, MS in the Bancroft Library (microfilm in the University of Washington Library), p. 54; Applegate, Views of Oregon History, p. 71.

[108] Salem *Oregon Statesman*, November 9, 1858.

[109] Salem *Oregon Statesman*, November 17, 1857; Joseph Lane to LaFayette Grover, January 31, 1858, Salem *Oregon Statesman*, March 16, 1858.

Southern Democrats were reluctant to add another free state to the union, while the Republicans were loath to admit a state that promised to be Democratic in politics. For a while it looked as if Oregon's bid for statehood would be rejected. In February, 1859, however, the statehood bill was passed by the narrowest of margins and Oregon took its place in the Union.[110]

The proslavery agitation in Oregon, however, died hard. While Congress debated the admission of Oregon to statehood, efforts were renewed in the territorial legislature to legalize slavery in Oregon Territory. Many of the proslavery advocates thought that, if slavery were legalized in the territory, Congress would reject Oregon's free state constitution, giving them another opportunity to push through a slave constitution. Consequently there was an urgency about this new movement; slavery must be legalized before Congress admitted Oregon.

Hardly a month after the election in which slavery had been decisively defeated, William Allen of Yamhill County asked for the appointment of a committee "to report what legislation is necessary to protect the rights of persons holding slaves in the Territory."[111] In the event that Congress should reject Oregon's bid for statehood, Allen pointed out, the area would remain a territory for a long time. By the enaction of legislation to protect slave property, immigration would be encouraged. Allen's resolution touched off a protracted debate among the members of the lower house. Several of them objected to the question's being introduced at all, since it had been settled in the election of the previous month. J. W. Mack refused to accept this as a criterion. He flatly asserted that there were men in the territory who owned slaves; these men, he declared, should be protected in their slave property even if this protection should cease the day Oregon became a state. Other members testified to the existence of slaves in Oregon; one of them predicted that Oregon's slave population would be doubled before another year was out. The majority of the members, however, felt that further discussion of the slavery question was useless. Allen's resolution was indefinitely postponed.[112] Less than a month later, however, Allen renewed his

---

110 Henry H. Simms, "The Controversy over the Admission of Oregon," *Mississippi Valley Historical Review*, XXXII (March, 1946) , 355-374.

111 Territory of Oregon, *House Journal*, 1857-1858 (Salem, 1858) , pp. 51-53.

112 Portland *Weekly Oregonian*, December 26, 1857; Territory of Oregon, *House Journal*, 1857-1858, p. 53.

efforts. In early January, 1858, he presented a petition to the legislature, signed by forty-seven residents of Yamhill County, asking for the protection of slave property.[113] The petition was followed in a few days by a formal bill. Mack expressed the hope that the bill would not be gagged, especially since it applied to the most valuable type of property in the territory.[114] Debate continued, during the course of which Allen stated that there were Negro slaves in Benton, Lane, Polk, and Yamhill counties.[115] Toward the end of the session, a vote was taken and the bill was lost. Thomas J. Dryer reported that the bill had "kicked up quite a stir" among the Democrats.[116]

Agitation reappeared in the following session of the territorial legislature. Early in January, 1859, W. W. Chapman, a representative from Lane County, and William G. T'Vault, of Jackson County, presented four petitions from citizens of Lane County, Clackamas County, and others, asking for the recognition of slave property in Oregon.[117] The petitions were referred to the judiciary committee, of which Chapman was chairman. Two days later he submitted a bill, accompanied by a report confirming the right, as established by the Dred Scott decision, of slaveholders to be secure in their property in the territories of the United States.[118] This bill, like the earlier one, failed to pass. The position of the territorial legislature during this session was an anomalous one. The first state elections had been held, and the state government had actually been put into operation for a brief period. When it was learned that Congress had not yet admitted Oregon, the territorial legislature was convened. The knowledge that this was probably the last session of the territorial legislature gave the efforts of the proslavery faction a "now or never" character.

While the subject was debated in the territorial legislature, the

[113] Petition of Mr. Crisp & Other Citizens of Yamhill, In Relation to Slavery, Oregon Provisional and Territorial Government Papers, Oregon State Archives (microfilm in the Oregon Historical Society Library), #9152.

[114] Portland *Weekly Oregonian,* January 16, 1858; Oregon Provisional and Territorial Government Papers, #8661

[115] Portland *Weekly Oregonian,* January 30, 1858.

[116] Territory of Oregon, *House Journal,* 1857-1858, p. 270; Portland *Weekly Oregonian,* January 23, 1858.

[117] Territory of Oregon, *House Journal,* 1858-1859 (Salem, 1859), pp. 111, 112, 118; Oregon Provisional and Territorial Government Papers, #10964, 10973, 10974.

[118] Territory of Oregon, *House Journal,* 1858-1859, p. 129; Portland *Weekly Oregonian,* January 15, 1859; Oregon Provisional and Territorial Government Papers, #9671, 11601.

argument continued in the columns of the newspapers. George H.
Williams defended himself against frequent attacks that he was an
abolitionist by emphatically stating his opposition to the Wilmot
Proviso as an outrage upon the rights of the South.[119] Other arguments, both pro and con, were heard from time to time.[120] Agitation
of the subject in its practical relation to the Pacific Northwest ended
with the admission of Oregon as a state in February, 1859.

[119] Two letters, George H. Williams to the Portland *Standard,* quoted in Salem
Oregon Statesman, November 9, 23, 1858. Williams claimed that his "Free State
Letter" merely tried to prove that "in a country situated like Oregon, thousands
of miles from slaveholding states, with a divided public sentiment, with all the
unfavorable circumstances of position, climate and productions . . . slavery would
be an impracticable, unprofitable and troublesome institution." Williams had no
objections to slavery in general but opposed its introduction into Oregon.

[120] Corvallis *Oregon Weekly Union,* April 2, 1859; Eugene *People's Press,* October 1, 1859; Oregon City *Oregon Argus,* February 19, 1859.

> *seeds of*
> *political discord*

THE ADMISSION OF OREGON TO
statehood in February, 1859, marked a turning point in local Pacific
Northwest politics. Prior to that time, local politics had been characterized by factional struggles. National issues often played a role
in the local election campaigns, but the underlying political drive
was generally a simple struggle for power. After Oregon became a
state, however, the local political parties became increasingly involved in the issues of national politics. By the end of the decade,
the chaotic party situation that marked national politics during the
fifties was reflected on the local scene. The party divisions in the
Pacific Northwest conformed more closely to the national political
groupings.

At the same time, there were significant differences between local
and national political alignments and issues, particularly with respect to the Republican party in Oregon, which adopted a position
contrary to that of the national party. The increasing intensity of
the sectional controversy during the decade, particularly as manifested in the split between President Buchanan and Senator Stephen
A. Douglas, contributed to the national orientation of Pacific
Northwest political activity. Popular sovereignty, an issue that was
considered to be of local as well as national significance, continued

to dominate the political discussions. Although popular sovereignty had no practical importance in Oregon after 1857, when the slavery question was settled by the electorate, it remained as a matter of principle with the pioneers, who earnestly recommended it as the most equitable solution of the sectional controversy.

Both the similarities and the differences between political alignments and issues in the Northwest and those in the nation at large were revealed in the campaign and election of 1860. The presidential election of 1860 was considered the final test between the rival sections, and many, both in the Pacific Northwest and in the nation, hoped that it would result in a peaceful resolution of the sectional grievances. As early as 1858, the settlers in the Pacific Northwest began looking forward to this significant election. The lines of division manifested in the presidential election of 1860 had their roots deep in the local political struggles of the 1850's.

The Democratic party, the first to organize in the Pacific Northwest, remained the dominant political group in the region until the outbreak of the Civil War. Several fortunate circumstances contributed to its early organization and its rapid increase in strength. These same circumstances, however, provided the seeds of discord that wrecked the party by 1860. Democratic party organization had been encouraged by Oregon's first territorial governor, Joseph Lane.[1] Lane was a strong Democrat, experienced in the ways of party politics, a Mexican War hero and a frontiersman. This happy combination endeared him to the territorial settlers. Lane's removal from office in 1850 by the Whig president, Zachary Taylor, caused widespread resentment in the territory. This resentment increased when Taylor's choice for the governorship arrived in the territory. John P. Gaines, a pompous individual with an exalted opinion of his own importance, was the antithesis of Lane. Lane's popularity continued; following his removal as governor, he was elected to four terms as territorial delegate. In 1859, he became one of Oregon's first United States Senators.

Democratic party doctrines were popular on the frontier and contributed in large measure to party strength in the Pacific Northwest. The most important doctrine was popular sovereignty, interpreted in the Northwest to mean full and complete territorial self-govern-

[1] Joseph Lane to William M. King, August 16, 1852, Joseph Lane Papers, Oregon Historical Society Library.

ment. Even before the principle was defined by the national Congress in the Kansas-Nebraska Act, the Democratic party in Oregon Territory had agitated for a revision of the traditional "territorial system" in the direction of greater self-government. This movement appealed to all elements of society regardless of party background, thus bringing increased support to the territorial Democratic party. When the Kansas-Nebraska Act passed in 1854, it was hailed as a first step in the realization of the frontier demands. It became a Democratic party issue locally as well as nationally. The opposition found itself in an embarrassing position; endorsing the popular sovereignty features of the bill, it concentrated its attacks against the repeal of the Missouri Compromise. As a result, many Whigs drifted into the Democratic party.[2]

The Democratic party was further strengthened because of an issue of strictly local significance, the struggle over the location of the territorial capital. In 1850, the territorial legislature, dominated by Democrats, passed an act removing the capital from Oregon City to Salem and locating the territorial penitentiary and university. The Whig Governor Gaines immediately declared the law in violation of the territorial organic act and consequently null and void. His action was considered an unwarranted interference by the executive in the legislative processes; technically, the territorial governor had no control over the actions of the legislature. The fact that the governor was a Whig made the decision all the more onerous to a majority of the settlers. By the time the legislature met again in December, 1851, the controversy had become a major issue in local politics. The great majority of the legislature, all the Democrats and a few Whigs, met at Salem, while the remaining Whig members gathered at Oregon City. The question was submitted to the United States attorney general, who decided in favor of Governor Gaines. Congress, however, at the suggestion of Joseph Lane, countered with a resolution approving the removal of the capital. By thus opposing the appointed governor, the Democratic party enhanced its local reputation as the "watchdog" of territorial rights.[3]

One of the important reasons for the continued strength and

[2] Joseph N. Prescott to Lane, July 25, 1854, Lane Papers; Salem *Oregon Statesman,* April 4, December 26, 1854, January 16, 1855; Portland *Weekly Oregonian,* May 13, 1854, February 17, 1855.

[3] Charles H. Carey, *A General History of Oregon, Prior to 1861* (2 vols.; Portland, 1935-36), II, 470-473.

leadership of the Democratic party in Oregon Territory during the 1850's was the efficient and dictatorial control over the party's policies and membership that was exercised by a small, close-knit group of individuals known as the "Salem Clique." Clustered about Oregon's first and "official" Democratic newspaper, the *Oregon Statesman,* and recognizing the leadership of its editor, Asahel Bush, this group exercised a "benevolent despotism" over the rank and file of the territorial Democratic party.[4] The role of the "Salem Clique" in early Oregon politics has often been the subject of controversy. Because of its dictatorial methods, it has sometimes been described in abusive terms. One historian pictured the rule of the "Clique" as ruthless and coercive, maintained only by "befogging the real issues, by denouncing the opposition, [and] by threatening and abusing the recalcitrant."[5] A contemporary, however, looking back at the "Clique" over a distance of forty years, concluded that the rule of the "Clique" was "a good one for the masses of the people."[6] This group of local party politicians retained an effective hold on the Democratic party throughout most of Oregon's territorial period. The relationship of Joseph Lane to the "Clique" is not entirely clear. Lane at first seemed subservient to the dictates of the "Clique." He held one trump card, however, which the "Clique" was forced to respect—his great personal popularity with the settlers on this frontier.

The very circumstances that brought the Democratic party to a position of unchallenged leadership in territorial politics early in the decade also contributed to its decline in the years just before the crucial presidential election in 1860. The first signs of discord in the party ranks appeared during the struggle over the location of the territorial capital. Although slight and of little consequence at the time, these signs nevertheless forecast future party dissension. Early in 1853, Asahel Bush warned the readers of his newspaper against aiding and abetting a party split. A small group of Democrats, calling themselves "national Democrats," objected to the use of the capital controversy as a party measure and preferred to base their

---

[4] Walter C. Woodward, *The Rise and Early History of Political Parties in Oregon, 1843-1868* (Portland, 1913), p. 88.

[5] *Ibid.*

[6] John R. McBride, "Annual Address," *Transactions of the Oregon Pioneer Association,* 1897, p. 40. McBride compared the "Clique" to Andrew Jackson's "kitchen cabinet," p. 38.

beliefs on national principles.[7] A few months later, the terms "hards" and "softs" were introduced into the local political vocabulary. A correspondent in Yamhill County, the center of this early "national Democratic" movement, reported that members of this group, calling themselves the "softs," claimed to be the true Democracy.[8] Although this defection was not a matter for serious concern at the time, it was important enough to prompt a letter from Joseph Lane urging that Oregon's Democratic party remain united and avoid factional difficulties such as were then plaguing the party in New York State.[9]

More significant to the future of the Democratic party in Oregon was the growing dissatisfaction with the leadership of the "Salem Clique." Linked with this was a mounting hostility among the local party leaders toward Lane. The small group of "national Democrats," or "softs," began attracting Democrats who were too independent to submit to the dictates of the "Clique." Other individuals, motivated by a jealousy of the stranglehold which the "Clique" held on the local territorial offices, joined the defection. One Democratic member of the territorial legislature, James F. Gazley, was literally read out of the party in 1855 for having opposed the "Clique"-sponsored viva-voce election law.[10] Gazley became a leading member of the "national Democratic" faction. In the same year, the "softs" attempted to wrest control of the office of territorial delegate from the "Clique." In the Democratic convention, where the two factions were represented, the name of Orville C. Pratt, one of Oregon Territory's first associate justices and an ambitious local politician, was placed in nomination by the dissenting group. The "Clique" forces were marshaled behind the more popular Lane, and Pratt was swamped.[11]

[7] Oregon City *Oregon Statesman*, February 19, 1853. See also *ibid.*, March 5, 1853, for a hint that Democrats in Linn County were beginning to separate.

[8] "A Democrat" to the Editor, May 29, 1853, Oregon City *Oregon Statesman*, June 4, 1853.

[9] Joseph Lane to Asahel Bush, December 2, 1853, Asahel Bush Papers, Oregon State Library (photostats in the University of Oregon Library). Lane expressed confidence that "principle should and will . . . hold the democracy together at least on the Pacific side of the Rocky Mountains."

[10] Portland *Weekly Oregonian*, January 13, 1855; Salem *Oregon Statesman*, February 6, 1855. The viva-voce election law provided that the votes at all general elections must be given in an audible voice before the election judges and the voters. It was Bush's way of combating the Know-Nothings who enjoyed a brief popularity at about this time; it was also recognized as an effective weapon for keeping recalcitrant Democrats in line.

[11] Salem *Oregon Statesman*, April 17, 1855.

The split continued to widen in succeeding years. The supremacy of the "Clique," however, was not seriously threatened. The county organizations were controlled by this group, thus depriving the dissenters of a medium for public expression.[12] In 1857, the "Clique" took the initiative in trying to preserve intact the Democratic organization by attempting to slough off the dissatisfied element as so much deadwood and by binding the loyal members of the party with new and more stringent regulations. A caucus of the Democratic members in the territorial legislature met and officially pronounced the *Democratic Standard,* a Portland newspaper that had become the organ of the "national Democrats," as an opposition paper and no longer to be regarded as a spokesman for the Democratic party.[13] The extent of the party split at this time is evidenced by the fact that the resolution barely passed the caucus by a vote of fifteen to twelve. In the following issues of the *Statesman,* Bush denounced those who had opposed the resolution as "bolters" and hence unreliable Democrats.[14]

Further efforts to keep party members in line were made at the territorial Democratic convention that met in April, 1857. The tone of the convention was forecast by the decision of one precinct in Marion County that declared:

> Whereas, there are some persons who profess to belong to the Democratic party, and talk much about the true Democracy, and stigmatize the Democratic party now in power as a "clique"; Resolved, that we recognize none as democrats who do not support with their votes the present Democratic organization, and further, that those who "bolt," or countenance "bolting," should not be recognized as belonging to the regular organization.[15]

An attempt was made by the "national Democrats" to promote the candidacy of James K. Kelly for the delegateship. Kelly, however, declined to run, certain that he could not be elected.[16] Joseph Lane was nominated for his fourth term as delegate by an almost unanimous vote. The territorial convention drew up a long slate of

[12] *Ibid.,* May 27, June 10, 1856.

[13] *Ibid.,* January 27, 1857. The *Democratic Standard* had been founded in July, 1854, with Alonzo Leland as editor. Although Democratic in politics, it opposed the dictation of the "Salem Clique," doubted the advisability of statehood, and opposed slavery.

[14] Salem *Oregon Statesman,* January 27, February 3, 1857.

[15] Resolution of the Labish Precinct, Salem *Oregon Statesman,* March 31, 1857.

[16] Hubert Howe Bancroft, *History of Oregon* (2 vols.; San Francisco, 1890), II, 419.

resolutions, including several designed to prevent further defection from the party line. The fifth resolution

> repudiated the doctrine that a representative or delegate can, in pursuance of the wishes or fancied interests of the district he represents, go into or remain out of a caucus or convention of his party and refuse to support the nominations thereof and still maintain his standing as a democrat.

The sixth resolution declared that those who did assert an independence of the party caucus nominations were to be proscribed as disorganizers and enemies of the party. The seventh resolution made the expulsion of the *Democratic Standard* official. These three resolutions were the only ones that the convention did not pass by a unanimous vote.[17]

The passage of these three resolutions, instead of welding the party into a tighter organization, encouraged those who opposed the "Salem Clique." Following the convention, dissension increased in many of the counties. In Yamhill County, where disaffection was particularly strong, the "national Democrats" called a county convention of their own. They refused to support Lane for the delegateship unless he should repudiate the three controversial resolutions of the territorial convention. A separate legislative ticket was nominated.[18] G. W. Lawson, an independent, free state Democrat, announced his candidacy for the delegateship against Lane, receiving the support not only of the disaffected Democrats but also of the rather motley Whig–Republican–Know-Nothing opposition to the Democratic party. Lane won the election easily.

When the voters in Oregon ratified a state constitution in 1857, they were confident that the next few months would see them in the Union as a state. Steps were immediately taken for the election of a state government. The "national Democrats" planned to participate in this election. During the session of the territorial legislature that followed the ratification of the constitution, the "Salem Clique" received more than its usual share of abuse. One member of the legislature declared: "A political revolution is at your door. It is time for the people of Oregon to declare that this junto shall be put

---

[17] Salem *Oregon Statesman*, April 21, 1857. Some members of the opposition interpreted these resolutions as an attempt to force a slavery clause into Oregon's state constitution. See Wilson M. Tigard to James and Nancy Winn, June 28, 1857, Dorsey D. Jones, ed. "Two Letters by a Pioneer from Arkansas," *OHQ*, XLV (Sept., 1944), 233-234.

[18] Portland *Weekly Oregonian*, May 9, 1857.

down, and they are determined to do it."[19] Under the leadership of
James K. Kelly and James O'Meara, who had assumed the editorship
of the *Democratic Standard,* a new political party was launched,
known as the National Democrats of the State of Oregon. At a
meeting in Portland both O'Meara and Kelly spoke, according to
report, of the "duplicity, mendacity, treachery and arrogance assumed by the Salem *clique* to govern, control and direct the
democracy of Oregon."[20] Bush defended the "Clique" in an editorial
entitled "Good Faith in Politics." According to Bush:

> good faith and common honesty between man and man, as well as the well
> known rules and common usages of the party, dictate that they should abide
> the results openly and fairly arrived at. . . . We believe that a man's presence
> in a political meeting or convention is as good as his bond to secure good faith
> on his part in support of the nominations fairly made by such meeting or
> convention, in which he participates. . . . if he does not wish to abide the
> results of a nominating meeting or convention, no one wishes to see him
> assume the responsibility of taking part in such proceedings.[21]

At a meeting of Linn County Democrats, Delazon Smith sponsored
a resolution denouncing the "miserable, soft faction, self-styled
'National Democrats'" as political enemies.[22] Lane wrote a frantic
letter from Washington, D.C., urging that every effort be made to
heal the breach in the party.[23]

By the spring of 1858, however, separation was complete. Both
wings of the Democratic party scheduled conventions, and each
nominated a full slate of state officers. The breach in the party at
this time was based on issues of strictly local significance. Although
the Democrats had split over the domination of the "Salem Clique,"
both wings were united as far as national policy was concerned. The
fight was simply one between the "ins" and the "outs"—the fundamental issue at stake in this quarrel was who would get the offices.[24]

[19] James H. Slater, a representative from Benton County, Portland *Weekly
Oregonian,* February 6, 1858.

[20] Joseph W. Drew to Matthew P. Deady, January 31, 1858; Delazon Smith to
Deady, February 5, 1858, Matthew P. Deady Papers, Oregon Historical Society
Library; Portland *Weekly Oregonian,* March 13, 1858.

[21] Salem *Oregon Statesman,* March 9, 1858.

[22] Linn County Democratic convention, February 27, 1858, Salem *Oregon
Statesman,* March 16, 1858.

[23] Joseph Lane to Delazon Smith, March 18, 1858, Salem *Oregon Statesman,*
May 11, 1858.

[24] One "national" was disappointed with the platform of the National Democrats, having supposed that the split was one of principle rather than merely for

This picture was soon altered. The Bush faction overlooked one vital circumstance in its struggle against the "bolters"—the role of Joseph Lane.

Joseph Lane, a man of consuming political ambition, was not one to depend for political preferment upon a small group of local party manipulators, nor was he content to be the creature of a political machine he himself could not control. Lane was a born leader and recognized this quality in his character. A man of great principle, he nevertheless exhibited a political self-interest that was common to frontier areas. His efforts were bent toward the attainment of one goal—the elevation of Joseph Lane. Lane possessed all the qualifications for a popular frontier leader. He himself had been a part of the westward movement, born in North Carolina and moving to Kentucky and Indiana at an early age. In Indiana his qualities for political leadership were first recognized. Elected to the state legislature before he was twenty-one years of age, Lane had to wait until after his birthday before taking his seat. He remained in the Indiana state legislature almost continuously for twenty-five years. In 1846, at the outbreak of the Mexican War, Lane enlisted in the army as a private, was shortly thereafter elected colonel of his regiment, promoted to brigadier general, and brevetted major general by the president. He emerged from the war a popular hero, bearing the sobriquet the "Marion of the Mexican War." In 1848, President Polk appointed Lane first governor of Oregon Territory; from that time Lane's political fortunes were wedded with this frontier area. In 1852, he was seriously considered for the nomination for president by the Democratic party and enjoyed a brief role in the nominating convention as Indiana's favorite son.[25]

In Oregon Territory, Lane caught the enthusiasm of the settlers. His short term as governor was a popular one. When he was removed by President Taylor and replaced by a Whig, a wave of indignation swept over the territory, affecting Whigs and Democrats alike. The year following his removal, Lane was elected territorial delegate,

the "spoils of office" ("A Voter" to William L. Adams, [n. d.], Oregon City *Oregon Argus*, April 24, 1858).

[25] Sister M. Margaret Jean Kelly, *The Career of Joseph Lane, Frontier Politician* (Washington, 1942); Eldorah M. Raleigh, "General Joseph E. Lane," *Indiana History Bulletin*, IV (Dec., 1926; suppl.), 71-82. Of interest is the campaign biography of Lane written in 1852 when for a time he was considered a "dark horse" for the nomination for president ("Western," pseud. *Biography of Joseph Lane* [Washington, 1852]; "Western" has been identified as Robert Dale Owen).

receiving over 80 per cent of the total vote cast. He was re-elected to this office in 1853, 1855, and 1857, each time receiving more than 60 per cent of the vote.

During these early years, Lane occupied a subservient position in the minds of the local party leaders. He was considered a valuable political asset; as a member of the national Congress and a close acquaintance of both Pierce and Buchanan, he represented a strong link between the local and the national Democratic organizations. But, although there were outward appearances of harmony between Lane and the "Clique," many members of that group exhibited an increasing dissatisfaction with Lane. Much of this feeling toward Lane was due to political jealousy.[26] In spite of Lane's value to the party, members of the "Clique" grew jealous of his popularity, which barred any of them from the office of delegate, and of his influence over the territorial patronage. When Lane began to display a political independence in his actions, and it was realized that he was not primarily interested in maintaining the power and prestige of the "Clique" but rather in promoting his own political stock, relations between the two grew colder.

As early as 1854, Lane, in Washington, D.C., had heard rumors that his popularity with Oregon's local Democratic politicians was beginning to wane. In a letter to Bush in which he practically pleaded for the nomination for delegate in 1855, Lane observed, "They say I am strong with the people but the politicians are determined to put me down."[27] Lane's reaction to the growing split in the territorial Democratic party illustrated his political astuteness. While deploring the breach in the party and denouncing those who would split the ranks, Lane nevertheless curried favor with all elements, at times even crossing the party line. One member of the "Clique" complained that Lane was "too much inclined to listen to softs and whigs."[28] Although Lane criticized President Pierce for attempting to conciliate the various factions in the Democratic party,[29] he soon followed the same practice. He tried to preserve the

[26] Homer L. Owen, "Nesmith: Pioneer Judge, Legislator, Farmer, Soldier, Senator and Congressman," *Reed College Bulletin*, XXVIII (June, 1950), 156.

[27] Lane to Bush, September, 1854, Bush Papers. See also Lane to Bush, February 3, 1855, Bush Papers; and Lane to Bush, October 29, 1854, Salem *Oregon Statesman*, December 19, 1854.

[28] Joseph W. Drew to Bush, September 19, 1855, Bush Papers.

[29] Lane to Bush, December 2, 1853, Bush Papers.

broad base of popularity that had swept him into office for the first time in 1851. Too close an identification with the "Salem Clique," he thought, would damage this popularity.[30]

Lane's greatest weapon, next to his popularity, was his influence over the territorial patronage. When he exhibited an independent frame of mind regarding the dispensation of patronage, members of the "Clique" became increasingly annoyed. On one occasion it was seriously suggested that the "Clique" throw Lane "overboard."[31] Lane incurred the wrath of the local party manipulators in 1855 when he secured the appointment of an Indiana man to a position the "Clique" had promised to one of their number.[32] Later in the same year, Lane again aroused the hostility of the "Clique." Joel Palmer, one of Lane's early friends in the territory and superintendent of Indian affairs, was accused of joining the Know-Nothings and had apparently admitted his indiscretion. The demand for Palmer's removal was instantaneous. Lane's hesitance to comply with this demand brought further criticism from the local party leaders. By 1856, Lane was dispensing the few territorial offices at his disposal with an eye to building up his own machine.[33]

In spite of their dissatisfaction with Lane, the members of the "Clique" were forced to promote his candidacy again in 1857. Although they felt it time to "rebuke the damned Softs" whose support Lane was evidently courting, they were unable to find another candidate of Lane's stature.[34] One member expressed his feelings to Deady: "It looks now as though old Lane was bound to be the next nominee for delegate—But between us, I will be damned if I ever

[30] Charles Stevens to "Brother & Sister," March 10, 1856, E. Ruth Rockwood, ed. "Letters of Charles Stevens," *OHQ*, XXXVIII (June, 1937), 176. Stevens wrote, "Many of the people are tired of Old Jo Lane's being the only representative of the people, and under the jurisdiction of patent Durham democracy." The term "Durham democracy" was applied to the "Clique" during its early years.

[31] James W. Nesmith to Deady, September 14, 1855, Deady Papers.

[32] James W. Nesmith to Bush, April 13, 1855, James W. Nesmith Papers, Oregon Historical Society Library. Nesmith exploded at this utter disregard of the "Clique" by Lane, "God Dam all such appointments as this last batch, they would sink anybody to Hell but Old Joe."

[33] Drew to Deady, February 15, 1856, Deady Papers.

[34] Drew to Deady, March 19, 1857, Deady Papers. Drew commented: "I think the time is about coming when all the leading democrats here—the oligarchists—as Leland terms them will exercise their rights, powers and duties and nominate one of their kind. . . . It seems damned humiliating to be forced year after year to support a man, who affiliated and seeks support from those who . . . abuse all other leading democrats in the Territory."

vote for him again or for any other such a damned demagogue. My democracy shall never carry me that far again."[35] By 1857, Lane had acquired such a personal following among the minor local politicians that one member of the "Clique" feared the "Lanites" intended to prevent the election of any man to the constitutional convention who was not of their number.[36]

Lane, however, held aloof from the party break that occurred early in 1858. In Washington, D.C., Lane assumed the role of an innocent, but interested, bystander. He appealed to party members to preserve harmony in their ranks, calling attention to their common enemy, the rapidly rising Republican party. "I see, with much regret," he wrote, "that division and discord exists in the ranks of the democracy of Oregon, threatening in its character, and if persisted in, will result in defeat and overthrow. Fellow democrats of Oregon, *division in the democratic party will not do*."[37] Earlier he had admonished his constituents to follow his own example: "I believe in straight forward honest democracy[.] my life has been given to the support of democratic principles[.] I have never dodged nor never will."[38] Lane had good reason for anxiety over the unity of the party and for his failure to take sides in the factional quarrel. He concluded one of his letters to Oregon, "I would be very glad to be chosen one of the first Senators from our new State."[39] Rumors had reached Lane in Washington that the "Clique" intended to displace him for the Senatorship by promoting the candidacy of one of their number.[40] Although there was some effort to accomplish this among the members of the "Clique," Lane was assured by the "Clique" that the reports he had received were false, undoubtedly circulated by "soft" Democrats.[41]

[35] Drew to Deady, August 27, 1856, Deady Papers.
[36] Deady to Bush, April 21, 1857, Deady Papers.
[37] Lane to Bush, March 18, 1858, Portland *Weekly Oregonian*, May 1, 1858.
[38] Lane to Bush, May 30, 1856, Bush Papers.
[39] Lane to Bush, March 18, 1858, Portland *Weekly Oregonian*, May 1, 1858. See also Lane to ?, April 4, 1858, enclosed in E. C. Hibben to George H. Williams, May, 1858, Bush Papers; Lane to Bush, April 2, 1858, Bush Papers. In the latter, Lane concluded, "I must be permitted however to say, that I have not a particle of doubt about the feeling of the Democrats of Oregon in regard to myself, nine out of every ten of them would if the question was presented to them go for me for the Senate." A comparison of this with the tone of earlier letters indicates the extent to which Lane had succeeded in building up a following independent of the "Clique."
[40] Lane to Deady, April 17, 1858, Lane Papers.
[41] Drew to Deady, January 10, 1858, Deady Papers; Deady to Lane, February 7, 1858, Deady Papers.

The election for state officers in 1858 at first gave promise of being a three-cornered contest. Although the feature attraction was the factional quarrel in the Democratic party, the newly organized Republican party was busy preparing for its first major entrance on the stage of local politics. The efforts of the Republican party, however, were hampered by the uncertainty of many of its members. This uncertainty reflected the confusion that existed on the frontier following the breakdown of the Whig party in the East and the appearance of the Republican party. The Know-Nothing party made a brief appearance in the Pacific Northwest but found almost no support in territorial politics.[42] As early as 1855, one Whig politician wrote, "The Whig party is dead to all intents & purposes—as to the K. N.s they are 'dead without mourners & lie unburied without offence.' "[43] The following year saw the first signs of organization among Republicans in the territory; the nomination of Fremont and his campaign for the presidency undoubtedly gave impetus to Republican organization on the frontier. Many Whigs, however, distrusted this new movement. Deprived of a national organization, they found themselves in a quandary. One of them wrote: "The Whigs are all dead out here—they call themselves the *Republican party*—which means negro worshipers. I cant go the Locofocos and I'll see the Republicans to the Devil before I'll vote with them. I dont know what I am exactly, but anything but an abolitionist."[44] The *Oregonian* emphatically opposed the Republican organization. The editor, Thomas J. Dryer, clung tenaciously to the Whig party. Isolated from the national party councils by both time and geography, the Whig party survived on the frontier long after its national counterpart had expired.

In spite of these difficulties, the Republicans in Oregon met early in 1858 to draw up a platform and nominate candidates to the state offices. There was a general feeling of pessimism in the convention; few gave the party a chance for election, even with the Democrats divided. They felt, however, that participation in the election would aid the party in organizing for future contests. A lengthy platform was agreed upon, and a slate of candidates was nominated, including

[42] See Priscilla Knuth, "Oregon Know Nothing Pamphlet Illustrates Early Politics," *OHQ*, LIV (March, 1953), 40-53.
[43] David Logan to Mary Logan, November 28, 1855, Harry E. Pratt, ed. "22 Letters of David Logan," *OHQ*, XLIV (Sept., 1943), 269.
[44] Logan to Mary Logan, September 10, 1856, *ibid.*, p. 272.

John R. McBride for congressman and John Denny for governor.[45] The *Oregonian* reacted immediately. Concerning the resolutions adopted by the convention the editor commented: "We are unable to discover any new features or principles enunciated in it, or any particular objections to it. It is simply a rehash of stereotyped resolutions, often passed by conventions of this character." Dryer continued:

> We have thought from the beginning that this republican movement was premature and unwise, and we still think so. It seems to have originated from a few men in and about Oregon City, who without consultation with other portions of the territory, and without the knowledge or consent of those who have a right to *advise at least,* in matters of this kind, called the convention, adopted their platform and nominated their candidates. . . . The whole movement was conceived in error by those restless minds who lack the all important element necessary to ensure a political triumph over the Salem dynasty at the present time.[46]

The Republicans, influenced by William L. Adams and his Republican newspaper the *Oregon Argus,* took too extreme a position on the slavery question to suit the conservative Whigs. In the course of the campaign, McBride and Denny encountered a great deal of opposition from Republicans and former Whigs in the Willamette Valley. Many of those upon whom the candidates had counted heavily for support were actually working against them.[47] Consequently, over Adams' bitter opposition, both McBride and Denny withdrew from the campaign, carrying with them most of the Republican ticket.[48] Dryer immediately rejoiced. Although some of the Republicans had denounced a coalition with the "soft" element of the Democratic party,[49] Dryer urged every member of the opposition to vote the National Democratic ticket.[50]

[45] Oregon City *Oregon Argus,* April 10, 1858.

[46] Portland *Weekly Oregonian,* April 10, 1858. In a last desperate appeal to the Whigs of Oregon, Dryer wrote: "Have the principles . . . of the Whig party ceased to exist? We think not. . . . What though the organization of the old Whig party be broken up—its principles still live. . . . Is John J. Crittenden, the gallant standard bearer, left alone? Have you all deserted him? . . . Have you denied the faith? Are you willing, do you wish to lose your political identity? Will you sell your birthright for a mess of pottage? Shame! Shame!" (*ibid.,* April 17, 1858) .

[47] John Cummins to Henry Cummins, February 19, 1862, Henry Cummins Papers, University of Oregon Library.

[48] Oregon City *Oregon Argus,* May 22, 1858. Leander Holmes, Republican candidate for secretary of state, had withdrawn earlier because he thought there was no chance of Republican success (*ibid.,* May 15, 1858) .

[49] Marion County Republican Convention, Portland *Weekly Oregonian,* April 3, 1858.

[50] Portland *Weekly Oregonian,* May 22, 1858.

The Republicans were ignored by both factions of the Democratic party. Each concentrated on opposing the other, thrusting this family quarrel into the center of local politics. Asahel Bush hurled all the venom at his command at the disaffected Democrats. Constantly referring to the National Democrats as a wing of the "Black Republicans," Bush declared the issue at stake in the election was

> to decide whether Oregon, carrying the victorious banner of the Democracy, shall throw her weight into the scale of the Union, of conservatism, and peace, or whether, trailing the black flag of faction and fusion, it shall enter the lists of the country's foes and hiss on the war upon the country's constitution and the fair fabric of liberty which it shields.[51]

The National Democrats were defeated; their candidate for state governor, E. M. Barnum, received 4,407 votes to 5,545 for John Whiteaker, the "Clique's" candidate.[52] LaFayette Grover, a member of the "Clique," was elected to Congress over James K. Kelly. The margin, however, was closer than in elections of previous years. Members of the Democratic party failed to recognize the handwriting on the wall.

When the election was over, Lane redoubled his efforts to assume complete control of the Democratic party in Oregon. Lane's friends controlled the Democratic caucus in the first session of the new state legislature and easily secured his election as United State Senator. For his colleague, Lane expressed a preference for Delazon Smith, who had been persuaded earlier to break with the "Clique."[53] With

[51] Salem *Oregon Statesman,* March 30, May 25, 1858. One Democrat thought it was a grave error to consider the National Democrats as the opposition instead of the Republicans. By consistently attacking the Republicans, he thought, the Democrats might have induced the National Democrats to vote with the "regulars." Instead, the breach in the party was probably widened by the election campaign (W. W. Bristow to Bush, June 12, 1858, Bush Papers).

[52] Salem *Oregon Statesman,* July 6, 1858.

[53] Drew to Deady, July 20, 1858, Deady Papers. Some members of the "Clique" had worked hard to secure the defeat of Lane for the Senatorship (Drew to Deady, January 19, March 23, 29, July 5, 1858, Deady Papers). Delazon Smith, "The Lion of Linn," had had a stormy but interesting career in politics. Born in New York, Smith attended Oberlin College, from which he was dismissed in 1837. Following his dismissal he published a pamphlet, *Oberlin Unmasked,* in which he accused the faculty and students of Negro worship and miscegenation and charged that the men and women students were guilty of "practices more erotic than matriculating in the same classes." In following years he published newspapers in New York and Ohio; from 1842 to 1845 he was Special United States Commissioner to Ecuador. The following year he moved to Iowa Territory and became a Methodist minister, finally moving to Oregon in 1852. In Oregon he was a member of the territorial legislature and the constitutional convention and finally one of the first United States Senators (R. Carlyle Buley, *The Old North-*

this assumption of power by Lane's friends (and relatives),[54] the war between the "Salem Clique" and Joseph Lane commenced.[55] Some Democrats came to the tardy realization that Lane had built up his own "clique." An observer of the Senatorial election in the state legislature wrote:

> Some of the personal friends of General Lane, seemed to regard any opposition to his election as almost treason; they would hardly allow the right of opposition to him by members, whose constituents desired some other democrat to represent the State in the United States Senate.
>
> In other words there seems to be a personal party . . . wedded to the political interests of General Lane, who maintain that he must and ought to have what he wants. . . .[56]

Early in 1859, Bush exhibited genuine alarm at the increase in Lane's strength. The tables were turned; Bush sang a different tune in his editorials. Joseph Lane, the idol of Oregon's Democracy, was now *persona non grata* with the erstwhile party machinists. Bush wrote:

> Gen. Lane has, in Oregon, always cultivated outside support, and kept hanging about the democratic organization as *his friends*—"Lane men"—a class of men who never voted for any other democrat. . . . all Gen. Lane's acts have unmistakably pointed to the building up of *a Lane party* here . . . until by his mouthpieces . . . it is shamelessly avowed that the democrat who does not "swear by Lane" . . . shall be proscribed. . . . We believe that the successful formation of *any* mere personal party will sound the death knell of the democratic party. Man-worship and the support of principles and measures are incompatible.[57]

When Congress adjourned in 1858 without having passed the Oregon statehood bill, Bush blamed the delay on Lane.[58] The premature state organization gave way to the territorial government, which functioned until the early part of 1859.

The dissension in Oregon's Democratic party soon assumed a national as well as a local justification. In December, 1857, relations

west: Pioneer Period, 1815-1840 [2 vols.; Indianapolis, 1951], II, 405-406; *Biographical Directory of the American Congress, 1774-1949* [Washington, 1950], p. 1825).

[54] Three of the most zealous Lane party workers were L. F. Mosher and Aaron Shelby, two of Lane's sons-in-law, and Nathaniel Lane, his son. Shelby was a member of the state house of representatives that helped to elect Lane Senator. Mosher and Nathaniel Lane were members of subsequent sessions.

[55] Drew to Deady, July 20, 1858, Deady Papers.

[56] Letter to Bush, Salem *Oregon Statesman*, July 13, 1858.

[57] Salem *Oregon Statesman*, February 1, 1859.

[58] *Ibid.*, December 21, 1858.

between President Buchanan and Senator Stephen A. Douglas reached an open break. Although there had been previous signs of a feud between these men, the Supreme Court decision in the Dred Scott Case and the introduction of the Kansas question into Congress precipitated the final rupture.[59] Douglas and his followers viewed the Dred Scott decision as a threat to popular sovereignty; the administration, with the strength of a well-nigh united South behind it, stood by the decision, denied Douglas' popular sovereignty, and argued the right of protection for slave property in the territories. The breach was widened by the Kansas question. President Buchanan urged the approval of Kansas' Lecompton Constitution, a document ratified overwhelmingly by proslavery voters in an election boycotted by those opposed to the extension of slavery. Douglas denounced the election and the constitution as an outrage against the principle of popular sovereignty. The split between these two individuals spread to the members of Congress and eventually to the rank and file of the party throughout the country. The Democratic party had split in many areas, as in Oregon, over purely local matters, but without exception these local splits became identified with the national split during the years preceding the crucial presidential election of 1860.

News of the Buchanan-Douglas split over the Kansas issue reached the Pacific Northwest early in 1858. At first attempts were made by some of the local leaders to gloss over the division. Delazon Smith "regretted" the difference in opinion between the two national figures and remarked, "What a pitty the people of Kansas could not have acted as wisely, honorably and harmoniously in framing and adopting their Constitution as have the good people of Oregon!"[60] Under Smith's influence, the Democrats of Linn County declared that the "difference of opinion" between Buchanan and Douglas was "both honest and courteous," adding that "the members of the democratic party may everywhere differ in opinion to the same extent and upon the same subject, without impairing their standing as

[59] For studies of this split see Reinhard H. Luthin, "The Democratic Split During Buchanan's Administration," *Pennsylvania History,* XI (Jan., 1944), 13-35; Philip G. Auchampaugh, "The Buchanan-Douglas Feud," *Journal of the Illinois State Historical Society,* XXV (April-July, 1932), 5-48; Richard R. Stenberg, "An Unnoted Factor in the Buchanan-Douglas Feud," *Journal of the Illinois State Historical Society,* XXV (Jan., 1933), 271-284; and Roy F. Nichols, *The Disruption of American Democracy* (New York, 1948).

[60] Smith to Deady, February 5, 1858, Deady Papers.

democrats."[61] Bush also attempted to smooth over the national disagreement, declaring, "There is no difference between the President and Mr. Douglas in matter of any vital principle involved."[62] Privately, however, he expressed a preference for Douglas' position.[63]

The national split could not be kept out of local party ranks. Lane immediately took a strong stand in favor of the administration in the Kansas question. Throughout his sojourn in Washington, D.C., as Oregon's territorial delegate, Lane worked closely with the Southern group. His actions, while receiving the approbation of most of Oregon's Democrats, sometimes proved annoying to certain elements in the territory. In 1856, Lane's Southern sympathies in the sectional struggle were demonstrated when, on two occasions, he acted as Preston Brooks's second in challenging New England members of the Senate to duels.[64]

Much more important in forcing the national party break into local Democratic politics in Oregon was the constitutional disagreement between the Dred Scott decision and Douglas' concept of popular sovereignty. In the Pacific Northwest, popular sovereignty was more than a party doctrine. From the earliest days of territorial status, the frontiersmen in the region felt that the territories were entitled to govern themselves, a feeling motivated partly by the pioneer's own tradition of self-government and partly by the rigorous control exercised over the area by the "territorial system." This feeling was manifested first of all in a movement toward revision of the nation's long-standing territorial policy. When this failed, statehood seemed the only alternative. The passage of the Kansas-Nebraska Act by Congress in 1854 was hailed in the Pacific Northwest as an opening wedge in the campaign against the "territorial system." While they recognized that the act granted only a limited form of self-determination, the settlers hoped that more legislation would follow, eventually accomplishing the revision they had so urgently demanded. Stephen A. Douglas was regarded as a national hero, not only because of his sponsorship of the Kansas-Nebraska Act but also because in his arguments he consistently took the point of view of

[61] Linn County Democratic Convention, Salem *Oregon Statesman*, March 16, 1858.
[62] Salem *Oregon Statesman*, March 2, 1858.
[63] Woodward, *Rise and Early History of Political Parties in Oregon, 1843-1868*, p. 140.
[64] Portland *Weekly Oregonian*, July 19, September 20, 1856.

the frontiersmen in favor of territorial self-government. Just as the desire for self-government on this frontier transcended party lines, so did the support of the Kansas-Nebraska Act and the principle of popular sovereignty.[65]

With the inclusion of the Kansas-Nebraska Act and the principle of popular sovereignty in the national Democratic platform of 1856, Democratic prestige in the Pacific Northwest was strengthened. By this time, however, there were some signs of disagreement over the application of the principle. The "Cincinnati" platform was highly ambiguous concerning the precise point in territorial experience when popular sovereignty could be applied. President Buchanan, following the lead of the Southerners in Congress, interpreted the act to mean that territorial settlers could only exercise their power when the area applied for admission as a state and denied the authority of the territorial legislature to legislate over the "domestic institutions." Douglas, on the other hand, maintained that the power resided in the territorial legislature. The implications of this disagreement were lost on the settlers in the Pacific Northwest; by this time, the citizens of Oregon had taken the first steps toward the adoption of a state government.

The argument consequently had little practical application in this area. The exclusion of both slave and free Negroes by Oregon's voters, at the same time that they ratified their state constitution, was hailed as a vindication of the Kansas-Nebraska principle.[66] The warfare being waged in Kansas over exactly the same issue was deplored in the Northwest.[67]

Meanwhile, the decision of the Supreme Court in the Dred Scott Case upset the equilibrium. Surprisingly, the decision received almost no notice in the public press in Oregon until some eight months after it was handed down. Both the Democratic and opposition newspapers seemed reluctant to introduce this new issue into local politics. During the election campaign for the constitutional convention in 1857, however, two seemingly incompatible elements in the Democratic party appeared. Bush frantically tried to remove from his

[65] See Robert W. Johannsen, "The Kansas-Nebraska Act and the Pacific Northwest Frontier," *Pacific Historical Review*, XXII (May, 1953), 129-141.

[66] Lane to Bush, January 3, 1858, Bush Papers; Lane to LaFayette Grover, January 31, 1858, Salem *Oregon Statesman*, March 16, 1858.

[67] For example, see the message of John Whiteaker, first state governor, to the legislature, delivered July 8, 1858 (Salem *Oregon Statesman*, July 13, 1858).

party the stigma of proslavery by maintaining that the test of a person's Democracy was not dependent upon his attitude toward slavery. At the same time he made no secret of his own free state sympathies. Other spokesmen of the party declared that no man could be a Democrat and vote for a free state. Consequently, many of those who favored the introduction of slavery into Oregon drifted into the camp of the National Democrats or "softs." Others, who opposed slavery in Oregon but maintained that in principle Southerners should have equal rights in the territories, associated with the same faction. These elements adopted the Dred Scott decision as justification for their position. By the end of 1857, the division of the Democratic party in Oregon over the issue of slavery extension was forecast.

In December, 1857, Bush attempted to preserve party unity by reconciling the Dred Scott decision with the Kansas-Nebraska Act. The two, according to Bush, were not actually incompatible. Since the decision guaranteed the exclusive sovereignty and jurisdiction of a state within its own area, Bush argued, the question of slavery was to be decided by each state. He saw no difference between the people who were moving in the formation of a state government and those who were already organized as a state. By temporarily adopting Buchanan's interpretation of the Kansas-Nebraska Act, that only when the people of a territory were forming a state government could they act with regard to slavery, Bush felt that the two principles could be harmonized.[68]

Bush was joined in his attempt to straddle the fence by the two factions of the Democratic party in their conventions early in 1858. The platforms of both the Democrats and the National Democrats with regard to national issues were strikingly similar, further proof that the break up to this time was based almost exclusively on local issues and jealousies. The Democrats, meeting at Salem, endorsed the 1856 "Cincinnati" platform and expressed confidence in the administration of President Buchanan. The principles of the Kansas-Nebraska Act were re-endorsed; at the same time the Dred Scott decision was declared to be an "authoritative and binding exposition of the constitution." Bush, in commenting upon the platform, wrote, "The doctrine of popular sovereignty embodied in the Nebraska-Kansas act is declared a fundamental principle of our

[68] *Ibid.*, December 8, 1857.

political creed; and the Calhoun doctrine of States Rights is maintained."[69] The National Democrats, meeting in Eugene the following month, also endorsed the "Cincinnati" platform and Buchanan's administration. They expressed belief "in the cardinal principles of popular sovereignty and in the right of the people of the Territories as well as of the States, to frame and adopt their constitutions and all local laws for their own government." Going one step further than the Democratic convention, this group expressed full confidence in Joseph Lane.[70] It is significant that in these convention declarations the Bush faction adopted the Buchanan interpretation in its pronouncement on popular sovereignty, while the National Democrats took Douglas' side—the reverse of the stand each group was to take in succeeding months.

The issue between the Dred Scott decision and Douglas' popular sovereignty was joined in the late summer of 1858. At Freeport, Illinois, Stephen A. Douglas declared, in answer to a question from his opponent in the Senatorial contest, that the people of a territory could prohibit slavery by lawful means before the formation of a state constitution, despite the Dred Scott decision. Slavery, he maintained, could not exist unless supported by local police regulations, which only the territorial legislature could establish. Proslavery men suddenly found themselves deprived of the victory they had so recently celebrated in the Dred Scott decision. Douglas' "Freeport Doctrine" spurred Oregon's proslavery group to action in the territorial legislature. In December, 1858, William W. Chapman, chairman of the judiciary committee and a member of the Lane party, reported a bill for the protection of slave property based on the Dred Scott decision.[71] According to Chapman:

> The spirit of the constitution of the United States as pronounced by the Supreme Court in "The Dred Scott Decision" authorizes the holding of slaves in any of the Territories of the United States . . . that while a territory remains as a territory, that it is as much the property of a slaveholding State, as it is

[69] *Ibid.*, March 23, 1858.
[70] *Ibid.*, April 20, 1858.
[71] William Williams Chapman had many years of experience as a frontier politician. Born in Virginia, he was one of the first settlers in Burlington, Iowa, then a part of Michigan Territory. In 1836 he became prosecuting attorney for Michigan Territory, later in the year first district attorney of Wisconsin Territory, and when Iowa Territory was created he was elected to two terms as territorial delegate. After taking part in Iowa's first constitutional convention in 1844, Chapman moved to Oregon. Strongly proslavery, he was appointed surveyor general in 1858 (*Biographical Directory of the American Congress, 1774-1949*, pp. 967-968) .

of a non-slaveholding State, and that the citizens of a slaveholding State have the same constitutional right to carry their slaves to said Territory, and use them there, and be protected in their rights, as the citizen of a non-slaveholding state has a right to convey any chattel property he may be possessed of, to said Territory, and be protected in his right to said property.

Chapman denied that a territorial legislature could prohibit slavery because "the inferior cannot exercise power that is not granted to the superior."[72] Two members of Chapman's committee submitted minority reports. N. H. Craner, a man heretofore associated with the Bush faction of the Democratic party, argued that the Dred Scott decision, "a fair and just exposition of the Constitution," granted protection to slave property in all the territories; consequently, there was no need for special legislation. E. D. Shattuck, the lone Republican member of the committee, "acquiesced" in the Dred Scott decision but maintained that "the Territorial Legislature may act according to its discretion upon any rightful subject of legislation." Shattuck argued, in the spirit of Douglas' popular sovereignty, that a territory was a "civil organism, has a life of its own and a living principle, by virtue of which it grows and develops, with no limit to the exercise of its intrinsic powers but the laws of the United States."[73] This effort to recognize slavery in Oregon Territory, like all previous efforts, was unsuccessful. Oregonians had made their decision on slavery, and they saw no reason to alter it.

Events in 1859 spelled the doom of the Democratic party as a united organization. The National Democrats were considerably strengthened by the application of the national issues to the factional struggle. Joseph Lane and his retinue took over the leadership of the splinter group. The "Salem Clique" was further weakened by disaffection in its own ranks. Matthew P. Deady, one of the leaders of the "Clique" during its early years, became an outspoken pro-slavery advocate. He urged Lane to stand by the Lecompton Constitution and regarded Douglas' stand on the Dred Scott decision as marking his "political departure."[74] The editor of the *Oregonian* described the rivalry between the two wings of the Democracy: "The

[72] Portland *Weekly Oregonian,* January 15, 1859; Oregon Provisional and Territorial Government Papers, #9671.

[73] Territory of Oregon, *House Journal,* 1858-1859, pp. 173-179; Oregon Provisional and Territorial Government Papers, #7966.

[74] Deady to Lane, February 7, 1858, Deady Papers. By 1860 Deady's conversion to the Lane party was complete, much to the annoyance of his former comrades in the "Clique."

hards or *Salem clique* wing of the present 'organization' denounce the 'softs' or 'nationals' as traitors, villains, &c. The 'nationals' denounce the Salem banditti by every epithet which their ingenuity can conjure up, or the English language suggest."[75]

Lane, as a United States Senator, was zealous in his opposition to Douglas in the national Congress. With the aid of President Buchanan he attempted to weaken Douglas' strength in the Pacific Northwest. The federal patronage was one of the greatest weapons against the Douglas forces. Douglas men in Oregon were removed and replaced by unequivocal Lane men. James W. Nesmith, Oregon's superintendent of Indian affairs, gave way to Edward R. Geary. W. W. Chapman, Lane's "first lieutenant" in the territorial legislature, was appointed surveyor general. Matthew P. Deady received the appointment of United States district judge. Bush lamented the fact that all the influential federal offices in the territory were, by the spring of 1859, filled by Lane men.[76]

Final victory over the "Clique" was achieved by Lane's forces at the Democratic state convention in April, 1859. The most important task facing the convention was the nomination of a congressman to succeed LaFayette Grover, whose term had expired in March.[77] The initiative was first seized by the "Clique." Although expressing concern over the unity of the Democratic party, Bush nevertheless was able to control the apportionment of delegates to the convention to his own advantage. The apportionment was determined on the basis of the vote given to Governor Whiteaker in the state election held the previous year. Thus, all the National Democrats who had voted for Barnum were theoretically unrepresented in the convention. Out of a total of seventy-five delegates, thirty-nine were to be elected from six counties, those with the greatest "regular" Democratic strength. In addition, an attempt was made to allow only those Democrats who had voted for Whiteaker to participate in Democratic primary meetings.[78] Adopting this course of action, Bush maintained, would prevent any "ambitious and designing man" who wished to build up a personal party within the Democratic organiza-

[75] Portland *Weekly Oregonian*, February 12, 1859.
[76] Salem *Oregon Statesman*, May 17, October 18, 1859.
[77] Grover, a longtime member of the "Salem Clique," had been elected to represent the new state of Oregon in Congress in the election of 1858. His term expired with the end of the 35th Congress; consequently he held his seat only from February 14, the date Oregon was admitted to the Union, to March 3, 1859.
[78] Portland *Weekly Oregonian*, February 19, March 12, 1859.

tion from doing so. In words that forecast more than he realized, Bush concluded:

> We should grieve to see it [the party], by its own carelessness and laxity of vigilance, sowing the seeds of its own destruction. A single false step, at this time, may place the Democratic party of Oregon in a position from which it may take years to recover.[79]

Bush's triumph was short-lived. The Lane forces went into the convention determined to take control of the party machinery.[80] Their first success came with the election of W. W. Chapman as president of the convention over James W. Nesmith. This victory was quickly followed up. Although a minority of the convention, the Lane delegates held a secret caucus to nominate their candidate for congressman. They invited several Democrats not identified with their group to participate in the caucus, thus giving them a majority of the convention delegates. After requiring those present to pledge their support to the nominee of the caucus, the Lane forces nominated one of their number, Lansing Stout.[81] The Bush faction, meanwhile, had nominated LaFayette Grover, who expected to be re-elected to his post at Washington. The surprise came in the balloting, when Stout was elected by a vote of forty to thirty-three. Members of the "Clique" were furious. Nesmith attacked the proceedings, but to no avail. He wrote to a friend:

> You have doubtless heard of the Damnable outrage perpetrated by Lane & Smiths friends in our mis-called Democratic convention . . . they held a Secret caucus over Burnses Saloon, and united the discordant elements . . . men who came instructed for Grover, merged their instructions in the caucus, and voted for Stout in the convention. This is a remarkable triumph of "cawcuss Sovreignty." I boldly denounced the "dirty bargains" in the convention, laid the thing open to public gaze.[82]

The resolutions, drawn up by a committee appointed by the pro-Lane Chapman, took the administration point of view and for the

[79] Salem *Oregon Statesman*, February 8, 22, 1859.

[80] The most important part of this machinery was the Democratic State Central Committee, which up to this time had been controlled by the "Clique."

[81] Stout had only recently settled in Oregon. Born in New York in 1828, Stout became a lawyer, moving to California in 1852. He was a member of the California state legislature in 1855. Two years later he moved to Portland, Oregon *(Biographical Directory of the American Congress, 1774-1949*, p. 1874). It was maintained, and probably with some truth, that Stout had been elected to the California state legislature on the Know-Nothing ticket (Salem *Oregon Statesman*, April 26, 1859).

[82] Nesmith to Deady, April 25, 1859, Deady Papers.

first time made no mention of popular sovereignty. The 1856 "Cincinnati" platform was endorsed, and the Dred Scott decision was declared to be the correct interpretation of the Constitution on the question of slavery. Buchanan's administration was endorsed, and the members of Oregon's delegation in Congress were given official thanks. In one last stroke, the chair appointed the new Democratic State Central Committee, heavy with Lane men and headed by W. S. Brock, an unequivocal partisan of Joseph Lane.[83] Henceforth, the "Clique" or Douglas wing of the party was considered the splinter group. By seizing control of the party machinery, Lane "regularized" the National Democrats.

Thus the breach in the party widened. The implications of the split, however, were not readily recognized by many of the Democrats. One interested observer took the Douglas Democrats to task for their timorous policy during and following the convention. He suggested to one of them:

> . . . if you had withdrawn from the convention—repudiated its proceedings— declared in favor of the Douglas doctrines and named Mr. Grover as your candidate—you would have had two thirds of the people with you—but then of course you would have cut loose from the Administration. . . .[84]

Later, Bush was criticized for not pursuing a bold policy after the breakup and was urged to follow the example of John W. Forney, in Pennsylvania, who had embarked on a course of opposition to the Democratic administration:

> . . . the Statesman is making the *least* instead of the *most* of even this. Instead of showing its readers, that the scism as it truly is one, of irriconcilable principle, it still goes on trying to catch a Leviathan with a pin hook. . . . I have long seen that the Statesman sympathised with Douglas and his doctrines, had it boldly avowed them six months ago its enemies today would have been under its feet. . . .[85]

The Republicans in Oregon were not idle in the face of the Democratic party split. Having withdrawn from the state election in 1858 because of their imperfect party organization, they made plans for a

---

[83] Salem *Oregon Statesman,* April 26, 1859; Portland *Weekly Oregonian,* June 18, 1859.

[84] Jesse Applegate to Nesmith, April 25, 1859, Jesse Applegate Papers, Oregon Historical Society Library.

[85] *Ibid.,* May 12, 1859.

vigorous campaign in 1859. In November, 1858, came news of Republican victories in many of the Eastern states. Adams, in the *Argus,* greeted the news with enthusiasm, declaring that the recent elections were portents of a "triumph in 1860 that will mark a new epoch in the history of this government."[86] Extracts from John W. Forney's Philadelphia *Press* were liberally sprinkled throughout the issues of this month.[87] Shortly after the news of the Republican victories was reported in Oregon, J. R. McClure urged the immediate organization of the Republican party on the basis of a never-ending hostility to the extension of slavery.[88] The Republican party organization in the Pacific Northwest, however, differed markedly from its national counterpart. Formed late out of groups of conservative Whigs who had remained loyal to their old organization until all hope for a revival was gone, the party adopted much of the conservatism and little of the radicalism of the national organization.

Early in territorial history, Whigs as well as Democrats had worked hard to achieve a greater measure of self-government while yet retaining territorial status. When the Kansas-Nebraska Act was passed, it found many supporters in the territory among the Whigs. Following the Dred Scott decision, when the Buchanan administration departed from the principles of the Kansas-Nebraska Act, the old-line Whigs and the Republicans in Oregon adopted the act. The first public announcement of this policy came in 1858, when Republicans were preparing to enter an election for the first time. Republican county conventions not only endorsed the principles of the Kansas-Nebraska Act but also denounced abolition. Leander Holmes, later to become a prominent leader of the party in the Pacific Northwest, gave the reason for Republican support of the Kansas-Nebraska Act, contending

> that the democracy could not and did not intend to honestly apply the
> principles of the Kansas Nebraska bill to our territories, as was manifest by

[86] Oregon City *Oregon Argus,* November 27, 1858. The congressional elections of October and November, 1858, resulted in the defeat of the administration in many Eastern and Midwestern states. Control of the House of Representatives passed to the Republicans and Douglas Democrats.

[87] Extracts from Forney's *Press* were widely reprinted among the opposition newspapers in Oregon. Earlier Adams had urged all Democrats to read the *Press,* probably in the hopes that they might follow Forney's lead in turning against the Buchanan administration (Oregon City *Oregon Argus,* November 13, 1858).

[88] J. R. McClure to Adams, November 20, 1858, Oregon City *Oregon Argus,* December 4, 1858.

the course of the administration in trying to force the Lecompton constitution upon the people of Kansas, against their will.[89]

At the same time, Republicans declared that their party was a "white man's party."[90] The *Oregonian* went further in committing the Republican party to popular sovereignty and the Kansas-Nebraska Act:

> We were opposed to the Kansas bill, and the introduction of the Kansas-Nebraska doctrine, not because we believed the doctrine wrong, but because it was disturbing a well considered and well settled doctrine. When the Kansas doctrine was established, and the Missouri Compromise abolished, we favored the Kansas doctrine. . . . We were then, and are now in favor of the Kansas-Nebraska doctrine of popular sovereignty. We desire to see both established in their true spirit and meaning. We regard Douglas and Crittenden as the true exponents of and supporters of those doctrines. They have expressed the views we entertain. . . . This is *the* question of the day. We would cheerfully support, upon this issue, either of the two named men for President.[91]

Some Republicans saw in popular sovereignty a means for checking the spread of the South's "peculiar institution" and considered it a powerful weapon for freedom. The adoption of popular sovereignty by Oregon Republicans was partly a matter of political expediency, but it also had a strong foundation in the convictions of the settlers themselves. By taking a stand in favor of popular sovereignty and the Kansas-Nebraska Act, the local Republican party contradicted the position of the national organization. The national party had originally been organized as a protest against the Kansas-Nebraska Act.

Undismayed by their withdrawal from the state elections in 1858, Republicans made early preparations for the 1859 congressional election. Their adoption of popular sovereignty as a party issue gave them considerable encouragement. In the county Republican conventions, they took a strong stand in favor of popular sovereignty, declaring that "the people of every organized Territory are, and of right, ought to be perfectly free to establish, or to exclude slavery, and to settle according to their own pleasure all their domestic institutions." They disclaimed any connection with abolitionism and denounced the idea of racial equality.[92] In their state convention, Republicans urged Congress to recognize the sovereignty of the

[89] Portland *Weekly Oregonian,* March 27, 1858.
[90] *Ibid.,* May 1, 1858.
[91] *Ibid.,* May 8, 1858.
[92] *Ibid.,* March 12, April 2, 1859.

territories. The platform also favored a free homestead bill, the construction of a Pacific railroad, internal improvements of a "national character," and a tariff "which shall discriminate in favor of home industry." For congressman, the Republicans nominated David Logan, a long-time advocate of popular sovereignty.[93] The shifting alignment of political parties was reflected in Bush's reaction to the Republican convention. For the first time he reprinted the Republican proceedings in full and made the statement, startling for him, "There are some good things in their platform and some slightly colored things."[94] The appearance at this time of a Republican organization which argued that slavery could legally be extended into the territories, provided the people in the territories favored it, must have seemed anomalous to national Republican leaders.

David Logan typified the conservative attitude of these frontier Republicans. Born in Kentucky, Logan moved with his family to Springfield, Illinois, where his father, Stephen T. Logan, was Lincoln's law partner for a few years. After a short practice as a lawyer, he entered the Mexican War, serving under the command of Edward Dickinson Baker, a fellow Illinoisan who would cross his path again in Oregon. In 1849 Logan migrated to Oregon. He was active in territorial politics, serving both in the legislature and in the constitutional convention. A strong Whig, Logan favored popular sovereignty and territorial self-determination. When the Whig party declined, he was extremely reluctant to join the Republicans. As late as 1856, he branded Republicans as "negro worshipers," and it was he who declared, "I'll see the Republicans to the Devil before I'll vote with them."[95] In the constitutional convention, Logan opposed a resolution prohibiting slavery in Oregon as being "too radical."[96] In 1859, the year he accepted the Republican nomination, he described himself as

> an "old line Whig" holding to the "Kansas-Nebraska" doctrine rightly interprited, (which means interpreted my way) —and a "popular Sovreignity—non intervention Republican" . . . I intend so far as the "negro" question is concerned, to be identified hereafter, with that political party, that favors the

[93] *Ibid.*, April 30, 1859.

[94] Salem *Oregon Statesman*, April 26, 1859.

[95] Logan to Mary Logan, September 10, 1856, Pratt, ed. "22 Letters of David Logan," p. 272.

[96] John R. McBride, "The Oregon Constitutional Convention, 1857," *Proceedings of the Oregon Historical Society, 1902-1905*, p. 33.

submission of the question of slavery to the people of the organized Territories —and is opposed to any kind of Federal intervention therewith.[97]

By 1859, Logan had assumed a position of leadership in the new Republican party.

In contrast with the election of the previous year, the 1859 election was fought almost exclusively on national issues; local issues were submerged. It became a contest between the Buchanan administration, represented by the Democrat Stout, and the Douglas forces, represented by the Republican Logan. The manner in which Stout had been nominated by the Lane faction alienated a great number of popular sovereignty Democrats; Logan's espousal of popular sovereignty made him the logical choice of this group.[98] By taking a strong position in favor of popular sovereignty, Logan forced Stout to the opposite extreme. Stout maintained, during his campaign, that every slaveholder had a right to take his slaves into the territories; he argued that it was the duty of Congress to protect this slave property by a national slave code if necessary. Logan, on the other hand, maintained that "the true interpretation of the Nebraska-Kansas act was to give to the people the sovereign control over their own affairs." He pledged the support of the Republican party to this interpretation.[99] The *Oregonian* confirmed the Republican position by adding:

> If a majority of the people [in a territory] are in favor of slavery let them have *it*; if a majority are in favor of free labor let them have it, and let that settle the question, thereby taking the question out of Congress and making it a local question, confining it to the Territories where it is to be decided.[100]

One individual, after listening to both candidates on the stump, wrote, "The principle of non-intervention as declared in the Kansas-Nebraska act, is the true principle and is bound to win." Lurking in the back of this pioneer's mind was the all-important election of the forthcoming year: "Let *non-intervention* on the one side and a *slave code* on the other be the issue between the two great political

---

[97] Logan to Mary Logan, September 7, 1859, Pratt, ed. "22 Letters of David Logan," p. 277. One member of the Republican convention opposed Logan's nomination because he thought Logan's Republicanism doubtful (C. Hoel to William L. Adams, April 27, 1859, Oregon City *Oregon Argus*, May 7, 1859).

[98] Evidence that many Democrats were planning to cast their ballots for Logan on this ground may be found in the Salem *Oregon Statesman*, May 3, 10, 1859.

[99] Jesse Applegate to Bush, [May, 1859], Bush Papers; Portland *Weekly Oregonian*, April 30, 1859; Salem *Oregon Statesman*, May 31, 1859.

[100] Portland *Weekly Oregonian*, June 4, 1859.

parties in the United States in 1860, and the slave code would be buried so deep that it would never see the light again."[101]

The results of the election should have caused Democratic leaders to give serious thought to the future of their party. Out of a total vote of 11,276 cast, Stout was elected by the slim margin of 16 ballots. Logan carried nine counties, primarily in the northern part of the state, while Stout carried ten. Particularly surprising was the vote of Marion County, seat of the state government and private bailiwick of the "Salem Clique." For the first time since the organization of the territory, Marion County left the Democratic column, casting 1,062 votes for Logan and only 296 for Stout.[102] Logan's support of popular sovereignty was responsible for the large Republican vote. Although they had been defeated, one Republican congratulated the "non-intervention" Republicans and the "non-intervention" Democrats, stating, "We may be proud of this campaign as one contested upon principle."[103]

Not all the Douglas Democrats, however, voted for Logan. Many of them, particularly the leaders, were unable to cast their votes for a Republican under any circumstances. Although many actively opposed Stout in the campaign, they reluctantly gave him their votes.[104] Bush particularly found himself in an anomalous position. During the campaign, he withheld the support of his paper from Stout, although he did not publicly support Logan. After casting his ballot for Stout, Bush rejoiced at the results of the election, declaring rather prematurely that Lane had run his last election and that Laneism was now out of the way.[105]

The larger significance of this congressional election was immediately recognized. Many persons on the Pacific Coast urged Logan to contest the election. A California newspaper felt such an action was imperative in view of the fact that the presidential election of 1860 might be settled ultimately in the House of Representatives.

[101] Samuel T. McKean to the Editor, May 8, 1859, Salem *Oregon Statesman*, May 17, 1859.

[102] The complete election returns may be found in the Portland *Weekly Oregonian*, July 30, 1859.

[103] "A Conservative Republican" to the Editor, *ibid.*, July 2, 1859.

[104] James W. Nesmith to Benjamin Stark, June 30, 1859, Benjamin Stark Papers, Oregon Historical Society Library; Drew to Deady, July 15, 1859, Deady Papers; Richard H. Dearborn to Deady, June 28, 1859, Deady Papers; Stephen F. Chadwick to Deady, May 29, 1859, Deady Papers.

[105] Salem *Oregon Statesman*, July 12, 1859.

Logan, however, declined to do so.[106] Anson G. Henry summed up the situation and looked to the future with confidence, reiterating the local Republican position in favor of popular sovereignty. In Henry's opinion, the close election was

> the result of the attempt to cram down the throats of the masses of the [Democratic] party, the Dogmas of Southern Democrats, if this is persisted in by Genl. Lane & his friends, it will result in the permanent overthrow of the party, & the triumph of a conservative Republican party who will repudiate the Massachusetts foolery & adopt the Non-intervention plank as a part of their platform. If the *"conscientious fools"* in the Republican ranks, had let Dave alone, & staid at home instead of making speeches for him, he would have been elected by 500.

Henry, like Logan, looked forward to the Senatorial elections in 1860 and, with what proved to be accurate foresight, predicted the election of a popular sovereignty Democrat and a Republican.[107] Dryer, with an eye trained on the 1860 presidential election, renewed the pledge of the Republican party to support the principle of the Kansas-Nebraska Act:

> The republican party of Oregon stands firmly pledged to non-intervention on the subject of slavery. Upon that issue the party has fought the battle just passed. Upon that issue it stands ready to fight the coming political battles of the State. In the coming contest for president, the republican party of Oregon will be arrayed for this principle. No man can expect their support who ignores or denies this principle.... This was the leading cardinal principle in the late contest.[108]

The 1859 congressional election in Oregon forecast the issue over which the presidential election of 1860 was to be fought on this frontier.

The election year of 1860 was doubly significant because of the situation resulting from Oregon's attempts to fill its two United States Senate seats. When Oregon's first Senators were elected in 1858, Delazon Smith had drawn the short term which expired with the adjournment of Congress in March, 1859, while Lane's term extended two years longer. In order that Oregon might be repre-

---

106 San Francisco *Times,* October 5, 1859, quoted in Portland *Weekly Oregonian,* October 15, 1859; Logan to Mary Logan, January 24, 1860, Pratt, ed. "22 Letters of David Logan," p. 281; Simeon Francis to Abraham Lincoln, December 26, 1859, Robert Todd Lincoln Collection, Lincoln Papers, Library of Congress (microfilm in University of Washington Library).

107 Anson G. Henry to Lincoln, July 17, 1859, Lincoln Papers.

108 Portland *Weekly Oregonian,* August 6, 1859.

sented by a full Senatorial delegation when Congress met again in
the winter of 1859, Governor Whiteaker called a special session of
the state legislature in May. The growing enmity between the two
factions of the Democratic party, however, prevented the choice of
another Senator. The debate in this session over the Senatorial question was an additional manifestation of the divergent positions
within the Democratic party.[109]

As soon as the legislature met, a Democratic caucus met to nominate a candidate for the Senate seat. Because of the overwhelming
strength of the Democratic party in the legislature, nomination by
the party caucus was tantamount to election. Both Lane and Bush
Democrats participated in the caucus; Aaron Shelby, Lane's son-in-
law, was one of the chief wire-pullers. The caucus met for one week
without being able to decide on a candidate. One observer noted
that "both sides seemed afraid to approach the question."[110] On
the sixth day, however, Delazon Smith was nominated by a vote of
twenty-two to twenty-one, a close victory for the Lane forces. Smith's
nomination produced an open revolt by the Bush, or Douglas, Democrats. Benjamin F. Harding, one of their leaders in the legislature,
protested vehemently against Smith's nomination. Declaring that
Lane had destroyed the Democratic party in Oregon, Harding emphatically stated that Smith's nomination "is no more binding upon
me or the democracy—it is no more binding upon a member of the
democratic party, than the nomination made by the Republican
party. . . . I repudiate the whole action of the caucus." He threatened
to withdraw from the hall if this would prevent Smith's election.
One of the Lane members, R. B. Cochran, reminded the "Salem
Clique" of its earlier role in Oregon politics: "They used to be a
great party for order and submission to the will of the majority, and
all that sort of thing, which was proper enough when they got their
choice in the caucus, but now they exhibit a spirit of factiousness
worthy of a mob."[111] After many fruitless efforts to adjourn the state
house of representatives, a resolution to go into joint convention for
the election of a Senator was passed by one vote. As soon as the reso-

[109] Adams had earlier predicted that the split in the Democratic convention
between Stout and Grover would be carried over into the legislative session.
While he had no sympathy for Bush in his loss of the party leadership, Adams
could not rejoice at the change (Oregon City *Oregon Argus*, May 21, 1859).
[110] Portland *Weekly Oregonian*, June 4, 1859.
[111] *Ibid.*, June 11, 18, 1859.

AMES W. NESMITH *(Oregon Historical Society)*   LANSING STOUT *(Oregon Historical Society)*

DELAZON SMITH *(Oregon Historical Society)*   EDWARD DICKINSON BAKER

JOSEPH LANE

JOHN WHITEAKER *(Oregon Historical Society)*.

ISAAC I. STEVENS

lution was presented to the state senate, four senators walked out, thus preventing a quorum. After a great deal of wrangling, the entire legislature adjourned on June 4. No business had been taken up; with the split over the Senatorial question, many of the legislators realized the futility of remaining in session. As a result, Oregon was represented by only one Senator in the first session of the Thirty-sixth Congress.

By the middle of 1859, the Democratic party in Oregon was hopelessly divided; the party had indeed sown the seeds of its own destruction. The lines of division manifested in the election of 1860 were already drawn. The congressional election of 1859 had been fought almost entirely on the national issues that were to split the nation the following year. To both Democrats and Republicans in Oregon it served as a harbinger of the future.

The party situation in Oregon's northern neighbor, Washington Territory, was by this time developing in the same direction. With a much smaller population and with no direct voice in national affairs, the territory nevertheless expressed a vital interest in national politics. As in Oregon, the Democratic party in Washington Territory split during the middle 1850's over a local issue; by 1859 the local split had become identified with the national Buchanan-Douglas split.[112]

Democratic party politics in Washington Territory centered about the figure of Isaac I. Stevens. Stevens, a professional soldier, veteran of the Mexican War, and a stanch Democrat, had been appointed governor of Washington Territory in 1853 as a reward for having campaigned for Franklin Pierce. With the help of the *Pioneer and Democrat,* he had built up a political machine known locally as the "Olympia Clique." As in Oregon, the rigid control over local politics exercised by the Democratic machine created some dissension in the ranks. Of greater significance, however, in the splitting of the party was Stevens' policy and action during the Indian wars.

In April, 1856, Stevens, as territorial governor, proclaimed martial law in two of the territory's counties on the ground that the emergency of the war situation warranted such an action. His proclamation was immediately challenged by the judicial authorities of the

[112] See Robert W. Johannsen, "National Issues and Local Politics in Washington Territory, 1857-1861," *PNQ,* XLII (Jan. 1951), 3-31.

territory. By May, the proclamations were withdrawn, but the controversy continued to rage.[113] The voters of the territory took sides in the contest. Party lines were blurred in the struggle that ensued. The Whigs, and later the Republicans, tended to oppose the governor, although after the breakup of the Whig party some Whigs shifted their support to Stevens. The Democratic party itself was badly split over this issue. Many prominent Democrats had been alienated by the governor's action and at once formed an anti-Stevens group within the Democratic party.

The opposition to the Democratic party in Washington Territory was not in such a confused state as it was south of the Columbia River. By early 1856, the Whig party was recognized as defunct and obsolete by most elements in the territory. A small Free-Soil movement, based on the national party of the same name, had been organized in Thurston County in 1855; by the following year, its ranks included many former Whigs. During the winter of 1856-57, members of this movement held organizational meetings, dropped the old name "Free-Soil," and henceforth designated their party as the Republican party. In 1857, this small Republican movement ran a candidate for territorial delegate, a full two years before Oregon's Republican party felt itself strong enough to enter an election.

Stevens left the governorship in 1857 and announced his intention to run for the office of territorial delegate, partly in an attempt to vindicate his actions as governor. Although there were bitter struggles in some of the county conventions between the Stevens and anti-Stevens Democrats, the delegates to the territorial convention nominated Stevens with little difficulty.[114] In its resolutions, the Democratic party placed more emphasis than usual on local issues. The "Cincinnati" Platform and the Kansas-Nebraska Act were endorsed, but the remainder of the platform dealt principally with the Indian wars and the Hudson's Bay Company possessory rights in the territory.[115] The Republicans, inviting the participation of all who "would save the soil bearing the name of the great and good Washington from the pollution of slavery," had some difficulty find-

[113] For the martial law episode, see Roy N. Lokken, "The Martial Law Controversy in Washington Territory, 1856," *PNQ,* XLIII (April, 1952), 91-119.
[114] Winfield Scott Ebey Diary, No. 5, April 11, 14, 1857, University of Washington Library; Harry N. M. Winton, ed. "The Death of Colonel Isaac N. Ebey, 1857," *PNQ,* XXXIII (July, 1942), 326; Olympia *Pioneer and Democrat,* April 17, 1857.
[115] Olympia *Pioneer and Democrat,* May 15, 1857.

ing a man willing to lead the party in the election campaign. The choice finally fell on Alexander Abernethy, a member of the territorial legislature. Like the Democratic organization, the Republicans devoted most of their platform to local issues. Their only excursion into national politics lay in an endorsement of the 1856 national Republican platform and a scathing denunciation of the Dred Scott decision.[116]

The election was fought and won by the Democrats in Washington Territory largely on the strength of the Indian war issue.[117] Stevens began a four-year period as territorial delegate that was to lead him into the arena of national politics. The election of 1857 also marked the introduction of Selucius Garfielde to the voters of the territory. Garfielde had come west with a national reputation as an orator and stump speaker, having campaigned in many of the Midwestern states for Buchanan in the election of 1856. He was rewarded with appointment to the land office in Washington Territory. Garfielde had a reputation for political opportunism, for varying "his politics according to the winds of fortune."[118] He accompanied Stevens during the campaign; while Garfielde spoke and argued the national issues, Stevens concentrated on the local issues.

The election of Stevens in 1857 did little to heal the schism in the Democratic party. The controversy was carried on with as much bitterness as before. As in Oregon, however, the final blow came with the national split between President Buchanan and Senator Douglas. Stevens, like Lane, remained loyal to the president. In fact, in Lane and Stevens President Buchanan counted two of his stanchest supporters.[119] The two representatives from the Pacific Northwest, each one the leader of the local Democratic organization, presented a rather formidable partnership in both local and national politics.[120] The two joined forces in their attempts to secure legislation for the Pacific Northwest and concentrated their efforts

[116] Steilacoom *Washington Republican,* April 3, May 29, 1857.

[117] Alexander S. Abernethy to Elwood Evans, August 11, 1857, Elwood Evans Papers, 1843-1894, Yale University Library (microfilm in University of Washington Library).

[118] Hubert H. Bancroft, *History of Washington, Idaho and Montana* (San Francisco, 1890), p. 280.

[119] Philip G. Auchampaugh, "James Buchanan and Some Far Western Leaders, 1860-1861," *Pacific Historical Review,* XII (June, 1943), 169-180.

[120] Lane to Stevens, August 16, 1857, Ronald Todd, ed. "Letters of Governor Isaac I. Stevens, 1857-1858," *PNQ,* XXXI (Oct., 1940), 418.

on keeping their local Democratic organizations in power and loyal to Buchanan.

The national split gave impetus to the local breach in the territorial Democratic party. Early in 1859, the Olympia *Pioneer and Democrat* publicly recognized this situation:

> For near one year—since the unfortunate difference between President Buchanan and Senator Douglas on the Kansas question, there has evidently been a steady and fixed determination on the part of the *outs,* claiming to belong to the democracy, to ignore the present administration, create a Douglas movement, and construct a party here whose issue with the democracy would be placed upon the ground of differance that existed between the President and that Senator at the last session of Congress.

Alarmed at this new development, the Democratic Central Committee in Washington Territory declared, "We wholly *ignore* the Kansas issue of the last session of Congress, because it is a matter which in no sense affects the people of this territory." However, almost in the same breath, the committee endorsed the measures of the administration on this question.[121] The complaints of the Douglas Democrats north of the Columbia were reminiscent of those in Oregon. One Douglas Democrat in Washington Territory referred to the area as a "haven of softs," and accused Stevens of appealing to all elements in order to stay in power:

> The Dem. party here now is in the hands of broken-down whigs, defunct Know Nothings, and soft Democrats—A pretty conglomeration isn't it? . . . The Stevens party have possession of the sham democratic organization which *seems* to be the Dem party. . . . By the power of patronage and a muzzled press he keeps that control.[122]

The year 1859 was an important election year for the territorial voters. Stevens' first term as delegate was up, and there was little doubt that he would seek re-election. The identification of the local Democratic split with the national split encouraged the Republicans to adopt a rather unusual campaign strategy. The Republican organization determined that no convention should be held in the territory and that no nomination should be made. Instead, early in May, William H. Wallace, a former Whig candidate for the delegateship and by this time a leading Republican, announced himself as an independent candidate. Unfettered by any formal partisan

[121] Olympia *Pioneer and Democrat,* February 18, 1859.
[122] Butler P. Anderson to Bush, March 8, 1859, Bush Papers.

resolutions or principles, Wallace hoped to gain support from the anti-Stevens or Douglas Democrats.[123] The Democrats easily renominated Stevens. Dissension, however, was apparent when the Democratic convention turned to the adoption of a platform. One Douglas Democrat, Daniel F. Brownfield, introduced a series of resolutions approving popular sovereignty as advocated by Douglas and affirming the right of the territories to regulate their own domestic affairs, declaring that "if the people of a Territory are in favor of slavery, they have an undoubted and constitutional right to make laws to establish and protect it." These resolutions, according to Brownfield, constituted the "great question upon which the Democratic party must either stand or fall in 1860." Brownfield's resolutions were rejected. In their place, the convention adopted a series of meaningless resolutions, "a long string of *thanks* and *praise*—empty platitudes."[124] The adoption of this unique platform by the Democratic convention was an attempt to counteract the Republican strategy by presenting the Democratic candidate equally untrammeled by party principles, a contradiction of the oft-repeated Democratic watchword, "Principles, not men."

Republican aspirations received a rude shock when Stevens was elected by 60 per cent of the total vote cast.[125] Their efforts to woo the disaffected Democrats to their side were unsuccessful, although Selucius Garfielde, a new convert to Douglas Democracy, abandoned Stevens and took the stump for Wallace.[126] The Democratic vote, however, exaggerated Stevens' actual strength. One Republican wrote:

> One half or more, that voted for him [Stevens] protested against his construction of the Dred Scott case, & the policy of the present administration—but they could not swallow the *Black* Republican nominee, although they agreed with him in opinion—Such men ought to be owned by a Southern planter & be worked on their plantation awhile.[127]

Stevens returned to Washington, D.C., where he was destined to play a leading role in the crucial election of 1860.

[123] Olympia *Washington Standard*, February 2, 1861; Steilacoom *Puget Sound Herald*, May 6, 1859; Olympia *Pioneer and Democrat*, June 10, 1859.

[124] Steilacoom *Puget Sound Herald*, May 27, 1859; Olympia *Pioneer and Democrat*, May 20, 1859.

[125] Election Returns, 1859, Washington Territory.

[126] Olympia *Pioneer and Democrat*, August 12, 1859.

[127] Anson G. Henry to Lincoln, July 17, 1859, Lincoln Papers.

By the end of 1859, the stage was set in the Pacific Northwest for the presidential election of 1860. In spite of the isolation of the region from the centers of political activity in the East, and in spite of the small population, the people on this far Northwest frontier expressed a vital interest in the national issues that threatened to disrupt the Union. The settlers made a determined effort to acquaint themselves "thoroughly with the real questions at issue between the two great parties" in order that they might vote with understanding and a "full conviction of the right."[128] Although some deplored the almost exclusive discussion of "nothing but *party, party, party*,"[129] the pioneers of the Pacific Northwest nevertheless attempted to understand, over the distance of thousands of miles, the issues that were disturbing the national calm. With this intense interest in the national issues went a growing feeling that the nation was approaching a crisis of serious proportions. One newspaper editor wrote early in 1859:

> We are no alarmist, and do not wish to be considered as such, but we cannot shut our eyes to that fact that our country has reached that crisis which must be met by the Democracy, or that fate, deprecated by the Father of his country, and against which he warned the succeeding generations, in tones the most solemn, will have been realized, and we, his unworthy countrymen, before the first century of our existence as a free people will have been reached, will live in a divided confederacy.[130]

In the words of one Oregon pioneer, written to a friend whose role in the election year of 1860 was not then suspected, "things are terribly mussed up every where politically, & morally & no human Eye can see the results that will follow or foretell the consequences. We can only hope for the best."[131]

128 Salem *Oregon Statesman,* January 4, 1859.
129 Portland *Weekly Oregonian,* December 3, 1859.
130 Corvallis *The Democratic Crisis,* February 9, 1859.
131 Henry to Lincoln, February 16, 1859, Lincoln Papers.

the realignment
of parties

THE SPRING AND SUMMER OF
1860 witnessed a realignment of political parties, both on the
national scene and in the Pacific Northwest. The national nominating conventions occupied the political spotlight during the first
part of the year. The Democratic party split into Northern and
Southern wings, a split that was reflected soon afterward in local
politics throughout the country. The Republicans, determined to
take full advantage of the Democratic discord, purposely weakened
their stand on slavery and appealed to Douglas Democrats for support. In the Pacific Northwest, the close similarity between Republicans and Douglas Democrats with regard to popular sovereignty was
carried to a new extreme. On the eve of the presidential election, the
two groups united in opposition to the Breckinridge wing of the
Democratic party. The union was immediately successful and laid
the foundation for the close cooperation that characterized the Civil
War years. Behind the realignment of political groups in 1860 was
the mounting sectional crisis.

All parts of the country sensed that a national crisis was approaching. The fears expressed in 1859 increased in 1860. One frontier
newspaper indicated that the anxiety and tension had penetrated to
the remotest parts of the nation.

There never was a period in the history of this country when we were at peace or free from party excitement, in which there was manifested such absorbing interest in National affairs as at the present time. It pervades all classes and conditions of society. . . . It is the firm settled conviction of the public mind that we are approaching, nay, have reached a crisis in political affairs, compared with which all former ones were as gentle gales to the destroying whirlwind.[1]

On the floor of the United States Senate, Joseph Lane declared, "We have been drifting towards disunion faster than we permitted ourselves to believe." Lane's view of the crisis was optimistic, however, and he called upon his colleagues not to "despair of the Republic."[2] In December, 1859, the *Oregon Statesman* recognized the crisis as a conflict between "sectionalism and fanaticism on the one hand, and conservative nationalism on the other." While the paper did not think that the election of a Republican would result in the dissolution of the Union, it felt that the breach between the North and the South would be considerably widened, adding to the

already too long list of encroachments, insults and provocations, which have inflamed the passions, estranged the affections, and alarmed the fears of our southern brethren, and which, if not checked, may finally result in the . . . violent disruption of the confederacy, with the horrors of civil war and servile insurrection.[3]

The Republican organization in the new state was the first to anticipate the national nominating conventions of 1860. In April, 1859, when the Republicans met to draw up a platform and to nominate a candidate for the congressional election, they also turned their attention to the forthcoming national convention of their party. Although the apportionment to the national convention was not known, three delegates were elected, A. G. Hovey, Dr. W. Warren, and Leander Holmes. On the motion of Byron J. Pengra, editor of the newly founded Republican newspaper *The People's Press,* the delegates to the national convention were instructed to support William H. Seward for the presidential nomination. Seward's endorsement by the convention came as a shock to many Republicans in Oregon. Seward was considered a radical on the slavery question; his "irrepressible conflict" and "higher law" doctrines were ideas which these frontier Republicans refused to accept. The endorse-

[1] Olympia *Pioneer and Democrat,* March 2, 1860.
[2] *Cong. Globe,* 36 Cong., 1 Sess., p. 567.
[3] Salem *Oregon Statesman,* December 20, 1859.

ment was carried after preparations for adjournment had begun and after many of the members of the convention had departed for their homes. One influential Republican asserted that a majority of Republicans in the state disapproved of the Seward endorsement, a "useless and mischievous" resolution, and blamed Logan's defeat in the 1859 congressional race partly on that endorsement.[4]

Because of Seward's unpopularity among Oregon Republicans and because of the irregularity of his endorsement by the convention, the party did not support the New York Senator.[5] In the fall of 1859, William L. Adams, through his newspaper, announced his support of Edward Bates for the Republican presidential nomination. In an editorial, Adams maintained that Bates was best qualified to lead the party of "conservative Republicanism" to success. Identified with none of the controversial questions of the day, Bates could unite the old-line Whigs, Americans, Free Democrats, and conservative Republicans. The radical element in the Republican party could easily be placated by the choice of the vice-presidential candidate from among their number. Bates's nomination, Adams thought, would be hailed with enthusiasm throughout the West. On the first page of the same issue appeared an extract from the Springfield *Republican* in which Bates's views on various questions were told in detail.[6] Following Adams' declaration, sentiment in favor of Bates gained momentum. Jesse Applegate wrote, "Mr. Bates is the only living man for whom I have that veneration amounting to man worship which Napoleon 1st seems to have inspired [in] his soldiers."[7]

Bates's popularity among Oregon Republicans may be attributed partly to the fact that a large number of Oregonians had migrated from homes in Missouri.[8] However, the Bates movement had deeper roots. A citizen of a frontier state, Bates had much in common with frontiersmen. A Whig without a party, he represented a conservative viewpoint, appealing to the pioneers' abhorrence of political extremes. Southern born and bred, he had allied himself with the

[4] Oregon City *Oregon Argus*, April 30, October 29, 1859.

[5] A Republican wrote in December, 1859, that efforts were being made to change the Seward instructions (Simeon Francis to Lincoln, December 26, 1859, Robert Todd Lincoln Collection, Lincoln Papers, Library of Congress [microfilm in University of Washington Library]).

[6] Oregon City *Oregon Argus*, October 1, 1859.

[7] Applegate to Deady, January 15, 1862, Jesse Applegate Papers, Oregon Historical Society Library.

[8] Portland *Weekly Oregonian*, July 14, 1860.

forces of free soil, believing that Congress had the right to prohibit slavery in the territories. Slavery itself, he thought, was a social relation and a domestic institution, dependent upon local law for its existence; its agitation could have no other purpose than to "stir up the angry passions of men, and exasperate the unreasoning jealousy of sections."[9] He shared the Westerner's attitude toward free Negroes, favoring their colonization in Central America.[10] A Western man, Bates strongly urged the construction of a Pacific railroad and the passage of a national homestead bill.

Many influential persons in the national Republican party, including Abraham Lincoln,[11] considered Edward Bates the best choice for the presidential nomination. He was the only candidate, they thought, who would receive Southern support. His nomination not only would remove the fear in the South of hostile purposes on the part of the Republicans but also would check the radical tendencies of the Republican party itself. Bates's support was strongest in the border states, both slave and free. Maryland, Delaware, and Missouri early declared for Bates, joined later by parts of the population in Illinois and Indiana. Bates lost in Kentucky only because of the strong ambitions of Cassius Clay for the presidency. Oregon's support of Bates added to the Western character of the movement.[12]

In April, 1860, the Republicans in Oregon met again in convention, readopted their platform of the preceding year except for the Seward instructions, and elected three presidential electors.[13] Although there was no formal endorsement of Bates's candidacy, there was a tacit understanding that Oregon's delegates would work for his nomination in the national convention. The State Republican Committee sent Bates a letter in May informing him that he was the choice of Oregon's Republicans for the presidential nomination.[14]

[9] Howard K. Beale, ed. *The Diary of Edward Bates, 1859-1866, Annual Report of the American Historical Association,* 1930 (Washington, 1933), IV, xii, 1-2, 112-114.

[10] Floyd A. McNeil, Lincoln's Attorney General: Edward Bates, unpublished Ph.D. dissertation, State University of Iowa, 1930, p. 191.

[11] Theodore C. Pease and James G. Randall, eds. *The Diary of Orville Hickman Browning* (2 vols.; Springfield, Ill., 1925), I, 395.

[12] For a discussion of the Bates movement, see Reinhard H. Luthin, "Organizing the Republican Party in the 'Border-Slave' Regions," *Missouri Historical Review,* XXXVIII (Jan., 1944), 138-161, and *The First Lincoln Campaign* (Cambridge, Mass., 1944).

[13] Portland *Weekly Oregonian,* April 28, 1860. The three electors were Thomas J. Dryer, Byron J. Pengra, and William H. Watkins.

[14] Beale, ed. *Diary of Edward Bates,* p. 124.

Leander Holmes, one of the delegates who was unable to make the trip to Chicago, empowered Horace Greeley, a leader in the Bates movement, to act in his stead and vote for Edward Bates.[15]

Abraham Lincoln was first mentioned for the presidency in the Pacific Northwest in February, 1860. Simeon Francis, a personal friend of Lincoln who had moved from Illinois to Oregon in 1859, wrote a lengthy article to the *Argus* outlining Lincoln's life and career and urging his nomination. Francis publicly agreed with Adams' estimate of Bates—"your views in regard to Edward Bates, and your high appreciation of the man, are my own"; privately he wrote, "I hate that Bates movement."[16] Lincoln's proposed candidacy was not taken seriously by Oregon's Republicans. A month after Francis first mentioned Lincoln's name, a correspondent of the *Oregonian* took Lincoln to task for his campaign against Douglas in Illinois. If "Abram Lincoln" had "taken and presented the sound, national, catholic and common sense view of the question of slavery in all its bearings," the correspondent felt that Douglas could have been easily defeated. Instead Lincoln chose to concentrate his campaign on abstract issues.[17]

There was remarkable agreement among the Republicans of Oregon regarding their choice for the presidential nomination. The opening of the national Republican convention in Chicago in May, 1860, found the Oregon delegation arrayed on the side of Edward Bates. No such unanimity of opinion was found in the Democratic camp, in spite of the fact that a favorite son, the leader of one wing of the local party, was a strong contender for the nomination.

Joseph Lane's name had been linked with the presidency for many years by Democrats in Oregon. In 1852, Lane had been presented to the national Democratic convention as Indiana's favorite-son nomination. At that time, many Western Democrats suggested Lane as a compromise in case the convention deadlocked.[18] In the convention,

---

[15] Oregon City *Oregon Argus,* March 31, 1860.

[16] *Ibid.,* February 11, 1860; Simeon Francis to Lincoln, December 26, 1859, Lincoln Papers.

[17] W. H. C. (San Francisco correspondent) to the Editor, March 3, 1860, Portland *Weekly Oregonian,* March 17, 1860.

[18] Thomas D. Harris to Howell Cobb, February 2, 1852, Ulrich B. Phillips, ed. *The Correspondence of Robert Toombs, Alexander H. Stephens, and Howell Cobb, Annual Report of the American Historical Association,* 1911 (Washington, 1913), II, 277-278; Jesse D. Bright to William H. English, May 15, 1852, "Some Letters of Jesse D. Bright to William H. English (1842-1863)," *Indiana Magazine of History,* XXX (Dec., 1934), 377.

Lane carried only Indiana's thirteen votes, but he carried them throughout twenty-nine ballots.[19] In 1856, Lane was again mentioned for the presidential nomination.[20] It was natural, then, that Lane should emerge as a contender for the nomination in 1860.

Early in 1859, Lane's chances for the presidential nomination seemed good. He had been elected United States Senator from Oregon after serving eight years in the national capital as delegate from Oregon Territory. Delazon Smith, his mate in Oregon's Senatorial delegation, wrote back to Oregon: "At this present writing his [Lane's] chances for the Charleston nomination are *better* than those of any other living man! . . . These suggestions may be 'simply laughed at' in Oregon, but they are *not* laughed at in the Atlantic States."[21] Oregon's representative in Congress was somewhat less optimistic: "Judging from evidences about the City of Washington Gen Lane has as good a chance as any one to be the nominee at Charleston."[22] Difficulties, however, soon developed. Lane's position in Congress and his alignment with President Buchanan over the Kansas question raised serious doubts concerning his popularity among Northern Democrats. Democracy in the North was, according to one correspondent, "fast narrowing down to Douglasism."[23] Lane's chances for the nomination were often linked with the close election between Logan and Stout in 1859. One Eastern newspaper commented:

> For a time the redoubtable Gen. Jo. Lane of Oregon appeared to be the chosen favorite, and he was lauded to the skies as a sort of humbug hard-cider candidate who would be pretty sure to win. But the result of the election in Oregon has pretty effectually disposed of his pretensions.[24]

The near rejection of Lane's candidate in his own state caused Democrats nationally to think twice about his "availability."

[19] Sister M. Margaret Jean Kelly, *The Career of Joseph Lane, Frontier Politician* (Washington, 1942), pp. 96-99.

[20] Orville C. Pratt to [Lindsay Applegate], October 19, 1854, Oliver Cromwell Applegate Papers, University of Oregon Library; Joseph W. Drew to Deady, June 29, 1856, Matthew P. Deady Papers, Oregon Historical Society Library.

[21] Delazon Smith to Asahel Bush, February 2, 1859, Asahel Bush Papers, Oregon State Library (photostats in the University of Oregon Library).

[22] LaFayette Grover to Nesmith, February 16, 1859, James W. Nesmith Papers, Oregon Historical Society Library.

[23] Edward J. Allen to Isaac I. Stevens, June 11, 1859, Isaac I. Stevens Papers, University of Washington Library.

[24] Philadelphia *Press*, [n. d.], quoted in Oregon City *Oregon Argus*, October 29, 1859.

The Democrats in Oregon scheduled their state convention for the middle of November, 1859, at which time they planned to elect delegates to the Charleston convention and to instruct them for a presidential candidate. On the eve of the convention, one administration newspaper in Oregon declared that Lane not only was an available candidate for the presidency but also would be an acceptable one. The South, the paper argued, would certainly prefer Lane to Douglas, and the North would prefer him to Davis or Wise. It seemed logical that Lane would be the best compromise. "To favor his elevation can harm no one," the editor wrote, "not even his bitterest enemy; to oppose him, may be opposing the best interests of Oregon." He urged the Democrats of the state to pledge their delegates to Joseph Lane, if for no other reason than to enhance Oregon's position in the Union:

> It is important that Oregon should clearly define her preferences, as she *may* hold the nominee in her hands. California and Oregon united, may, in any event, exercise an influence in the Charleston convention far greater than numerical strength; and if successful, that influence would be correspondingly felt throughout the next administration.[25]

Since the Democratic party was divided in Oregon as well as in the nation, it was expected that other candidates would be presented in Oregon to challenge Lane. One of these was Daniel S. Dickinson of New York. Dickinson had many qualifications to recommend him to these Western Democrats. A lawyer, he had been a lifelong Democrat and an active participant in New York State politics. From 1844 to 1851 he was a member of the United States Senate, where he allied himself with the expansionists, favoring the annexation of Texas and the acquisition of all of Oregon to 54°40'. In December, 1847, he introduced several resolutions on the acquisition of territory and the formation of territorial governments in which the principle of popular sovereignty was first publicly enunciated. In spite of his belief in popular sovereignty, Dickinson broke with Douglas over the Kansas issue and remained loyal to the administration. Although he was not active in public life during the fifties, his name was prominently mentioned throughout the country for the Democratic nomination in 1860.[26]

[25] Corvallis *Oregon Weekly Union*, November 12, 1859.
[26] There is no adequate biography of Dickinson. For the details of his life see John R. Dickinson, ed. *Speeches, Correspondence, etc., of the Late Daniel S. Dickinson, of New York* (New York, 1867), pp. 1-17.

The first expression for Dickinson in the Northwest was made in July, 1859. A Democrat, writing from Vancouver, blamed Lane for the sharp increase in Republican strength in Oregon and urged the Democratic party to endorse Dickinson for the presidency. Dickinson, with an "uncompromising and fearless devotion to the Union," would be the choice of conservative national Democrats everywhere and if nominated would most likely carry all of the South and the Pacific Coast in addition to many of the Northern states.[27] Two county conventions, Multnomah and Yamhill, endorsed Dickinson, at the same time taking a strong stand in favor of popular sovereignty and territorial self-government.[28]

Although Stephen A. Douglas was the favorite of a large proportion of Oregon's Democrats, there was surprisingly little sentiment expressed in his favor before the meeting of the state convention. The Bush faction and the *Statesman* had earlier supported Douglas, and they continued to give publicity to their national leader. Oregon's Democracy was not united on a preference for the presidential nomination, as was evidenced by the county conventions that met prior to the state convention. Two counties were instructed for Daniel S. Dickinson; Jackson County supported Lane; and Josephine County endorsed Douglas for the presidency and Breckinridge for the vice-presidency.[29]

The same disruptive tendencies that had characterized previous Democratic party meetings were carried into the state convention that met at Eugene on November 16. The first struggle, centering about the question of the apportionment of delegates, developed long before the convention met. The Lane faction, controlling the State Central Committee, favored the use of Lansing Stout's vote as a basis for the apportionment. Since many Douglasites had withheld their votes from Stout, the party split was further aggravated. Bush declared that those Democrats who had withheld their votes from Stout would never consent to a convention on that basis.[30] Other members of the Douglas wing backed up this contention. W. W. Bristow believed that if a convention were called on the basis of Stout's vote the Republicans would most certainly carry the next

[27] "Union Democrat" to the Editor, July 1, 1859, Salem. *Oregon Statesman,* July 12, 1859.
[28] Salem *Oregon Statesman,* November 15, 29, 1859.
[29] *Ibid.,* November 15, 22, 29, 1859.
[30] *Ibid.,* July 19, 1859.

election.[31] Joseph W. Drew suggested an alternative. He urged the
Douglasites to call a separate convention, based upon Governor
Whiteaker's vote in 1858, thus excluding from representation large
numbers of the Lane group. Such a convention could instruct
unanimously against Lane. Drew was not unaware of the national
implications such an open split might have. He asked, "Would not
the moral effect of a convention of democrats instructing against
Lane have some influence abroad and at home also?"[32]

The Democratic State Central Committee met late in September.
W. S. Brock, an unequivocal Lane man and chairman of the committee, appointed Nathaniel Lane secretary of the meeting. Lafayette
Mosher, Joseph Lane's son-in-law, offered a resolution to base the
representation of the convention on Stout's vote. Drew immediately
objected, but his counterresolution was refeated. At this moment,
the delegates from six counties, led by Drew, walked out of the
committee meeting. Mosher's resolution was passed without a dissenting vote. The withdrawing members met together and issued an
"Address to the Democracy of Oregon" in which they bitterly condemned "the system of persecution and proscription for the purpose
of building up a Lane party" and the disfranchisement of lifelong
Democrats. They recommended the election of delegates to the
convention on the basis of Whiteaker's vote in defiance of the committee's action.[33] James W. Nesmith feared that Oregon would be
represented at Charleston by a double set of delegates as a result of
this action. He was satisfied, however, that the "sentiment of oposi-
tion to Joseph is daily becoming stronger, and however much you
may regrett it . . . his career of humbugging, dishonesty, and deception, is rapidly drawing to a close."[34]

The editor of the *Oregonian*, assuming the role of a bystander
watching his rivals rush to their own destruction, announced the
forthcoming Democratic convention and commented, "considerable
fun is anticipated."[35] With an almost diabolic interest, Dryer sent a
stenographer to the convention and published the most complete
account of the proceedings. W. W. Chapman, the newly appointed

31 W. W. Bristow to Bush, August 18, 1859, Bush Papers.
32 Joseph W. Drew to Bush, August 15, 1859, Bush Papers.
33 Salem *Oregon Statesman*, October 4, 1859.
34 Nesmith to Deady, October 7, 1859, Nesmith Papers.
35 Portland *Weekly Oregonian*, November 5, 1859. Dryer, indeed, saw no reason
for a Democratic convention in the first place, maintaining that Lane had undoubtedly already chosen the delegates to the Charleston convention.

surveyor general of Oregon, was selected chairman pro tem of the convention. Almost at once, Ralph Wilcox proposed that the Committee on Credentials be instructed to seat delegates according to Whiteaker's vote. The committee met and decided in favor of the Lane position; delegates were admitted on the basis of Stout's vote in the last congressional race.[36] LaFayette Grover thereupon announced to the convention: "I am authorized by *eight counties* here, to say to the Convention, on behalf of these counties, that they retire from the Convention upon this decision. . . . They do not do so on any feeling. They are present here without authority to sit longer in the Convention." The delegates promptly walked out "amidst much laughter." The convention then organized by electing Delazon Smith president. Three delegates, Lane, Matthew P. Deady, and Lansing Stout, and three alternates, J. K. Lamerick, John Adair, and John F. Miller, were elected to represent the Democratic party at the convention in Charleston. These delegates were instructed for Joseph Lane.[37]

The withdrawing members of the convention prepared a statement in which they set forth their arguments for basing the apportionment on Whiteaker's vote. At Grover's suggestion, they passed a resolution pledging the Democracy of the seceding counties to support the nominee of the Charleston convention whoever he might be.[38]

This action of the seceders proved a great disappointment to those who had expected a separate convention, a second set of delegates, and instructions for Stephen A. Douglas. Dryer was particularly furious at what he termed the "absence of back-bone" in those who withdrew from the convention.[39] Joseph Hooker, a Douglas Demo-

[36] Attempts to compromise the apportionment issue had been made in the weeks preceding the meeting of the convention, notably by Governor Whiteaker. Brock, however, refused to entertain such notions, declaring that anyone who favored compromise was not and never had been a Democrat (W. W. Bristow to Bush, November 17, 1859, Bush Papers; Eugene *People's Press,* November 19, 1859).

[37] Portland *Weekly Oregonian,* November 26, 1859. The choice of Lane as a delegate and the instructions for Lane provoked no little comment. One Democrat declared that the convention "made a d——d ass of itself in instructing Lane to go for himself" (Joseph Hooker to Nesmith, December 19, 1859, Nesmith Papers). Nesmith commented, "Lane is pretty *shure of his own vote,* which is more than any other candidate for the presidency can say" (Nesmith to James O'Meara, December 4, 1859, Nesmith Papers).

[38] Salem *Oregon Statesman,* November 22, December 6, 1859.

[39] Portland *Weekly Oregonian,* December 10, 1859.

crat and resident of Douglas County, was also bitter. Writing to Nesmith, Hooker declared:

> The Resolution introduced by Grover & passed committing them to the nominee of the Charleston convention is damnable, virtually undoing all that was expected to be gained by the division. The issue, if persisted in, as I hope it will be, must be fought on broader grounds than is furnished by the records of our state convention. It must embrace the *atrocities* of the present administration & perhaps those of the Charleston Convention itself.[40]

Party leaders, however, still hoped for a party reunion. Nesmith, writing to James O'Meara, a member of the Lane faction, declared:

> I think with you that there should have been an adjustment of difficulties in the convention, I know that those who withdrew are willing for any honorable compromise, but the stronger party would neither make, or listen to any terms. . . . My only hopes now are, that the Charleston convention will disregard the instructions for *"Joseph"* and present a ticket that will restore harmony and united action.[41]

Bush himself expressed the hope that the party would be reunited, and he refused to counsel active opposition to the existing party organization.[42] Democratic party leaders began to realize that without a united party there would be no hope for success in 1860.

A new issue arose in the spring of 1860 to drive the two factions of the Democratic party even farther apart. The Lane group, through the formal party machinery, decided to hold a congressional election in the summer of 1860 and made plans for the nomination of a candidate. This decision immediately aroused a storm of protest from the Douglas wing. An election for congressman had to be held sometime in 1860 so that Oregon would be represented in the House of Representatives after the end of the Thirty-sixth Congress on March 4, 1861. The Lane faction believed the election should be held in June, when the regular state election was scheduled.[43] The *Statesman,* on the other hand, argued that an election in June would be both illegal and inexpedient. Bush suggested the election be held in November and hoped the state legislature would pass a special law to that effect.[44] There was more to this controversy than merely

[40] Hooker to Nesmith, December 19, 1859, Nesmith Papers. A surveyor and West Point graduate, Hooker was soon to achieve national fame as the commander of the Army of the Potomac during the dark days of the Civil War.
[41] Nesmith to O'Meara, December 4, 1859, Nesmith Papers.
[42] Salem *Oregon Statesman,* December 6, 1859.
[43] Corvallis *Oregon Weekly Union,* February 4, 1860.
[44] Salem *Oregon Statesman,* February 14, 1860.

the election of a congressman. The election for members of the state legislature, regularly scheduled for June of even-numbered years, had a special significance in 1860. Members of the new legislature were to elect two United States Senators. If the Lane faction was to retain control of the Senatorships, the composition of the new legislature was all important to its success. If a congressman were nominated in June, Laneites thought that enough Lane legislators would be pulled through to insure the Senatorship for another term. On the other hand, if an election were deferred until November, the new Senators might already have been chosen. Other considerations, doubtless, were important in the minds of Lane men. While they still controlled the Democratic party machinery, the election of one of their number to Congress seemed likely. This might not be the case if they waited until after the national nominations were made and after the national presidential campaign had been fought.[45]

Accordingly, a Democratic state convention met in April, 1860. The Douglas wing refused to cooperate; consequently, six of the eight counties that had seceded from the November convention were still unrepresented. Five ballots were taken, finally resulting in the nomination of George K. Sheil, a Salem lawyer and ardent pro-Southern Democrat.[46]

Further friction developed at the April meeting of the Democrats over the decision of the Lane group to choose presidential electors. Because of the split in the party and the uncertainty over the results of the Charleston convention, many Democrats thought this was going too far. According to one Douglas Democrat, "The assurance of these party despots is becoming more and more reckless and their effrontery has never been equalled." He went on to write:

The whole Lane Society and all his office-holders are cursing Douglass as a Black Republican and "worse nor that." Nearly all his office holders and their tools swear they will not vote for him, if he gets the nomination and yet this crowd, in advance of the Charleston Convention, intend to nominate an electoral ticket—In the event of the nomination of Douglass at Charleston, are *genuine* Douglas men intending to vote for men as electors who are selected by an *anti* Douglas Convention? I should think it would require a vast amount of

[45] This election for congressman is treated in more detail by Lester Burrell Shippee, "An Echo of the Campaign of Sixty," *OHQ*, XII (December, 1911), 351-360.

[46] Salem *Oregon Statesman*, April 24, 1860.

cheek for me to aspire to be an elector on the Dem. ticket, if Lane is the nominee at Charleston. . . .[47]

The Lane men, themselves, realized that to nominate electors before knowing what kind of party platform these electors would be pledged to support would be politically inexpedient. Consequently, no electors were chosen. Resolutions were passed declaring the Cincinnati platform to be a satisfactory statement of the principles of the party. Joseph Drew moved to add the words, "as advocated and enunciated by Stephen A. Douglas." His motion was voted down by the overwhelming vote of sixty to four, an indication of the one-sided character of the convention.[48] Dryer pointed out that "Stephen A. Douglas had few friends in the convention."[49]

In spite of the arguments of the Douglasites that a congressional election in June would be illegal, the Republicans met in the spring and nominated David Logan to oppose Sheil, thus giving an air of legality to the election.[50] Drew, one of the most vociferous of Douglas Democrats, exploded:

> The damned fool republicans have called a convention for the 19th of Apr. I hoped they would keep still and, if they saw fit in June to vote for a Congressman, they would vote at least for some independent candidate—possibly a Douglas democrat. They are a damned impracticable brainless set of asses to attempt to push a man on a republican platform just at this time.[51]

The centers of attention in the early part of 1860, to Oregonians as well as to others in the country, were the national nominating conventions. Following the endorsement of Joseph Lane by the state Democratic convention, speculation mounted regarding his chances for the presidential nomination. In January, 1860, Adams declared that the two most likely nominees were Edward Bates and Joseph Lane and thought the chances good that these two individuals would oppose one another for the presidency in November.[52] Lansing Stout, writing from Washington, D.C., was certain that Lane would be on the Democratic ticket, either as president or vice-president. He did, however, give Douglas a good chance for the nomination.[53]

[47] Drew to William J. Beggs, February 20, 1860, Bush Papers.
[48] Salem *Oregon Statesman,* April 24, 1860.
[49] Portland *Weekly Oregonian,* April 28, 1860.
[50] *Ibid.*
[51] Drew to Bush, March 11, 1860, Bush Papers.
[52] Oregon City *Oregon Argus,* January 21, 1860.
[53] Lansing Stout to Nesmith, January 28, 1860, Nesmith Papers.

Judge Deady, also writing from the national capital, reported that "Lane's room is full from morning till night with accomplished knee-benders who look upon him as a sure card for the Presidency. He has a kind and acceptable word for them all and they go away thinking him the greatest man in the nation."[54]

Lane's candidacy received nation-wide recognition. The governors of Indiana and Tennessee and a former governor of California were reported as favoring his nomination.[55] One Memphis newspaper enthusiastically described Lane as

> the embodiment of the great characteristics of our people—energy, enterprise and perseverance. He possesses the iron will of Jackson, and the ability and judgment necessary to make a useful and popular President.—He is peculiarly the type and representative of the Great West, whose claims should be considered by the Convention.[56]

Even the *Charleston Mercury* was forced to admit that "The star of Jo. Lane, of Oregon, for the Charleston nomination, is in the ascendant in many portions of the country."[57] Men high in the national administration regarded Lane's candidacy favorably. John B. Floyd, Buchanan's secretary of war, wrote:

> If Lane's friends make no mistake, his prospects will be better than those of any other man I know. There is a feeling of great kindness expressed for him by everyone, and those to whom the idea of his candidacy is new are strongly impressed with his availability.[58]

Finally, it was reported that President Buchanan himself favored Lane for his successor.[59]

[54] Deady to Nesmith, January 4, 1860, Deady Papers.

[55] *Charleston Mercury*, [n. d.], quoted in Corvallis *Oregon Weekly Union*, December 17, 1859; Portland *Weekly Oregonian*, February 11, 1860.

[56] Memphis *Avalanche*, [n. d.], quoted in Corvallis *Oregon Weekly Union*, December 17, 1859. This was not the only instance in which Lane's name was linked with that of Andrew Jackson. Another Southern newspaper commented during the campaign of 1860: "General Lane is nearer what our imagination has ever conceived General Jackson to have been than any man that we ever have or expect to see. He is a tall, muscular, bony man of sixty, possessed of all the vigor of thirty, with a high full forehead, and well developed organization; very plain and very agreeable" (Raleigh [N.C.] *Standard*, July 25, 1860, quoted in Kelly, *Career of Joseph Lane, Frontier Politician*, p. 165).

[57] *Charleston Mercury*, [n. d.], quoted in Corvallis *Oregon Weekly Union*, December 17, 1859.

[58] John B. Floyd to James Buchanan, August 8, 1859, in Philip G. Auchampaugh, *James Buchanan and His Cabinet on the Eve of Secession* (Privately printed, 1926), p. 58.

[59] Edgar Eugene Robinson, ed. "The Day Journal of Milton S. Latham, January 1 to May 6, 1860," *California Historical Society Quarterly*, XI, 13 (entry for March 24, 1860).

Although Lane had won the control of the party machinery in Oregon, however, the state's Democrats were by no means united in support of their favorite son. Asahel Bush reiterated his preference for Stephen A. Douglas. Douglas, he maintained, was the only Democrat who could be nominated and elected, and the only candidate who could save the country from catastrophic civil war. He was a living embodiment of popular sovereignty, and his position and service to the party, thought Bush, entitled him to the nomination.[60] The size of the Douglas group in Oregon was variously estimated. One member of the group declared that a vote for Douglas in the Charleston convention would "receive the approbation of two thirds of the people of Oregon."[61] Another was confident that "a *large* majority of the party in the State prefer Douglas over all others named in connection with the office."[62] Joseph Hooker, soon to win the sobriquet "Fighting Joe," thought Douglas was the ablest man in the party: "Whether he sinks or swims his bitterest enemies must admit that he is of the stuff of which heros are made."[63]

On April 23, 1860, the Democratic National Convention in Charleston began its deliberations amidst an atmosphere of tension and ill-concealed hostility. The Oregon delegation contained six members by allotment of the national Democratic organization. Only two of the members originally chosen by the state convention were present: Lansing Stout, Oregon's representative in Congress, and John K. Lamerick, formerly a brigadier general in the Oregon militia. Lane remained in Washington, D.C., but kept in constant touch with the delegation by telegraph. The remaining positions in the delegation were held by proxies: Isaac I. Stevens, Washington Territory's delegate in Congress and close friend of Joseph Lane; Justus Steinberger, an agent of the Pacific Mail Steamship Company and also a resident of Washington Territory; R. B. Metcalfe, a former Indian agent in Oregon Territory and now a resident of Texas; and A. P. Dennison, an Indian agent in Oregon and a member of the Lane faction. On the second day of the convention, A. P. Dennison was chosen one of the vice-presidents and Isaac Stevens was appointed to the Committee on Resolutions and Platform.[64]

60 Salem *Oregon Statesman*, December 20, 1859.
61 James M. Pyle to Deady, February 1, 1860, Deady Papers.
62 William H. Farrar to Nesmith, November 18, 1859, Nesmith Papers.
63 Hooker to Nesmith, December 19, 1859, Nesmith Papers.
64 Murat Halstead, *Caucuses of 1860; a History of the National Political Con-*

The Oregon delegates aligned themselves with the anti-Douglas forces. The Pacific Coast delegations were in a strategic position in the convention since there were fifteen slave states and sixteen free states represented exclusive of the Pacific Coast. In almost every instance, the decision of the two Pacific states tipped the balance in favor of the South. Thus, the Southern group organized the convention and elected the anti-Douglas Caleb Cushing to the permanent chairmanship.[65] Similarly, the South was able to muster a majority on the all-important Platform Committee. Stevens, with the representative from the California delegation, voted with the South in favor of amending the Cincinnati platform in such a way as to repudiate the Northern or Douglas interpretation. The committee remained in session for several days, unable to unite on a single set of resolutions. In the meantime, the convention was flooded with resolutions from the floor in a vain and confused effort to aid the committee in its deliberations.

On the fifth day of the convention, April 27, the Committee on Platform presented three reports to the delegates: the majority report embodying the Southern point of view, the minority report of the Douglas members, and a third plan suggested by Benjamin F. Butler which simply reaffirmed the Cincinnati platform of 1856. Debate raged for the next few days over the adoption of these reports. On the day following the presentation of the reports, Isaac Stevens made a speech before the convention urging the adoption of the majority, or anti-Douglas, report. Balloting on the platform began on Monday, April 30, after much behind-the-scenes week-end negotiation. Butler's platform was defeated first. The Douglas, or minority, report, supported by a majority of the individual delegates, was then taken up by the convention. After the adoption of the first resolution, the convention was thrown into disorder and seven Southern states refused to vote further. On the following day, the Southern delegations withdrew from the convention. Immediately after the walkout, a delegate from California, according to a convention reporter, proceeded to "pour hot shot into the Popular Sovereignty camp." Purporting to speak for the entire Pacific Coast, the Californian declared that the South had been maltreated and

ventions of the Current Presidential Campaign: Being a Complete Record of the Business of all the Conventions (Columbus, Ohio, 1860), pp. 24, 29.
[65] Roy F. Nichols, *The Disruption of American Democracy* (New York, 1948), p. 297.

warned that "if the aggressions of the North continue, and the Union should be dissolved, the Pacific States have, thank God, the domain upon which to build up a splendid empire of their own."[66]

The remaining delegates turned to the election of a presidential candidate. The names of six individuals were placed in nomination: Stephen A. Douglas, James Guthrie, Daniel S. Dickinson, Robert M. T. Hunter, Andrew Johnson, and Joseph Lane. Stevens made the nomination address for Lane. What was at first considered an easy victory for the Douglas forces turned into a losing battle. The winning candidate, it was decided, must receive two-thirds of the total vote of the convention, not two-thirds of the remaining delegates. A deadlock ensued. On the first ballot, Douglas received 145½ votes, far short of the required two-thirds. Lane received the vote of the Oregon delegation plus three votes from Pennsylvania. Fifty-seven ballots were taken before the delegates realized the futility of continuing unless the Douglas group should agree to drop their candidate. Douglas at no time received more than a bare majority of the full convention. Lane's vote reached a high of twenty and one-half votes but dwindled to fourteen votes by the fifty-seventh ballot.[67] At this point, the delegates adjourned for six weeks to meet again in Baltimore on June 18, 1860. Provision was made for the replacement of those delegations that had withdrawn from the convention. By this maneuver the Douglas supporters hoped that their candidate might yet be nominated.[68]

The Oregon delegation remained in the convention but continued to side with the anti-Douglas forces. For a time it looked as though Lane might emerge as a compromise choice. On April 21, the *New York Times* correspondent at Charleston reported that orders had arrived from Buchanan urging the nomination of Lane.[69] Stout later revealed that a movement to compromise the difficulties by nominating Lane had met with favor from both sides. After the disruption of the convention over the platform, Stout wired Lane in Washington for instructions. Lane immediately replied: "Your dispatch is received. Stand by the equality of States, and Stand by those

[66] Halstead, *Caucuses of 1860*, pp. 33, 41, 56, 79; Austin L. Venable, "The Conflict Between the Douglas and Yancey Forces in the Charleston Convention," *Journal of Southern History*, VIII (May, 1942), 226-241.

[67] Halstead, *Caucuses of 1860*, pp. 85-91.

[68] Nichols, *Disruption of American Democracy*, pp. 307-308.

[69] *New York Times*, April 25, 1860.

States that Stand by the Constitutional rights of all. By all means go with them—go out and Stand by them."[70] Although Stout attempted to keep the contents of the dispatch secret, a leak in the telegraph office revealed Lane's sentiments to the Douglas managers. The movement in Lane's favor, according to Stout's report, immediately collapsed.[71] The correspondent of the *New York Herald,* an administration newspaper, however, adopted a different view of Lane's chances:

> Gen. Lane's despatch to Mr. Stout . . . urging the Oregon delegation to remain firm in maintaining the equality of the States, has created a strong feeling in his favor. He would have had the best chance of being nominated if the democratic convention had held together . . . Stout kept back Lane's friends, some think, too long. No organized band of politicians worked for him, but he provoked, on that account, the less hostility.[72]

In the weeks before the convention at Baltimore in June there was a great deal of scrambling among the Douglas delegates and their opponents to build up sufficient strength to carry their programs. The seceders from the Charleston convention scheduled a meeting in Richmond early in June, but most of them decided to take no action there and proceeded on to Baltimore. The chances for an amicable settlement of party difficulties were no greater in Baltimore than they had been in Charleston. Lane, himself, wrote: "One thing, however, is certain, that is Douglas cannot nor will not be nominated, or if he should be the south will bring out a candidate and run him with the certainty of giving him the entire south." Lane aptly summed up the situation: "We are in a muss, and I can hardly see how we can get out with whole bones, but we will see."[73] The *New York Herald* still thought Lane's chances were good. Lane's name and that of Jefferson Davis were most prominently mentioned among the Southern group; if a Southern man should be nominated

[70] San Francisco *Daily Evening Bulletin,* June 18, 1860; Washington *Star,* [n. d.], quoted in Salem *Oregon Statesman,* July 3, 1860.

[71] James O'Meara, "The Pioneer Days" [newspaper clipping, dated November 30, 1890], Scrap-Book #48, Oregon Historical Society Library. Stout's story was told to O'Meara following the convention. O'Meara concluded that "General Lane had prevented his own nomination for president by the indiscretion of that dispatch. His nomination at Charleston at the time would have prevented the fatal split in the democratic party. . . . The destiny of the Union was involved in that brief dispatch."

[72] *New York Herald,* [n. d.], quoted in Salem *Oregon Statesman,* June 12, 1860.

[73] Lane to Deady, May 13, 1860, Joseph Lane Papers, Oregon Historical Society Library.

for president, it was almost certain that Lane would receive the second place on the ticket.[74]

The Oregon delegation appeared in the Front Street Theatre, Baltimore, on June 18, and, to the delight of Southerners, continued to act with the Southern states.[75] On the second day of the meeting, Isaac Stevens was appointed to the Committee on Credentials.[76] A bone of contention appeared at the very beginning in the decision to seat a number of contested delegations, particularly from those Southern states that had withdrawn at Charleston. The Douglas forces this time had everything their own way. The majority report of the committee, seating all the Douglas delegations, was presented and adopted by the convention. Stevens presented the minority report, which maintained that the withdrawal of delegates from the Charleston convention did not constitute resignation and that they still were the accredited delegates from their states.[77]

The climax came after the acceptance of the majority report by the convention. The Virginia delegation, large portions of the delegations from North Carolina, Tennessee, and Maryland, and the California group walked out. At this point, Isaac Stevens took the floor and declared that he had "a most melancholy duty to perform." He went on to say:

> We did hope, when this Convention reassembled at Baltimore, that it would bring together the Democratic party in every sovereign State. We find ourselves grievously mistaken. By your action to-day, gentlemen as much entitled to seats as ourselves, in our opinion, are excluded from the floor. We do not mean to impugn the motives of others, but are conscious that a most grievous wrong and insult has been given to sovereign States. These States are the weak parties in this contest, and we have resolved to stand by them and assert their rights. I now announce that the delegation from Oregon have come to the conclusion to withdraw from the deliberations and take no further part in them.[78]

The Oregon delegation thereupon walked out of the hall, followed by individual members from other states. Following the withdrawal, the remaining delegates nominated Stephen A. Douglas for presi-

[74] *New York Herald,* [n. d.], quoted in Salem *Oregon Statesman,* June 12, 1860.
[75] *Richmond Enquirer,* May 8, 1860, Dwight L. Dumond, ed. *Southern Editorials on Secession* (New York, 1931), p. 79.
[76] Halstead, *Caucuses of 1860,* p. 177.
[77] *Minority Report of Mr. Stevens, Delegate from Oregon, Showing the Grounds upon which the Regular Southern Delegation were entitled to Seats in the Convention at the Front Street Theatre, Baltimore* (Breckinridge and Lane Campaign Documents, No. 2, Washington, 1860).
[78] Halstead, *Caucuses of 1860,* p. 199.

dent. Benjamin Fitzpatrick, the original choice of the convention
for vice-president, declined. Herschel Johnson of Georgia was later
chosen to fill his place.

The Oregonians assembled in Market Hall with the rest of the
seceding delegates. Representing 105 votes out of the old convention,
the group unanimously adopted the majority platform of the
Charleston convention. Stevens again placed the name of Joseph
Lane in nomination for president, declaring, "We have tried him
and know him as a statesman, and as a man of honor—we know him
as a man of experience, and we know him as a man ruled by the
Constitution under which we live."[79] Lane, however, received no
votes for the presidency. Breckinridge was nominated over Daniel S.
Dickinson by a vote of eighty-one to twenty-four, the Oregon delegation casting its ballot for the former. Lane's name was then placed
in nomination for vice-president by a delegate from North Carolina,
seconded by the California delegation, and unanimously approved.[80]
Anticipating the presidential campaign, Caleb Cushing, chairman of
the Market Hall convention, appointed a sixteen-man Democratic
National Executive Committee to be headed by Isaac I. Stevens.

Thus, the final and complete disruption of the national Democratic party was accomplished. Two presidential tickets were presented to the American people, each group claiming to be the regular
party organization. Compromise had failed, an unpleasant indication that the political issues between the two sections had now
reached a point where compromise was impossible. There was little
rejoicing over the results of the Democratic conventions. The possibility of a Republican victory in 1860 loomed larger than ever.

On June 30, 1860, Joseph Lane, now a candidate for vice-president,
sent to Caleb Cushing his letter of acceptance, in which he expressed
the spirit and principles that had actuated the Southern delegates.

> Compromises of constitutional principles are ever dangerous, and I am
> rejoiced that the true Democracy has seen fit to plant a firm foot on the rock
> of truth, and to give the people an opportunity to vindicate their love of jus-
> tice and fraternal regard for each other's rights.
> Non-intervention on the subject of Slavery, I may emphatically say, is that
> cardinal maxim of the Democracy—non-intervention by Congress and non-

[79] *Ibid.,* p. 224.
[80] Breckinridge was considered a conservative man. He had already assured
the delegates of his devotion to the cause of reuniting the party and his disavowal
of the Southern threats to secede should the Republicans win (Nichols, *Disruption of American Democracy,* p. 319).

intervention by Territorial Legislatures, as is fully stated in the first resolution of the adopted platform.

In vain should we declare the former without insisting upon the latter; because, to permit Territorial legislatures to prohibit or establish Slavery, or by unfriendly legislation to invalidate property, would be granting powers to the creature or agent, which, it is admitted, do not appertain to the principal, or the power that creates; besides which, it would be fostering an element of agitation in the Territory that must necessarily extend to Congress and the people of all the States.

If the Constitution establishes the right of every citizen to enter the common territory with whatever property he legally possesses, it necessarily devolves on the Federal Government the duty to protect this right of the citizen whenever and wherever assailed or infringed. The Democratic party honestly meets this agitating question, which is threatening to sever and destroy this brotherhood of States. It does not propose to legislate for the extension of Slavery, nor for its restriction, but to give to each State and to every citizen all that our forefathers proposed to give—namely, perfect equality of rights, and then to commit to the people, to climate, and to soil, the determination as to the kind of institution best fitted to their requirements in their constitutional limits, and declaring as a fundamental maxim, that the people of a Territory can only establish or prohibit Slavery when they come to form a constitution, preparatory to their admission as a State into the Union. . . .

Our Union must be preserved! But this can only be done by maintaining the Constitution inviolate in all its provisions and guaranties. The Judicial authority, as provided by the Constitution, must be maintained, and its decisions implicitly obeyed, as well in regard to the rights of property in the Territories as in all other matters.[81]

Lane, a Western man with strong Southern sympathies, expressed a constitutional principle that had been at stake in the Democratic national convention, and one which would be finally decided in the forthcoming election. His statement prompted Horace Greeley to describe him as "the poorest stick ever set up for so exalted a station," and to accuse him of "unbounded servility to the extreme Pro-Slavery faction."[82]

News of the split in the Charleston convention was carried by pony express from Missouri to California, and from San Francisco to Portland by the steamer "Panama." The arrival of the steamer brought out crowds anxious to learn the result of the national convention. The first passenger ashore was seized and asked the outcome of the convention. When the people found out that no nomination

[81] Joseph Lane to Caleb Cushing, June 30, 1860, Horace Greeley and John F. Cleveland, eds. *A Political Text-Book for 1860: Comprising a Brief View of Presidential Nominations and Elections* . . . (New York, 1860), p. 212.
[82] *New York Tribune*, June 26, 1860.

was made and the meeting had broken up, they moved on to the newspaper depot, where the San Francisco newspapers were torn open and read. The editor of the *Oregonian* described the scene that followed:

> Some politicians went home with their copies, to read in solitude the sad particulars. Others stood around speechless, to hear the comments, and, like the boy who had suffered a personal disaster, had not a word to say. We saw an editor standing with his face toward the Willamette, staring at vacancy. It was a sad scene. The streets were never more quiet than they were an hour after the steamer's arrival.[83]

The presence of a few "irreverent" Republicans in the crowd added insult to injury. The *Statesman* blamed the split on "the talent and restlessness of John Caldwell Calhoun," who had raised a school of Southern politicians dedicated to the unholy ambition of founding a Southern republic.[84] The *Oregonian* expressed surprise that the North had finally stood its ground and forced the convention either to accept a Northern platform or split. The disruption, it was thought, stemmed from an "irrepressible conflict" within the Democratic party.[85]

The nominations of the Baltimore conventions were not received in Oregon with the jubilation that had characterized earlier days. Both the Lane and Douglas groups were satisfied that their candidates had been nominated by the regular Democratic party, and both considered their opponents as "bolters." The disruption of the national party had dashed all hopes for reunion on the state level, and the period of Democratic domination in both national and local politics was rapidly coming to an end. The nomination of Breckinridge and Lane was received with some enthusiasm by Democrats in Washington Territory. When the news arrived citizens of Olympia, the territorial capital, fired sixty guns to celebrate the occasion. The *Pioneer and Democrat,* preoccupied with party regularity, at first cast a few doubts on the legality of the convention that nominated Breckinridge. These doubts were dismissed with the observation that, even if all the states were not represented in the convention, the delegates did represent people "who entertain views upon the question of slavery similar to those we hold to."[86] More typical,

[83] Portland *Weekly Oregonian,* May 26, 1860.
[84] Salem *Oregon Statesman,* May 29, 1860.
[85] Portland *Weekly Oregonian,* May 26, 1860.
[86] Olympia *Pioneer and Democrat,* July 27, 1860.

however, was the attitude of one Island County Democrat who, upon hearing of the split in the national convention and the nomination of two tickets, wrote, "This is a pretty *kettle of fish* indeed[.] God only knows how it will come out."[87]

While the Democrats were sealing their doom at Charleston and Baltimore, the Republicans prepared to nominate their standard-bearer. The Chicago convention was characterized by an atmosphere of enthusiasm and optimism. Most of the delegates realized, especially after the initial disruption in the Democratic party at Charleston, that they would in all likelihood be nominating the next president of the United States. They were determined to nominate a man and draft a platform that would appeal to as many groups and areas of the nation as possible. With the presidency almost within their grasp, Republicans did not wish to reduce their chances by acceding to the radicalism that was inherent in their organization. The sentiment of a large number of the delegates was expressed by Horace Greeley, who wrote:

> Now about the Presidency: I want to succeed this time, yet I *know* the country is not Anti-Slavery. It will only swallow a little Anti-Slavery in a great deal of sweetening. An Anti-Slavery man *per se* cannot be elected; but a Tariff, River-and-Harbor, Pacific-Railroad, Free Homestead man, *may* succeed *although* he is Anti-Slavery; so I'll try to get a candidate who will fairly and readily unite votes to win.[88]

Greeley became a leader in the convention and used the opportunity to carry his plans into action.

The Republican convention opened in Chicago on May 16, 1860. Oregon's delegation was completed by the appointment of three additional delegates, Joel Burlingame, Henry W. Corbett, and Frank Johnson.[89] Joel Burlingame, the father of Anson Burlingame, was the only delegate to make the trip East for the convention. Frank Johnson, a young divinity student at Hamilton, New York, was appointed because he was already in the East. Leander Holmes had assigned his proxy to Horace Greeley, a singular piece of good fortune for the Republican cause, and Corbett assigned his proxy to Eli Thayer, a Republican congressman from Massachusetts. Either

[87] Winfield Scott Ebey Diary, No. 6, p. 334 (July 23, 1860), University of Washington Library.

[88] Greeley to Mrs. Whipple, April, 1860, quoted in William Harlan Hale, *Horace Greeley, Voice of the People* (New York, 1950), p. 215.

[89] Oregon City *Oregon Argus*, February 25, 1860.

A. G. Hovey or Dr. Warren gave his proxy to Henry Buckingham, a resident of Salem and the fifth member of the Oregon delegation. The sixth member was unrepresented in the convention.[90]

As an official member of the convention, Horace Greeley directly exerted his influence on the Republican deliberations. Greeley had personal reasons for defeating the aspirations of Seward; on the other hand, he sincerely believed the nomination of Edward Bates would be the best choice for the party. In this he was in perfect accord with the Oregon delegation. Greeley had said, on one occasion, that Bates was the "only Republican whose election would not suffice as a pretext for civil war."[91]

The greatest task that faced the Republican convention was the preparation of a platform that would appeal to all the groups comprising the Republican organization. On the first day of the convention, the Committee on Resolutions was appointed, including Greeley of Oregon. When his name was announced, according to an eye witness, the convention experienced its first great outburst of applause and enthusiasm. Amidst the din were many cries, "When did you move?"[92] That same day, Greeley and Thayer drew up a resolution, referred to as the "Oregon Platform," which they hoped to include in the formal party platform. The resolution, "nearest to real popular sovereignty," according to one observer, declared that slavery could only exist where it had been established by laws constitutionally enacted, and opposed the introduction of slavery into the territories through the intervention of the national government.[93] The platform finally adopted by the convention contained seventeen resolutions, "the most perfect and unequivocal statement of Republican faith ever written," according to one member of the Oregon delegation.[94] It was marked by an obvious attempt to play down the radical tenets that had given birth to the Republican party, and less than one-third of the platform had to do with slavery. Statements urging economy in government and favoring a protective tariff, a free homestead policy, river and harbor improvements, pro-

[90] Leslie M. Scott, "Oregon's Nomination of Lincoln," *OHQ,* XVII (Sept., 1916) , 201-203.
[91] Quoted in Francis Brown, *Raymond of the Times* (New York, 1951) , p. 184.
[92] F. J. [Frank Johnson] to Adams, June 1, 1860, Oregon City *Oregon Argus,* July 14, 1860.
[93] Halstead, *Caucuses of 1860,* p. 130.
[94] F. J. [Frank Johnson] to Adams, June 1, 1860, Oregon City *Oregon Argus,* July 14, 1860.

tection to immigrants from foreign lands, and the construction of a Pacific railroad were included in the platform.[95] The section on slavery in the territories, as one historian has said, was weak and colorless, an attempt to evade one of the vital issues of the day. The power of Congress to exclude slavery from the territories was not affirmed, perhaps in an effort to avoid taking an interventionist position; the authority of Congress, of a territorial legislature, or of any individuals to give legal existence to slavery in the territories was denied.[96] The platform was a conscious attempt to broaden the base of the Republican party, not only to appeal to as many interest groups as possible but also to hold together the heterogeneous groups that composed the party.

The platform was speedily adopted, and on the third day of the convention the members were ready to consider the nomination of candidates. Seward led the first ballot, with Edward Bates polling only forty-eight votes and trailing four other candidates. On the second ballot, Bates's strength dropped to thirty-five. On both ballots he received Oregon's five votes plus a scattering of support from the border states. The third ballot was the last. When the fourth state in the roll call, Massachusetts, was called, the avalanche for Lincoln was apparent. Bates was abandoned, and Oregon cast four votes for Lincoln and one vote for Seward. In the final result Lincoln was only one and a half votes away from the nomination; Ohio promptly switched four votes from Chase to Lincoln, and the Illinoisan was nominated.[97] Hannibal Hamlin of Maine was nominated for vice-president on the second ballot.

Although Republicans received the news of Lincoln's nomination enthusiastically, some held a few reservations. Orville Hickman Browning, a member of the Illinois delegation, still thought that Bates should have been nominated and that the choice of Lincoln might prove a mistake. Had the struggle been prolonged, he felt, Bates would have been nominated.[98] Bates himself thought that a

[95] Greeley and Cleveland, eds. *Political Text-Book for 1860*, pp. 26-27.
[96] Emerson D. Fite, *The Presidential Campaign of 1860* (New York, 1911), pp. 124-125.
[97] Halstead, *Caucuses of 1860*, pp. 146-148; Allan Nevins, *The Emergence of Lincoln* (2 vols.; New York, 1950), II, 259-260. There is a belief that the switch of four of Oregon's votes from Bates to Lincoln on the third ballot started the Lincoln landslide; it has often been said that Oregon "nominated" Lincoln at Chicago (Scott, "Oregon's Nomination of Lincoln," pp. 201-214). There is no evidence in the official proceedings of the convention to support this belief.
[98] Pease and Randall, eds. *Diary of Orville Hickman Browning*, I, 408-410.

fatal blunder had been committed and the party would soon break into pieces.[99] Publicly, however, Bates lauded the nomination of Lincoln as the elevation of a Western man with Western principles. His Western origins and frontier affiliations made him a national candidate. "He could not be sectional if he tried," Bates wrote. "All his feelings and interests are identified with the great valley of the Mississippi, near whose center he has spent his whole life. That valley is not a section."[100]

Lincoln's nomination was warmly praised by the Republican papers in the Pacific Northwest. Adams enthusiastically acclaimed the Western character of the candidate and of the platform upon which he had been placed. He called upon Oregonians to unite with their brethren of the Old Northwest in support of the great principles enunciated by the party:

> in favor of freedom as national—of preserving the territory of the nation pure from the stain of slavery—of extending liberal and just institutions—of protecting free labor—of developing and magnifying the resources of our vast country, and of extending our systems of internal improvements.[101]

Dryer announced the nomination of Lincoln and Hamlin with more restraint.[102] The rank and file of the party in Oregon immediately held a "ratification meeting" at Lafayette, in Yamhill County, at which John R. McBride, Anson G. Henry, Adams, Medorem Crawford, and George L. Woods spoke. James McBride, the father of John, declared that the policy of the Republican party was identical with that of the Democratic party in former times, and hence would receive his support. Henry, one of Lincoln's old friends in Illinois, spoke of his close friendship with the party's candidate. As a frontiersman, Henry maintained, Lincoln was familiar with the needs of the Pacific Coast.[103] The Douglas Democrats viewed Lincoln's nomination with a good deal more equanimity than might have been expected. The *Statesman* declared that Lincoln's fame rested upon his opposition to Douglas in Illinois in 1858. Although he had proved no match for Douglas, Lincoln did show himself possessed of a good deal of "political tact." The paper was a little puzzled, how-

[99] Beale, ed. *Diary of Edward Bates,* pp. 128, 131.
[100] Bates to Browning, June 11, 1860, Pease and Randall, eds. *Diary of Orville Hickman Browning,* I, 416-417.
[101] Oregon City *Oregon Argus,* June 23, 1860.
[102] Portland *Weekly Oregonian,* June 23, 1860.
[103] *Ibid.,* July 14, 1860.

ever, that the Republicans had discarded all their old leaders in favor of this prairie politician.[104]

One more political convention completed the four-cornered presidential contest. In early May, a group of unreconstructed Whigs met at Baltimore and organized the Constitutional Union party. The delegates, drawn mainly from the border states, nominated John Bell of Tennessee for president and Edward Everett of Massachusetts for vice-president. Convinced that party platforms had misled and deceived the American people, in addition to encouraging the creation of sectional political parties, the group formulated no platform. The Pacific Coast states and eight others, from the South, New England, and the Midwest, were not represented in the convention. The Bell ticket received some support in California but was given little attention by her northern neighbor. In August, 1860, however, an effort was made to organize a Bell-Everett ticket in Oregon.[105] When Bell was nominated, an electoral ticket was formed, but there is no evidence of an active campaign in Oregon. One observer later reported, "It is equivalent to a quest at Pompeii at this time to dig from the depths of time the evidences of their existence."[106]

Before the nominations of the Chicago and Baltimore conventions were known in Oregon, the voters in that state went to the polls to choose a congressman and state legislators. The selection of the latter was significant since the new legislature would elect two United States Senators in its fall session. The Republicans realized that they held the balance of power between the two warring factions of the Democratic party and were determined to exploit fully this opportunity. Their first step was to invite Edward Dickinson Baker, known in the West as the "Grey Eagle of Republicanism," to move to Oregon, campaign for Lincoln, and finally run for United States Senator.

Baker, born in England, had migrated early in life to Illinois, where he studied law and practiced in Springfield as a partner of Stephen T. Logan, the father of David Logan. Baker and Lincoln became lifelong friends. In 1843, they were both defeated for the Whig nomination to Congress. Baker was elected to the following

[104] Salem *Oregon Statesman,* June 26, 1860.
[105] Oregon City *Oregon Argus,* August 4, 1860.
[106] Salem *Oregon Statesman,* September 11, 25, 1860; James O'Meara, "Our Pioneer Days," Scrap-Book #48, Oregon Historical Society Library.

term but resigned midway through the session to participate in the Mexican War. Although a Whig, Baker supported President Polk's expansionist policy and stanchly defended this expression of America's manifest destiny. Following the Mexican War, Baker was again elected to Congress. In 1851 he moved to San Francisco, where he practiced law and entered politics, becoming one of the organizers of California's Republican party. During the late fifties his association with the Douglas faction of the Democratic party grew very close. Baker himself was a champion of popular sovereignty and advocated it as a Republican measure in his campaigns. When David C. Broderick, a leader of the Douglas wing and Senator from California, was fatally shot in a duel, Baker was chosen to deliver the funeral oration. Although Baker consistently sought election to public office in California throughout the fifties, he was not successful in his attempts to challenge the power of the strong Democratic machine in that state.[107]

Oregon's Republicans had considered inviting Baker to canvass the state during the local elections as early as April, 1858, when the first state election was in the offing. The following year, T. J. Dryer and David Logan privately asked Baker to move to Oregon not only to campaign for the Republicans but also to run for Senator.[108] The invitation was extended without publicity because of the fear that older Republicans might resent it, as indeed they did. In December, 1859, Baker arrived in Oregon ostensibly to see the "country" and greet many of his old friends. The San Francisco correspondent of the *Oregonian,* however, let the cat out of the bag when he announced, "Col. Edward D. Baker . . . is about removing to Oregon. . . . [Oregon] will gain one of the most eminent champions of free-

---

[107] There is no adequate account of Baker's life. His career has inspired eulogistic treatment rather than critical and balanced study. For the details of his life, see John P. Snigg, "Edward Dickinson Baker—Lincoln's Forgotten Friend," *Lincoln Herald,* LIII (Summer, 1951) , 33-37; William D. Fenton, "Edward Dickinson Baker," *OHQ,* IX (March, 1908) , 1-23; James H. Matheny, "A Modern Knight Errant—Edward Dickinson Baker," *Journal of the Illinois State Historical Society,* IX (April, 1916) , 23-42; John J. Hay, "Colonel Baker," *Harper's Magazine,* XXIV (December, 1861) , 103-110; Milton H. Shutes, "Colonel E. D. Baker," *California Historical Society Quarterly,* XVII (December, 1938,) , 303-324; Edward A. Dickson, "Lincoln and Baker: The Story of a Great Friendship," *Historical Society of Southern California Quarterly,* XXXIV (September, 1952) , 229-242; and *Biographical Directory of the American Congress, 1774-1949* (Washington, 1950) , pp. 805-806.

[108] Salem *Oregon Statesman,* April 6, 1858; Oregon City *Oregon Argus,* October 27, 1860.

dom and the rights of man in the Union."[109] That same month, Lincoln was informed that Baker had hired a house in Salem and was making arrangements to bring his family to Oregon.

> *Sub Rosa*—He is coming here on a political mission. His object is to go to the Senate. The prospects now are that he will get one third or more of the Representatives and Senators at the election in June—and that the Anti-Lecompton democrats will get about the same number, and that together they will elect the two Senators—of which he is likely to be one. His ambition is to be a Senator.[110]

Baker's arrival in Oregon filled out the roster of Illinoisans who were active in Oregon politics. Anson G. Henry, David Logan, Simeon Francis, and Edward D. Baker had all been close friends in Illinois.

The Republican party in Oregon also considered the possibility of a coalition with other political groups since Republican strength was insufficient in itself to elect a United States Senator. Aid from outside the party was necessary. Some Republicans, fearing that such a move was in the wind, strongly opposed the idea of fusion. As early as March, 1859, one Republican declared that he preferred defeat to an entangling alliance with another political group.[111] The *Oregonian* declared its opposition: "Better, far, to suffer a defeat than a partial victory acquired at the sacrifice of honor and principle."[112] Jesse Applegate thought a coalition with either branch of the Democratic party would result in a loss of self-respect; the Republican party was a party of principle, not of price.[113] In spite of these protestations, Republican leaders seriously considered a fusion with the anti-Lane Democrats as a means of ending Lane's leadership in Oregon politics and of securing a foothold for their own party. One of the leaders of the movement undoubtedly was Baker himself, who brought to Oregon politics a long career marked by compromise and concession. An alliance with the Douglas Democrats was not the sacrifice many Republicans thought. The two groups had much in common. Working closely together in national

109 Portland *Weekly Oregonian,* December 17, 1859; W. H. C. [San Francisco correspondent] to the Editor, December 19, 1859, *ibid.,* December 24, 1859.
110 Simeon Francis to Lincoln, December 26, 1859, Lincoln Papers.
111 G. W. Hunt to the Editor, February 25, 1859, Oregon City *Oregon Argus,* March 12, 1859.
112 Portland *Weekly Oregonian,* October 29, November 5, December 10, 1859.
113 Oregon City *Oregon Argus,* March 31, 1860.

politics, both parties locally advocated popular sovereignty and shared a strong antagonism against their common enemy, the Lane Democrats.

The first move toward a fusion of Republicans with Douglas Democrats took place during the state election campaign of 1860. The principal object of both groups was the defeat of the Lane faction in the struggle for legislature seats, thereby assuring the election of a Republican and a Douglas Democrat to the United States Senate in September. The fusion was not a well-directed state-wide policy but was expressed on the county level. In Marion County, strongly anti-Lane, the Republicans, on the advice of Baker, nominated no ticket, leaving the field entirely to the two wings of the Democratic party. Republicans were advised to support the Douglas Democratic ticket.[114] A more concerted effort was made in Linn County, Delazon Smith's home county, often referred to as the "Gibraltar of Oregon Democracy." The Republicans of Linn, normally standing no chance for election, were favorable from the beginning to an alliance with the Douglas Democrats.[115] A mixed caucus was held, and an opposition ticket, consisting of two Republicans and two Douglas Democrats, was agreed upon. Both George H. Williams and James W. Nesmith supported this fusion ticket.[116]

The fusion game paid off for both the Republicans and the Douglas Democrats. The new legislature contained nineteen Lane Democrats, eighteen Douglas Democrats, and thirteen Republicans. The Republicans clearly possessed the balance of power; a Republican leader predicted that one of the new Senators would be a Republican or there would be no election.[117] The election for congressman was not so encouraging. Bush, maintaining up to the last minute that the election was an illegal one, ignored the fight for Congress. Logan, the Republican nominee, encouraged by the differences in the Democratic ranks, was confident that he would be elected.[118] The election, as in 1859, was a close one. Sheil, the

114 *Ibid.*, June 9, 1860.

115 John Conner to [Elisha Applegate], December 23, 1859, Oliver Cromwell Applegate Papers. Conner was the leader of the Republican party in Linn County.

116 Salem *Oregon Statesman*, February 21, 1860; Deady to Nesmith, June 29, August 4, 1860, Deady Papers.

117 Amory Holbrook to Lincoln, July 21, 1860, Lincoln Papers.

118 Salem *Oregon Statesman*, May 29, 1860; Logan to Mary Logan, January 22, 1860, Harry E. Pratt, ed. "22 Letters of David Logan," *OHQ*, XLIV (Sept.,

Lane Democratic candidate, was narrowly elected by a margin of only 103 votes.[119]

Although a larger vote had been cast than in any previous year, Bush maintained more strongly than ever that the election had been without constitutional authorization. The new legislature, he hoped, would provide for a new election.

> Should the legislature fail, at the coming session, to make legal provision for a Congressional election, we then advise and urge that candidates for Congress be voted for at the Presidential election in November. . . . One illegal election is as good as another; but the latest expression of the people is entitled to the most consideration. Let us choose a Congressman in November, in any event.[120]

Logan was bitterly disappointed at his defeat. Adams, however, was not disheartened. He was certain that Oregon was potentially a Republican state. Adams was confident that, if a Republican president should be elected in 1860, the Douglas Democratic votes would become Republican votes and the fusion between the two groups would prove to be a lasting one.[121]

The election attracted a good deal of national attention. Joseph Lane, a candidate for vice-president, was by this time a national figure, and many eyes were turned toward his home state. The fact that the election would determine the political complexion of Oregon's two United States Senators gave it national significance. One San Francisco newspaper declared, before the results of the election were known:

> It was one of the most important political contests to the country at large that will be held this year in the Union. It has determined which side of the principal question that agitates the nation, two United States Senators shall occupy during the ensuing six years—Whether they shall be classed as Northern or Southern men.[122]

When it was learned that the Republicans and Douglas Democrats had achieved a decisive majority over Lane's followers, the same newspaper spoke of the results as a "political revolution" and predicted that Oregon would never again vote a James Buchanan Demo-

---

1943), 280. Bush referred to the Lane ticket as the "guerilla ticket." He never raised the names of the candidates to the masthead of his paper and urged Democrats to vote the Democratic ticket on the county level only.

[119] Portland *Weekly Oregonian*, July 14, 1860.

[120] Salem *Oregon Statesman*, August 14, 1860.

[121] Oregon City *Oregon Argus*, July 7, 1860.

[122] San Francisco *Daily Evening Bulletin*, June 7, 1860.

cratic ticket. Republicans and Douglas Democrats in California were hopeful that a similar "revolution" would occur in their own state.[123] Horace Greeley, in his *Tribune,* was enthusiastic. In an editorial entitled, "Hail, Oregon!" Greeley wrote that the election was a forerunner of the "great purifying tornado of next November." He was confident that two anti-Lane Senators would be chosen by the state legislature.[124]

Republicans in Washington Territory had little cause for enthusiasm. An election for members of the territorial legislature was held almost simultaneously with the Oregon election. The results were encouraging to many Democrats who had been apprehensive of their party's future. The Democrats made a clean sweep, electing twenty-four members of the legislature against nine Republicans. In jubilation, the *Pioneer and Democrat* reported that the "democracy were never before so united."[125] The Democratic majority, however, was a deceptive one, for it obscured the split between the Stevens forces and the anti-Stevens, or Douglas, group. One Republican saw the results as "the handwriting on the wall to Stevensocracy."[126]

The Democratic party in Oregon still remained rather tenuously united under one organization, in spite of the fact that the national party had already split into two distinct units. The final split of the local party was accomplished on August 18, 1860, when the Democratic State Central Committee met to schedule a state convention for the nomination of presidential electors. As soon as the committee meeting opened, Riley E. Stratton, a Douglas Democrat, declared that the time for the separation had arrived. In order to hasten the split, he offered a motion that the committee endorse Douglas and Johnson as the regular nominees of the Democratic party. Delazon Smith immediately countered with an amendment declaring that Breckinridge and Lane should be so recognized. Smith followed with a plea that Stratton's resolution be withdrawn and an attempt be made to compromise the differences in the party. Stratton, however, refused. Smith's amendment was upheld, and the Douglas members walked out of the meeting.[127] The withdrawing members

123 *Ibid.,* June 14, 1860.
124 *New York Tribune,* July 9, 1860.
125 Olympia *Pioneer and Democrat,* July 13, 20, 1860.
126 Alexander S. Abernethy to Elwood Evans, July 19, 1860, Elwood Evans Papers, 1843-1894, Yale University Library (microfilm in University of Washington Library).
127 Corvallis *Oregon Weekly Union,* August 21, 1860.

then met together and scheduled a Douglas Democratic convention to nominate three Douglas presidential electors.[128]

Both conventions met at Eugene in September, 1860. The Breckinridge convention endorsed their national platform and, in a fit of invective, resolved to "despise and loathe the vile treason, the gross personalities, and the hypocritical teachings of the *Oregon Statesman,* and those who furnish the Judas material for its weekly issues." Delazon Smith, James O'Meara, and D. W. Douthitt were chosen presidential electors. At the close of the session, an olive branch was held out to the Douglas Democrats. W. W. Chapman proposed that a committee be formed "to confer with any Committee that may be constituted by the Douglas Convention for the purpose of conciliation."[129] The Douglas convention, however, would not cooperate. Meeting in the same city and at the same time as the Breckinridge group, the Douglasites endorsed the principle of nonintervention and the speedy construction of a Pacific railroad. William H. Farrar, Benjamin Hayden, and William Hoffman were selected presidential electors. In the hope that the state legislature would declare the congressional election of June illegal and provide for a new election, the convention empowered the central committee to make all nominations necessary for such an election.[130] Thus, the two wings of the once-united Democratic party followed the pattern of the national organization. The final, formal split of the party in September, 1860, was the culmination of almost a decade of intraparty strife. The divorce resulted not only from national issues, which aided the local party split, but also from issues that were primarily local in character and origin.

The crucial session of the Oregon state legislature opened at Salem in the second week of September. All legislative business was insignificant compared to the election of the two United States Senators. Bush stressed the importance of this election. The next few years, he thought, would see "the most momentous political question of this or of any age—that of the permanent existence of this Union" settled, "definitely and irrevocably." The floor of the Senate would become a battlefield of liberty where Seward's "irrepressible conflict" would be fought. To prevent the Union from ending in disaster,

[128] Salem *Oregon Statesman,* August 28, 1860.
[129] Corvallis *Oregon Weekly Union,* September 22, 1860.
[130] Salem *Oregon Statesman,* September 25, 1860.

Bush thought it was imperative that two noninterventionist Senators be chosen by the legislature.[131] Republicans, Douglas Democrats, and Lane Democrats were all confident of victory.[132] Lane had more than a personal interest in the results of the election. The eyes of the nation were turned toward the far Northwest, closely observing the political trends in Lane's own state. Lane's repudiation in Oregon would damage the national Breckinridge ticket.

Partisan strife was evident from the day the legislature opened. The state house of representatives was organized by a coalition of Republicans and Douglas Democrats. Benjamin F. Harding, a Douglasite, was elected speaker. The state senate split in its vote for president of the senate between a Lane Democrat and a Douglas Democrat. Following the deadlock, six Lane members prepared to withdraw from the proceedings in order to prevent a quorum. Governor Whiteaker, a Lane Democrat, persuaded them to remain in the chamber in the hope that some reconciliation could be made. The next day, however, the six members walked out.[133] In spite of an earnest appeal by Whiteaker and the fruitless searchings of the sergeant-at-arms, the six members remained out of the session for almost two weeks.[134]

During the absence of the six senators, legislative business in the upper house was at a standstill. All parties were busy preparing for the Senatorial election. The Republicans were particularly active. Those who favored the election of Baker not only had to arrange a coalition with the Douglas Democrats, without which Baker could not be elected, but also had to contend with dissatisfaction in their

[131] *Ibid.,* September 4, 11, 1860.

[132] Baker to Lincoln, August 1, 1860, Lincoln Papers; Lane to Deady, July 13, 1860, Lane Papers.

[133] Salem *Oregon Statesman,* September 18, 1860; Amory Holbrook to "Dear Sir," [n. d.], Amory Holbrook Papers, Oregon Historical Society Library; State of Oregon, *Senate Journal,* 1860, pp. 4-5, 8-9. The withdrawal of the six senators was apparently carried out on the advice of Delazon Smith and had been planned for some time before the meeting of the legislature (Letter from Oregon, August 27, 1860, *Sacramento Daily Union,* September 10, 1860).

[134] The Breckinridge state convention, meeting in Eugene at this time, endorsed the action of the six senators who had withdrawn "for the purpose of preventing the consummation of a gross and infamous fraud upon the Democratic masses of this State, by the accomplishment of the election of a Black Republican to the Senate of the United States (as the fruit of a corrupt and infamous secret coalition)" (Corvallis *Oregon Weekly Union,* September 22, 1860). The Douglas convention linked the withdrawal with that of the Southerners from the national convention as part of a "great revolutionary scheme" (Salem *Oregon Statesman,* September 25, 1860).

own ranks. Some Republicans objected to Baker's election. David Logan and Amory Holbrook, both old residents of Oregon and each desirous of obtaining the election for himself, worked against the Baker forces in the Republican caucus meetings.[135] One Republican thought the election of Baker would injure Republican prospects in the November election. "Our enemies will charge that we have sold out to a California politician, and it will be used much to our injury," he wrote. Rather than elect Baker, he favored postponing the election altogether.[136] Another Republican thought an adherence to Baker would be suicidal because of his short residence in Oregon. He generously offered his own candidacy as that most likely to succeed.[137]

The Republican caucus succeeded in nominating Baker as its candidate for the Senate, although Holbrook and Logan refused to concur in the choice.[138] Jesse Applegate, not a member of the legislature but always an interested spectator, furiously opposed the action of the caucus:

> A more corrupt set of men never combined for an unrighteous purpose than the Republicans who made Baker the nominee of their party for the Senate. . . . My opinion of these mercinary and treacherous writches I have expressed freely to themselves and to others—and with my consent—neither the actors, aiders, or abettors of this plot against the rights of the people, and the interests of the State, shall ever enjoy an emolument, or abuse a trust.[139]

Negotiations between the Republicans and the Douglas Democrats continued. One member of the legislature reported on the opening day that there appeared to be some kind of an alliance between Baker and James W. Nesmith, the first choice of the Douglas group. Difficulties, however, constantly presented themselves. Some Douglasites declared they could not support Baker, while others

135 Henry to Lincoln, September 16, 1860, Lincoln Papers. Henry was one of the ringleaders of the pro-Baker forces.

136 W. V. Spencer to Medorem Crawford, September 13, 1860, Medorem Crawford Papers, University of Oregon Library. Crawford was a member of the legislature. It was thought that should Baker fail to be elected he would move back to California (Henry to Lincoln, September 16, 1860, Lincoln Papers).

137 J. Quinn Thornton to Crawford, September 18, 1860, Crawford Papers.

138 Henry to Lincoln, September 16, 1860, Lincoln Papers. Although Logan was instrumental in bringing Baker to Oregon, he had a change of heart when Baker was proposed as the Republican candidate. Holbrook thought the Republicans would lose out altogether because of the "engineering of Col. B. who thinks he runs it all & will take no advice. Our own folks begin to be sick of his management" (Holbrook to David W. Craig, [n. d.], Holbrook Papers).

139 Jesse Applegate to Harvey Gordon, September 24, 1860, Applegate Papers.

would support no other Republican. The situation became so confused that the sentiment of one member, "What will be the result cannot now be foretold," was soon the general feeling of the legislature.[140]

A week after the legislative session had begun, in the midst of the confusion resulting from all the party machinations, John R. McBride, one of the leading Republican members, made a special appeal to those blocking the proceedings. McBride complained that the family quarrel in the Democratic party had clogged the wheels of government. Rising above partisan bickerings, he maintained that Oregon could not afford to lose her representation in the United States Senate during such a crucial period; rather than deprive Oregon of two Senators just to secure a partisan success, he declared, he would even accept two respectable Breckinridge Democrats.[141] Balloting began for the Senators, in spite of the fact that the senate was not organized, and in the course of two days twenty ballots were taken without a result. In addition to the six absent members, a large number voted blank; consequently no candidates received the required number of votes, and balloting was abandoned.[142]

Two days later, the missing senators returned to their seats in the legislature and balloting resumed. After ten ballots were taken without result, a recess was called. When balloting began the next day, a noticeable change appeared in the lineup. Republican–Douglas Democratic cooperation was strengthened.[143] The Baker forces threw their support behind James W. Nesmith, the Douglas Democratic candidate, and elected him to the long term, while the Douglas Democrats joined the Republicans in electing Baker to the short term.[144]

For the first time since early 1859, Oregon had a full delegation

[140] Holbrook to "Dear Sir," [n. d.]; Holbrook to David Craig, [n. d.], Holbrook Papers.

[141] Portland *Weekly Oregonian*, September 29, 1860.

[142] State of Oregon, *Senate Journal*, 1860, pp. 17-18; Portland *Weekly Oregonian*, September 29, 1860. Anson G. Henry was confident that Baker would be elected Senator, even if not in a strictly legal manner (Henry to Lincoln, September 16, 1860, Lincoln Papers).

[143] Before the final ballot was taken, John R. McBride wrote, "Nesmith & Baker will be elected—*but keep it still*" (John R. McBride to David Craig, September 26, 1860, David W. Craig Papers, Oregon Historical Society Library).

[144] Proceedings, Oregon Senatorial Election, Oct. 1860, MS in the Oregon Historical Society Library. This document gives the details of all fourteen ballots and is signed by the presiding officers of the state senate and house of representatives. See also Salem *Oregon Statesman*, October 8, 1860.

in the United States Senate. The coalition of Douglas Democrats and Republicans not only indicated that the Douglasites were closer in principle and doctrine to the local Republican position than they were to their former brethren in the Democratic party, but also was an early sign of the realignment of political parties that followed the election of 1860. Some Republicans disliked the fusion with the Douglas group.[145] Holbrook considered Baker's election as much a "Squatter triumph" as a Republican victory and thought his election would lose the state for Lincoln. He was highly suspicious of Baker's close associations with the Douglas faction, both in California and in Oregon. Logan spread the story that Baker had sold out the Republican party in order to secure his election.[146] Republican leaders criticized the actions of Holbrook and Logan and accused them of "base treachery" to the party. McBride wrote that Holbrook "deserves nothing but curses at the hands of every true Republican." The *Oregonian,* now under the editorship of Simeon Francis, declared, "God may forgive Amory Holbrook for his treachery to the republican party, but the republicans of the Nation and of Oregon never will."[147]

The Douglas Democrats rejoiced at the results of the election, not only because the Lane faction had been decisively defeated but also because the new Republican Senator was pledged to the Douglas doctrine of popular sovereignty. Baker made no secret of his support of nonintervention, allowing the people of the territories to determine their own domestic institutions without interference by Congress. Even Republicans admitted that Baker's views were virtually identical with those of the Douglas Democrats.[148] Like the Republicans, not all Douglasites approved of the fusion. John C. Ainsworth, one of Portland's most prominent entrepreneurs, switched his allegiance from Douglas to Breckinridge because of the coalition. LaFayette Grover, former congressman and himself a disappointed candidate for the Senate, declared that the election of Nesmith and Baker would result in the "almost total destruction" of the Demo-

145 John A. Millard to Lindsay Applegate, October 3, 1860; R. S. Applegate to [Ivan D. Applegate], October 7, 1860, Oliver Cromwell Applegate Papers.

146 Holbrook to Craig, [n. d.], Holbrook Papers; Holbrook to Lincoln, October 2, 1860, Lincoln Papers; Simeon Francis to Craig, October 6, 1860, Craig Papers.

147 William L. Adams to Craig, [n. d.], Craig Papers; Henry to Lincoln, October 3, 1860, Lincoln Papers; McBride to Craig, October 2, 1860, Craig Papers; Portland *Weekly Oregonian,* November 24, 1860.

148 Portland *Weekly Oregonian,* September 29, 1860.

cratic party in Oregon. He was certain that Oregon would vote for Lincoln or Breckinridge in the November election.[149] The Lane Democrats were furious at the turn of events. One Lane newspaper branded every Democrat who supported the coalition as guilty of "moral and legal perjury" and urged the Lane members of the legislature to resign in order to prevent such a "corrupt and doubly infamous cabal" from doing any more harm to the people of Oregon.[150]

Following the election, both groups of Democrats justified their actions to the people of the state. An address by the Douglas members of the legislature appeared first. The Breckinridge Democrats, according to the address, had left the Democratic party and should therefore have no cause to complain if the "democracy combine with other parties against them as the common enemy." Rather than re-elect Delazon Smith or leave Oregon without Senators altogether, they had united with the Republicans in the election of Baker, by far the most palatable course to the Douglasites. The support given to Baker was not as much a sacrifice as many Democrats thought. The address declared, "In voting for Col. Baker, we were influenced, to some extent, by his well known position upon the question of slavery in the Territories—a position differing but little from that of our own party."[151] The Breckinridge statement was more bitter. Having elected thirty-seven out of the fifty members of the legislature, the Democratic party, it maintained, had a right to expect that two Democratic Senators would be elected. Instead a "perfidious and treacherous coalition" had engaged in a "wicked, nefarious attempt to disorganize, distract, and destroy the Democratic party in the State."[152]

The national reaction to Oregon's Senatorial election was immediate, almost as if the attention of the nation had been fixed on the proceedings at Salem. The California newspapers were first to comment. Republicans rejoiced that their favorite son had finally won his way to the United States Senate. One paper particularly exulted over the defeat of the Lane Democracy. The election of Baker and Nesmith, according to the paper, was the first fruit of "that political

[149] W. V. Spencer to Crawford, October 5, 1860, Crawford Papers; John A. Williams to "Friend Coon," October 3, 1860, Salem *Oregon Statesman,* October 15, 1860; LaFayette Grover to Bion F. Kendall, October 6, 1860, Bion F. Kendall Papers, University of Washington Library.
[150] Portland *Daily Morning News,* September 30, 1860.
[151] Salem *Oregon Statesman,* October 8, 1860.
[152] Corvallis *Oregon Weekly Union,* October 27, 1860.

revolution which we have warned the Democracy was going on upon this coast for the last three years." The Pacific coast would henceforth have two more votes in Congress that could be relied on to resist the "seductions of the ultra-South." A tremendous demonstration was held in San Francisco upon receipt of the news. The election, many thought, might swing the whole Pacific Coast into the Lincoln column.[153]

The news encouraged the antiadministration press in all parts of the nation. After the election, the *New York Times* wrote in an editorial, "If an alliance of Republicanism with Popular Sovereignty be practicable in Oregon, there is no reason why it should not prevail everywhere on the Pacific coast." The *Times* went on to characterize politics and political thinking in the Northwest:

> There [the Pacific Northwest] the doctrines of Mr. Douglas, freed from that narrow scrutiny which, to the more practiced sense of the civilized East, discloses their sophistry, are seen only in their results, which are recognized as being as hostile to the extension of Slavery as the extremest convictions of Gerrit Smith himself. And beyond the Rocky Mountains, political questions find liberty to adjust themselves upon their merits far more readily than here.[154]

The action of the Oregon legislature was significant in its possible influence on the coming presidential election. Lane was defeated in his own state, a circumstance that many hoped would injure the Breckinridge ticket nationally.

Thus the summer of 1860 witnessed the final split of the Democratic party on the Pacific Northwest frontier. While the split followed national developments, the alignment of the political parties differed from their national counterparts. The Republican party was controlled by popular sovereignty men and was therefore closely identified in principle with the Douglas Democrats. A situation was thus developing which, while it contained elements of aggressive Southern sympathies, contained other elements which produced a dominant Unionist nationalism. The fusion of Republicans with Douglas Democrats was a unique Western development, made possible only because the slavery issue had no potency to generate either a strong pro-Southern opinion or a vigorous antislavery sentiment.

[153] San Francisco *Daily Evening Bulletin,* October 8, 9, 1860; San Francisco *Daily Alta California,* October 9, 1860; *New York Times,* October 23, November 3, 1860.
[154] *New York Times,* October 25, 1860.

*the campaign
of 1860*

THE FUSION OF REPUBLICANS
with Douglas Democrats in the state of Oregon and its success in the
Senatorial election were a revolution in Pacific Northwest politics.
The domination of the Democratic party in Oregon politics was
finally broken by the election of a Republican and a Douglas Democrat to the United States Senate. The Democratic party suffered an
additional defeat in the election of 1860. The political developments
in the Pacific Northwest, however, were part of a far wider, more
significant revolution in American party politics, the campaign and
election of 1860. The frontier areas expressed a vital concern in the
national campaign; their interest was not lessened by isolation from
the center of political activity. One southern Oregon farmer wrote a
month before the election, "There is nothing in the world thougt of
heard or spoken of but polyticks."[1] Oregon's Governor Whiteaker,
in his message to the state legislature, reviewed the "unusual
spectacle" of four presidential candidates and concluded that it was
barely possible "that more angry strife or bitter feeling would be
manifest if the two sections of the country were engaged in actual
war."[2] The Pacific Northwest was brought closer to national politics

[1] R. S. Applegate to [Ivan D. Applegate], October 7, 1860, Oliver Cromwell
Applegate Papers, University of Oregon Library.
[2] State of Oregon, *Senate Journal*, 1860, p. 31.

in 1860 by the active participation of two "favorite sons" in the election campaign, Joseph Lane, the vice-presidential candidate on the Breckinridge ticket, and Isaac I. Stevens, the national chairman of the Breckinridge campaign committee.

Following the Democratic national conventions, Isaac I. Stevens settled down to months of hard work as chairman of the national Breckinridge and Lane committee. From his headquarters in the national capital, Stevens supervised the publication and distribution of campaign literature and scheduled campaign speeches and rallies. Months later he commented that his heart was always in his work; that he approached the task of presenting the Breckinridge ticket to the people with a crusader's zeal. "I believed that, in my humble sphere, I was striking a blow for the honor and renown of my country, and for the perpetuity of its institutions."[3] One of his duties was the preparation of an *Address to the Democracy and the People of the United States* in which the Breckinridge position was described in detail.[4]

In contrast with present-day campaigns, the presidential campaign of 1860 was a quiet one, an atmosphere that belied the tremendous importance of the issues involved. Abraham Lincoln made no speeches during the campaign. Douglas, the most energetic of the candidates, toured widely throughout the Midwest, South, and East. The first presidential candidate to make a concerted effort to carry the issues of a national election to the people, Douglas was on the stump from July up to the very day of the election in November.[5] Both Breckinridge and Lane planned to spend the summer quietly and looked with some disgust on Douglas' campaigning.

The popular reaction to Douglas' campaign roused the Breckinridge candidates from their lethargy. Lane made a series of excursions, in the course of which he delivered campaign speeches in Philadelphia and New York. Late in the summer he visited his birthplace in North Carolina, where he assured an audience that he would come to their defense if Southern rights were further invaded.[6] Lane's

[3] *Cong. Globe*, 36 Cong., 2 Sess., p. 207.

[4] *Address to the Democracy and the People of the United States* (Washington, 1860); Hazard Stevens, *The Life of Isaac Ingalls Stevens* (2 vols.; New York, 1900), II, 305. This *Address* was widely reprinted in the Breckinridge press throughout the country.

[5] Allan Nevins, *The Emergence of Lincoln* (2 vols.; New York, 1950), II, 277, 290-298.

[6] Portland *Weekly Oregonian*, October 13, 1860; Sister M. Margaret Jean

brief tour terminated in his old home state of Indiana, where he traveled in the company of Jesse Bright. Just across the river, in Covington, Kentucky, he delivered one of the most widely reported speeches of his campaign. The issue of the election was, according to Lane, "whether or not all the people should have equal rights in the common Territories." Popular sovereignty, he declared, was the "sheerest nonsense ever uttered by mortal man." He was for the preservation of the Union but warned that it could only be preserved by maintaining the Constitution and by refusing to allow the government to infringe on people's rights.[7] In Indianapolis, Lane promised he would not rebel if a Republican were elected; the next four years, he assured his audience, would pass quickly.[8] In his campaign speeches, Lane concentrated his arguments on the issue of slavery in the territories and gave little attention to other problems.

Isaac Stevens made few speeches in behalf of the Breckinridge ticket in the East. His most notable effort was at a "fusion" meeting at Cooper Union Institute in New York in October, 1860. There he maintained that the government could be saved only by the "inauguration of a new policy," a foretaste of his later belief in a "reconstruction" of the government as the only means for preserving the Union. The Republican party, he thought, was treasonable in its nature, and a Republican victory would mean the abolition of slavery and the complete overthrow of Southern rights. The inauguration of Lincoln, Stevens predicted, would be followed by a series of slave uprisings.[9]

The election campaign was fought with more vigor on the local level. In the Pacific Northwest news of the election monopolized the columns of the press throughout the summer and early fall. The election was recognized as more important to the Union than any preceding it.

The struggle in Oregon in 1860 was more a fight between the two wings of the Democratic party than between Democrats and Republicans. Not only had the local Douglas Democrats and Republicans demonstrated an ability to work together in state politics but also

Kelly, *The Career of Joseph Lane, Frontier Politician* (Washington, 1942), pp. 173-174.

[7] Cincinnati *Gazette*, September 12, 1860, quoted in *New York Times*, September 14, 1860; Portland *Daily Morning News*, October 16, 1860.

[8] Rome (Ga.) *Weekly Courier*, October 12, 1860, quoted in Ollinger Crenshaw, *The Slave States in the Presidential Election of 1860* (Baltimore, 1945), p. 28.

[9] *New York Times*, October 29, 1860.

their positions in the national presidential campaign tended to con-
verge. In other sections of the country where attempts were made
to fuse two or more of the four presidential tickets, the Republican
party was considered the common enemy of both wings of the Democratic party. Consequently, fusion attempts usually involved the
union of Breckinridge and Douglas tickets. In the Pacific Northwest,
however, a different situation prevailed. There, the Douglas Democrats and the Republicans coalesced against the Breckinridge Democrats. Local conditions were important in bringing about this coalition. The domination of the Lane party in Oregon politics during
the first year of statehood undoubtedly helped to unite the two wings
of the opposition, but the mere desire for office was not the sole, or
the most important, explanation. The foremost election issue in
1860 in Oregon, the issue that was fundamentally responsible for
the positions taken by the three parties, was that of popular
sovereignty. To understand the force this principle had in determining the direction of local politics in 1860, it must be borne in
mind that the Pacific Northwest was an isolated frontier, populated
by people strongly imbued with Jeffersonian-Jacksonian ideals and
jealous of their right of self-government.[10]

The issue of popular sovereignty was an important one in the local
state elections preceding the national contest. The congressional
election of 1859, in particular, was fought almost exclusively on
that issue, with the Republicans and Douglas Democrats uniting
behind a popular sovereignty Republican. The *Statesman* predicted
that popular sovereignty, or the doctrine of nonintervention by the
national government in the affairs of the territories, would be the
principal issue in 1860. Three proposals, the paper noted, had been
suggested as solutions of the problem of slavery in the territories: the
doctrine of the Senators from Mississippi, Jefferson Davis and Albert
Gallatin Brown, in favor of a congressional slave code for the territories; the position of the Buchanan administration, denying the
power of the territorial legislature to act on the question of slavery
and leaving the final determination to the Supreme Court (where

10 The issue of popular sovereignty in the election of 1860 has generally been
either minimized or ignored entirely. The standard accounts of the election
conclude that the Pacific railroad and the homestead issue were the ones most
appealing to Western areas. While other parts of the West have not been examined in this connection, this interpretation does not hold true for the Pacific
Northwest. See Reinhard H. Luthin, *The First Lincoln Campaign* (Cambridge,
Mass., 1944), pp. 220-227.

it had already been decided in favor of the administration) ; and the doctrine of popular sovereignty, as advocated by Stephen A. Douglas. In the *Statesman's* review of these proposals the national Republican position was curiously absent.[11]

Douglas Democrats had kept the principle of popular sovereignty before the people of the Pacific Northwest since receiving the news of the Kansas-Nebraska Act. As the presidential campaign approached, they argued their position with renewed intensity. Although four newspapers in Oregon took the side of Douglas, the *Oregon Statesman* remained the spokesman for the party. Popular sovereignty was not interpreted in its limited application, as originally provided in the Kansas-Nebraska Act, but was synonymous with the broader aspect of complete territorial self-government within the limits of the Constitution. A rigid construction of the Constitution, it was maintained, conceded no power whatever to Congress over the "domestic economy" of the territories.[12]

The Kansas-Nebraska Act was a preliminary expression of popular sovereignty. The Douglas party argued that, while the act had granted a limited form of self-government to the territories, a vote for Douglas was a vote for popular sovereignty in its broadest aspects. It was not proper that the national government, responsible for the welfare of thirty million people, should "fritter" away its time in the details of a municipal code for a few thousand territorial settlers, nor was it fair that these settlers should be governed by laws not of their own enacting and by officers not of their own choosing. Asahel Bush not only voiced the position of his party but also expressed a long-standing frontier grievance when he wrote:

> The power of self-government is the birthright of the American people, whether in large bodies or small. Still as the Atlantic States become fossilized, and conservative, they view with trembling distrust every exercise of power by a new and as they think, unstable community. They are inclined to settle any question of territorial policy by amplifying on the relations between beardless boys and fond parents.

An attempt was made to separate popular sovereignty from the slavery agitation. Nonintervention, declared Oregon's Douglasites, would be just as important if slavery were unknown on the continent. The extension of slavery was wholly within the interest of

[11] Salem *Oregon Statesman,* July 5, 1859.
[12] *Ibid.,* March 1, 1859.

those whom it directly concerned and therefore was not a legitimate issue in national politics.[13]

Through the campaign, the Douglasites took this broad point of view. Selucius Garfielde was invited down from Washington Territory to stump Oregon for Douglas. In one speech, he declared that the power of self-government was inherent in the people of both states and territories and that the Constitution granted Congress no power to interfere with the domestic concerns of either. The *Statesman* added:

> The "territory" or *land,* of the Territories belongs to the United States and is the common property of the citizens of all the States. But the *domestic* and *political institutions* of the Territories belong to the *people who inhabit the Territories* and to the citizens of no State.[14]

Douglas argued in favor of complete territorial self-government in many of his campaign speeches during the summer and early fall of 1860. Popular sovereignty was more than simply an adjustment of the slavery question. As a man "who has spent his whole life on the frontier," Douglas compared the demands for self-government in the territories to the American Revolution. "I have never claimed for the people of the territories any other right, or higher right, than our fathers maintained at the point of the bayonet for the colonies prior to the Revolution." The Wilmot Proviso was an attempt to violate the principle of self-government. Douglas informed one audience in North Carolina:

> Those of us who penetrated into the wilderness think that we know what kind of laws and institutions will suit our interests quite as well as you who never saw the country. . . . You cannot convince us that we are not as good as our brothers, who remain in the old states.[15]

The Douglas Democrats in Oregon did not accept the national platform of their party without qualification but, like the Republicans, modified the national stand. The Douglas convention at Baltimore had compromised its original position by adding a resolution designed, perhaps, to bring the two wings of the Democratic

[13] *Ibid.,* July 19, 1859; November 17, 1857.

[14] *Ibid.,* June 5, September 4, 1860.

[15] Speech at Raleigh, North Carolina, August 30, 1860; *Springfield Tri-Weekly Republican,* July 23, 1860; Newbern (N.C.) *Daily Progress,* [n. d.], all quoted in Emerson D. Fite, *The Presidential Campaign of 1860* (New York, 1911), pp. 276-300, 149, 150. For similar statements by Douglas, see Crenshaw, *Slave States in the Presidential Election of 1860,* pp. 80, 83.

party together again. The power of the territorial legislature, according to the resolution, was limited by the Supreme Court, a concession to the Southern position. This qualification was not accepted in the Pacific Northwest. Douglas Democrats argued in rather vague terms that the powers exercised by the territorial legislature were subject to the Constitution, at the same time maintaining that a strict interpretation of the Constitution forbade national governmental interference in the territories.

A few Douglasites in Oregon supported popular sovereignty as a solution to the slavery question. George H. Williams wrote that the national government should have nothing to do, either directly or indirectly, with slavery other than to enforce the fugitive slave law. The people of each state and territory should be free to form and regulate their domestic institutions in their own way. "On this ground alone," Williams thought, "can political parties be national."[16] One group felt that congressional interference with slavery in the territories would "lead to an 'irrepressible conflict' between north and south, which will finally end in turmoil, civil war and a dismemberment of these States."[17]

As the campaign progressed, the confidence of Douglas Democrats increased. In July, Bush had declared that Oregon was "as certain as fate" to cast its vote for either Douglas or Lincoln, but by October he wrote:

> At no time since the opening of the canvass have the supporters of Douglas and Johnson throughout the State, felt so strong assurance of carrying Oregon as during the past two weeks. Everywhere the word is, the cause is prospering, and our ticket gaining ground. . . . [Douglas] will carry Oregon by not one vote less than 1500 majority.[18]

He expressed great annoyance that the Republicans had also adopted popular sovereignty. When the Republican party first endorsed the principle of the Kansas-Nebraska Act in 1859, Bush sarcastically noted, "The next time they meet they will probably endorse the Lecompton Constitution." Democrats regarded the Republican endorsement as testimony in favor of popular sovereignty, "that opposing partisans have the intelligence to perceive and the inde-

[16] Salem *Oregon Statesman*, March 27, 1860; Oregon City *Oregon Argus*, March 24, 1860.

[17] Tillamook County Democratic Convention, Salem *Oregon Statesman*, September 18, 1860.

[18] Salem *Oregon Statesman*, July 31, October 15, 1860.

pendence to recognize the truth of the principle." They complained, however, that Republicans did not advocate the complete form of popular sovereignty implied by the Kansas-Nebraska Act, and accused the party of using popular sovereignty to disguise its real principles. Bush assured his readers that the adoption of popular sovereignty by the Republicans did not make that principle a "black republican" doctrine.[19]

Republicans were sincere in their support of popular sovereignty. The national Republican platform in 1860 was written to appeal to as many different groups and regions as possible in order to attract the largest amount of votes. To this end, the strong declarations of the party in 1856 regarding congressional power over the territories were purposely softened in 1860. Instead, the party made the vague declaration that slavery could not be legally and constitutionally established in the territories by either Congress or the territorial legislature. This left the door open to local interpretation. Actually Republicans recognized the hold which popular sovereignty had upon the masses, especially in the West, but feared that the principle might lead to the extension of slavery.[20] Republicans on the Pacific Northwest frontier, although opposing the extension of slavery into the West, admitted that under popular sovereignty a territory was free to adopt or protect slavery.

By admitting the possibility of an adoption of slavery, popular sovereignty was opposed in principle to the argument of the slavery restrictionists. Because of this opposition, there were some contradictions in the local Republican position. Thomas J. Dryer of the *Oregonian* accepted popular sovereignty with few reservations. William L. Adams of the *Argus* was more careful in his discussions. Early in 1859, he branded the Douglas doctrine as having been conceived to "hoodwink, blind, and deceive credulous people." Scarcely a month later, however, he endorsed the principle in its broadest application but continued to argue that the national government had the right to keep slavery out of the territories. Adams accused the Douglas Democrats of holding a limited point of view. Republicans, he claimed, believed in "securing to the people of the Territories the privilege of electing their own officers, and a Congressional

19 *Ibid.,* March 15, April 12, August 2, 1859.
20 Henry C. Hubbart, "Revisionist Interpretations of Stephen A. Douglas and Popular Sovereignty," *Social Studies,* XXV (March, 1934) , 103-107.

recognition of all the sovereignty in a Territory compatible with the Constitution and the laws of the land."[21]

Republicans sharpened and clarified their support of popular sovereignty in the campaign of 1860. Early in the campaign, county conventions endorsed the policy of allowing territories to elect their own officers and control their own local affairs, "to secure them in their rights and preserve them from the tyranny of a partisan and irresponsible executive and judiciary." At the same time, they opposed the extension of slavery—"it should not be extended where it does not exist." Adams attempted to demonstrate that Douglas did not favor popular sovereignty in its "pure" form and that the Kansas-Nebraska Act "contained no fraction of Popular Sovereignty." The paper declared there was

> no good reason why genuine popular-sovereignty men should not support the Republican nominees. . . . Although the Republicans have not been the avowed champions of "squatter sovereignty," it could be readily shown that they have been its only supporters in Congress from the birth of the Kansas-Nebraska bill to the present time.

On the eve of the election, this sentiment was repeated: "All good, honest, patriotic, free-soil, truly popular-sovereignty Democrats can very consistently vote for Lincoln and Hamlin and genuine popular sovereignty, instead of for the doubtful popular-sovereignty of Douglas and fire-eating Johnson."[22]

Edward Dickinson Baker was the foremost Republican advocate of popular sovereignty in Oregon. In a speech in May, 1860, he admitted that many Republicans differed over popular sovereignty but stated that he acted upon his own convictions. He had opposed the Kansas-Nebraska Act, but since then he had recognized popular sovereignty as the "mightiest engine ever devised for the extension of free institutions." Slavery, he said, could exist only under municipal law; if a territory should adopt slavery he would acquiesce in it, although he would use his personal influence against it. Popular sovereignty would result in freedom if the immigration of Northern whites were encouraged by the passage of a free homestead bill. Later, Baker declared that a congressional measure granting territories the power to establish their own domestic institutions "would

---

[21] Oregon City *Oregon Argus*, February 19, March 26, 1859.
[22] Portland *Weekly Oregonian*, April 11, 1860; Oregon City *Oregon Argus*, April 7, 14, August 25, September 1, 8, November 3, 1860.

secure free institutions for all our territories, now and henceforth."[23]

In October, Baker left Oregon for the national capital to assume his new duties as United States Senator. On his way, he stopped in San Francisco long enough to deliver a campaign speech. The speech was widely reported throughout the nation. The *New York Times* described it as the greatest political demonstration of the season in California. For two and a half hours, Baker held his audience in rapt attention. He declared:

> I am a popular sovereignty Republican. . . . I believe in popular sovereignty, not as a principle, but as a policy—as a measure. And I don't believe in it because I don't care about slavery. I *do* care about slavery—I *do,* so help me God! . . . But since the experiment in Kansas, I believe more in the capacity of the people to govern themselves. The people will not tolerate slavery on free soil. . . . We will make it a great weapon for freedom. . . . Southern men claim the right to go wherever they choose with their property. I say in reply that the negro is not property in the general sense; he is property only in a sort of qualified sense. A negro can be property only in the fact of the common law . . . when he gets away from your local law, he is free by every instinct of humanity. . . . The normal condition of the Territories is freedom.[24]

Baker carried his fight for popular sovereignty into the United States Senate where he declared, "I hold myself bound . . . to vote in favor of what is called popular sovereignty . . . I believe the best way is to allow the people of the Territories to govern themselves, slavery or no slavery."[25]

Republicans in Oregon doubted that their ticket could win the state in 1860. One Republican writing to Lincoln expressed the belief that Douglas would run stronger than the Lane ticket and that the split in the Democratic party might give the state to Lincoln. The Republican party, he reported, was a hopeless minority in Oregon; victory depended upon the support of free-soil Democrats.[26] Lincoln was more confident. In early August he predicted he would carry all of the states that had voted for Fremont, in addition to many others where the Democratic party was divided, Oregon included.[27] Anson Henry urged the electorate to vote for Lincoln,

[23] Portland *Weekly Oregonian,* May 12, October 20, 1860.

[24] *New York Times,* November 14, 1860; San Francisco *Daily Evening Bulletin,* October 27, 1860.

[25] *Cong. Globe,* 36 Cong., 2 Sess., p. 1206.

[26] Holbrook to Lincoln, July 21, 1860, Robert Todd Lincoln Collection, Abraham Lincoln Papers, Library of Congress (microfilm in the University of Washington Library).

[27] Lincoln to Simeon Francis, August 4, 1860, in "Letters," *OHQ,* VIII (March, 1907), 76-77.

who, he assured them, would restore harmony between the North and the South and would carry out in good faith all the compromises of the Constitution. For two months prior to the election, the *Oregonian* reprinted on its back sheet a speech by Henry Clay against the extension of slavery; the Republican national platform; "Yancey's Plan for Disunion" (pointing out that William L. Yancey was a close friend of Joe Lane) ; and an item entitled "Joe Lane for Whipping White Men and Women," which stated that Lane had voted against disallowing a New Mexico territorial law forbidding courts from interfering in the correction of a servant by his master.[28]

By October, the election of Lincoln was considered "morally certain." The *Argus* closed the campaign with an appeal to the Douglas Democrats spread across one of the pages in large type:

> It is now positively certain that Douglas will not receive the Electoral vote of *one* single State.—Why not, then, vote for Lincoln, and thus aid in putting under your feet the men who slaughtered your favorite Douglas at Charleston and Baltimore, and murdered the Patriot Broderick in California, for their gallant and noble resistance to the unjust demands of a corrupt, tyrannical, and slavery-extending Administration. You could not better meet the wishes of your great leader, than by aiding to crush out, in this far corner of our beloved country, the rising spirit of Secession and Disunion.[29]

This argument had a telling effect on the outcome of the election.

Arrayed against the Douglas Democrats and the Republicans was a third interpretation of popular sovereignty. The Breckinridge Democrats, or Lane Democrats as they were called in the Pacific Northwest, argued that the Dred Scott decision had altered the original principle of popular sovereignty. Daniel S. Dickinson, one of the most active of Breckinridge campaigners in 1860, labeled this modification, "qualified popular sovereignty." According to this view, the people of "the States and the Territories should be left, while a Territory, to enjoy just such rights as to carrying their slaves with them when removing into the Territories, or exclusion therefrom, as it should be held by the courts belonged to them."[30] Breckinridge Democrats carried the principle of nonintervention further than the Douglasites were willing to go. Not only did they deny the

---

[28] Portland *Weekly Oregonian,* August 11, September 1, 8, 15, 1860.

[29] *Ibid.,* October 6, 1860; Oregon City *Oregon Argus,* November 3, 1860.

[30] *Speech of Hon. Daniel S. Dickinson of New York, Delivered at the Cooper Institute, New York, July 18, 1860* (Breckinridge and Lane Campaign Documents, No. 6, Washington, 1860) , p. 11.

power of the national government to establish or prohibit slavery in the territories but they also denied the power of the territorial legislature to take such action. "Non-intervention on the part of Congress with Slavery in the Territories," wrote President Buchanan, "unless accompanied by non-intervention on the part of the Territorial Legislatures, amounts to nothing more in effect than to transfer the Wilmot Proviso from Congress to these Legislatures."[31] The final arbiter was the Supreme Court, which had already ruled in favor of the Southern position. The principal objection to Douglas' point of view, according to Dickinson, was his "Freeport doctrine" showing how a territorial legislature might circumvent a Supreme Court decision.

According to Breckinridge Democrats, popular sovereignty could not be exercised until a territory moved into statehood. At that point, and at that point only, could the people in a territory make a decision on the slavery question. The leading Breckinridge paper in Oregon summarized its position:

> . . . the question of slavery [must be left] in the Territories, where the constitution leaves it, to enjoy such rights as shall be declared to exist by the judiciary of the country, under such protection as the local legislature may feel disposed to extend to it, and to be finally determined by the people in their own way when they form their State institutions, without interference from any source whatever.[32]

The question was examined at great length by the Corvallis *Oregon Weekly Union* in April, 1859. The conclusions of James H. Slater, the editor, occupied three full newspaper columns. Slater argued that Congress had the power neither to introduce nor to exclude slavery in any of the territories. Without this power, Congress could not delegate it to the territorial legislature. Consequently, there was no power in existence that could determine the status of slavery in an area that was under territorial organization. The right to carry slavery into a territory existed and could be exercised; it could not be restricted by any power other than that of the state government which superseded the territorial government.[33] Lane supported this

---

[31] Buchanan to C. Comstock, July 5, 1860, John Bassett Moore, ed. *The Works of James Buchanan, Comprising His Speeches, State Papers, and Private Correspondence* (12 vols.; Philadelphia, 1910), X, 457.

[32] Corvallis *Oregon Weekly Union*, April 30, 1859. See also Stevens' statement in his *Address to the Democracy and the People of the United States*, p. 12.

[33] Corvallis *Oregon Weekly Union*, April 10, 1859.

position, maintaining that the inhabitants of a territory could not, by unfriendly legislation, infringe upon the rights of people from any state in the Union. Any man had a right to carry into a territory that property which was recognized in the state from which he migrated. Only when forming a state constitution could the people of a territory adopt or reject slavery.[34]

This position was defined in seven resolutions presented by Jefferson Davis to Congress early in 1860, not only declaring that slaveholders had an equal right in the territories with persons from free states, but also stating that it was the duty of Congress to protect the slaveholder in this right. Lane agreed with Davis and argued at length in favor of the resolutions.[35] Although the Southern demand for a slave code had appeared in the Oregon congressional campaign in 1859 when Stout urged its adoption, many Lane Democrats were loath to accept this new element of the Southern position. Intervention on behalf of slavery was as bad, they thought, as the kind of intervention advocated by the national Republican leaders. Slater did not deny the constitutionality of a slave code but considered its enactment highly inexpedient. Later he scouted the whole idea, declaring that it never "had any existence in any body's brain but that of Senator Douglas, and he only made use of it for the purpose of arousing the prejudices of the North."[36] However, the advocacy by some of the Breckinridge Democrats of a congressional slave code gave the Douglasites an additional campaign argument. Bush reported: "There are but two sides to this question. There is Congressional intervention *for* or *against* slavery, upon the one side, and popular sovereignty upon the other. The one is the doctrine of fanatics, both northern and southern; the other is the doctrine of the people."[37]

For two months preceding the election, almost every issue of the *Union* contained editorials on popular sovereignty. Douglas' popular sovereignty was declared in terms reminiscent of Calhoun to be little more than the "absolute rule of unrestricted, dominant majorities"; because it disregarded the property rights of Southern slaveholders, popular sovereignty was tyranny and despotism. Property rights were secured by constitutional guarantees. "What folly is it then,"

[34] *Cong. Globe*, 36 Cong., 1 Sess., pp. 184-185.
[35] *Ibid.*, pp. 2321-2350.
[36] Corvallis *Oregon Weekly Union*, May 29, October 20, 1860.
[37] Salem *Oregon Statesman*, May 31, 1859.

Slater exclaimed, "to assert that they may be made to depend upon the will of a capricious majority of a legislative body, or by the people of a newly settled country." Two weeks before the election, he summarized the position of Oregon's Breckinridge Democrats:

> Local [territorial] government emanating from Congress, instead of the people, can exercise only such powers as may be constitutionally conferred upon it, and is in fact the government of the United States in the Territories and its whole duty is to protect, not to create or destroy the rights of the citizens. If, therefore, slaves are property . . . the same as other property, by what process of reasoning can it be shown that they are entitled to less protection than any other class of property? The whole question hinges right here.[38]

Joseph Lane did not return to Oregon during the election campaign. Stevens also, by virtue of his duties with the national Democratic organization, remained in the East throughout the summer and fall of 1860. The brunt of the campaign in Oregon was borne by the local party leaders. Delazon Smith, one of the most tireless campaigners, frequently argued that a civil war might follow the defeat of the Breckinridge ticket. Most of the state officers used their influence on behalf of Breckinridge and Lane. Governor Whiteaker, with strong proslavery sympathies, maintained that, if Douglas had denied the power of the territorial legislature as well as the power of Congress to interfere with slavery in the territories, he would have sided with him. Whiteaker wrote, "I want *no* interference by legislation, but let the courts say whether slavery exists or not, and I will abide the decision." Matthew P. Deady, also strongly proslavery, believed that popular sovereignty was the "essence of anarchy lawlessness and mob rule." Deady supported Breckinridge and felt that his candidate stood an even chance for election but, like President Buchanan, thought that neither of the Democratic candidates could claim a regular nomination.[39]

Southerners were confident that both Oregon and California would cast their ballots for Breckinridge and that with the help of these states they could win the election. Such confidence was not shared by all members of the party. Lane, for example, seems to

---

[38] Corvallis *Oregon Weekly Union,* September 4, October 20, 1860.

[39] Drew to Bush, August 4, 1860, Asahel Bush Papers, Oregon State Library (photostats in the University of Oregon Library) ; Whiteaker to Bush, September 8, 1860, Salem *Oregon Statesman,* September 11, 1860; Deady to George E. Cole, July 31, 1860, Matthew P. Deady Papers, Oregon Historical Society Library; Moore, ed. *Works of Buchanan,* X, 458-459.

have lost hope for victory late in the campaign. He practically conceded Lincoln's election and thought that the difficulties between the North and South would increase.[40] One Breckinridge Democrat in Washington Territory concluded that "Politicks is very much mixed up."[41]

Although popular sovereignty was the most important issue on this frontier in 1860, it was not by any means the sole issue of the election. Many other questions were mentioned both by individuals and by the press; in varying degrees the stand taken by the parties on these questions contributed to the final result.

Of particular importance to the West were the construction of a Pacific railroad and the passage of a national homestead act. The Republican party championed both of these measures, partly in an effort to win support for their party in the West. The inclusion of railroad and homestead planks in the national Republican platform in 1860 was part of the design to broaden the base of party appeal. In some areas, these questions were argued to the exclusion of other issues. In Minnesota, Iowa, and Wisconsin, for example, the homestead issue monopolized the campaign; in California, the Pacific railroad issue was a prominent one.[42] In Oregon, the influence of these issues was diminished by the fact that both the Republicans and the Democrats endorsed the measures.[43] The Republicans however, held an advantage over their opponents; they pointed out that the Democratic party, controlled largely by its Southern wing, had been responsible for the defeat of both homestead and railway legislation during the past decade.

The differences between the parties over the construction of a Pacific railroad involved the manner of financing construction and the choice of route over which the railroad was to pass. In the Northwest the support of a Pacific railroad transcended these party considerations. Westerners were not particular how the railroad was built or by what agency. In fact, the Breckinridge Democratic press

---

[40] Crenshaw, *Slave States in the Presidential Election of 1860,* pp. 61, 28, 72; Eldorah M. Raleigh, "General Joseph E. Lane," *Indiana History Bulletin,* IV (Dec., 1926, suppl.), 77.

[41] William M. Morrow to Isaac I. Stevens, October 10, 1860, Isaac I. Stevens Papers, University of Washington Library.

[42] Verne E. Chatelain, "The Federal Land Policy and Minnesota Politics, 1854-1860," *Minnesota History,* XXII (Sept., 1941), 227-248; Luthin, *The First Lincoln Campaign,* p. 178.

[43] Oregon City *Oregon Spectator,* September 30, 1853.

took the view that without government aid the railroad might never be built, a position contrary to that held by the national organization.[44] In 1859, a Pacific Railroad Convention met in San Francisco to recommend routes for a transcontinental railway. The meeting, attended by delegates from Washington Territory, Oregon, and California, was not marked by partisanship, and both Republicans and Democrats were invited. Rather, the convention split along sectional lines, the delegates from Washington Territory and Oregon favoring a northern route, those from northern California a central route, and those from southern California a southern route.[45]

A similar situation existed with regard to the homestead issue. Westerners of both parties generally supported the demands for homestead legislation. Douglas had always worked for free homesteads, as had other influential Democrats. However, as in the case of the railroad issue, the Democratic party was held responsible for the defeat of homestead legislation during the fifties. The Southern Democrats, with the support and approbation of Joseph Lane, had defeated homestead legislation in the Senate, and the Republicans used this action to demonstrate Democratic hostility to the measure. Just before the election, the *Oregonian* emphatically declared that a vote for Breckinridge would be a vote against the Homestead Act,[46] although few of Oregon's Breckinridge Democrats were opposed to the free homestead principle. Lansing Stout, for example, strongly supported it in the House of Representatives.[47] The sentiment in the Pacific Northwest in favor of both a transcontinental railroad and a homestead act undoubtedly operated to the advantage of the Republican party. While the local Democratic organizations united with the Republicans in support of these measures, they were betrayed by the actions of many of their national leaders. The overland mail issue had some effect on the election in California, but in Oregon it remained in the background, possibly because Lane was, with Senator William Gwin, a strong advocate of regular overland mail service to the Pacific Coast.

Two additional issues that influenced the election of 1860 in the

44 Corvallis *Oregon Weekly Union*, October 22, 1859.
45 Portland *Weekly Oregonian*, October 8, 15, 1859; Robert R. Russel, *Improvement of Communication with the Pacific Coast as an Issue in American Politics, 1783-1864* (Cedar Rapids, Iowa, 1948), pp. 273-276.
46 Portland *Weekly Oregonian*, October 27, 1860.
47 *Cong. Globe*, 36 Cong., 1 Sess., p. 1115.

Pacific Northwest were the question of corruption in government and the controversy over the Oregon war debt. The corruption issue received a great deal of space in the local Republican press. Before the election, the Covode Report, a voluminous summary of irregularities in the Buchanan administration, was issued by a special congressional investigating committee. This report was given wide publicity in the Far West. Republicans complained that the public money had been placed in the pockets of "unprincipled partisan toadies" instead of being applied to such worthy projects as the construction of a Pacific railroad. The *Oregonian* concluded that eight years of Democratic rule were enough; it was time for a change.[48]

The question of the payment of the Oregon war debt was a potent force in local politics during the latter years of the decade. The debt had been created by both Oregon and Washington Territory in 1855-56, when local troops were raised to combat an Indian uprising. Amounting to six million dollars, the debt was supposed to be met and repaid by the national government. Congress, alarmed at the large amount due, had begun a series of investigations which proved highly annoying to the Pacific Northwest. Although Lane worked hard throughout his terms in Congress to secure the payment of the war debt, his efforts were always blocked. By 1860, voters in the region were ready to turn elsewhere for satisfaction. In January, it was felt that only a Republican would be able to secure congressional approval for the payment of the debt.[49] The issue was discussed a great deal during the year and may have been one of the reasons for the coalition between the Republicans and the Douglas Democrats in the state legislature.[50] It undoubtedly was one of the considerations which many of Oregon's voters carried with them to the polls in November, 1860.[51]

[48] Oregon City *Oregon Argus*, November 27, 1858; Portland *Weekly Oregonian*, November 3, 1860.

[49] Logan to Mary Logan, January 24, 1860, Harry E. Pratt, ed. "22 Letters of David Logan, Pioneer Oregon Lawyer," *OHQ*, XLIV (Sept., 1943), 281.

[50] Henry to Lincoln, July 17, 1859, Lincoln Papers; Matthew P. Deady to the San Francisco *Bulletin*, November 1, 1863, Scrap-Book #112, Oregon Historical Society Library.

[51] Another issue was summarized in the latter part of 1859: "The Republican party is opposed to the governments of aristocracies and monopolies, and so long as the Democracy draws its vital breath from the worst of all systems of aristocracy, it has little to commend itself to the free laboring masses of America" (Eugene *People's Press*, November 19, 1859) .

As election day drew near, the feeling grew that none of the four presidential candidates would get a majority of the electoral vote, and thus the House of Representatives would be forced to make the choice. One Douglas Democrat, upon hearing of the initial split in the Democratic party, lamented the fact that the election would probably go to the House, where Breckinridge stood the best chance. A Breckinridge Democrat was confident that, if his ticket were not elected by the people, "Surely the House will not Falter in such a trying imergency."[52] The Republicans, however, had organized the House of Representatives; the election of any one of the Democratic candidates would prove difficult. One prominent Southerner thought that if the election were thrown into the House the Republicans would immediately unseat Lansing Stout, whose close victory in 1859 had been seriously questioned, thus giving them a majority of the state delegations.[53]

The difficulty of electing a president either at the polls or in the House of Representatives, some thought, would give Joseph Lane his long-awaited opportunity to sit in the White House. Should the House be required to elect a president, then the Senate would be obliged to select a vice-president. If the House failed to agree on any one of the four candidates, then the Senate choice for vice-president would become president.[54] There was a widespread belief that this man would be Joseph Lane. "Joseph," according to one Oregonian, "will doubtless be next 'Old Public Functionary.' "[55] Many national Republican leaders claimed during the campaign that the choice for president really lay between Lincoln and Lane. Henry J. Raymond and David Dudley Field both sounded the alarm, "Lincoln or Lane!" in their campaign speeches. Horace Greeley pointed out that there was no middle ground between Lincoln or Lane, an honest Republican or a corrupt Democrat. The Constitutional Unionists in Indiana all but abandoned their ticket because they thought the defeat of Lincoln would mean the election of

---

[52] Winfield Scott Ebey Diary, No. 6, p. 334 (July 23, 1860), University of Washington Library; Morrow to Stevens, October 10, 1860, Stevens Papers.

[53] J. Henly Smith to Alexander H. Stephens, June 26, 1860, quoted in Crenshaw, *Slave States in the Presidential Election of 1860*, pp. 68-69.

[54] Port Townsend *Register*, quoted in Portland *Weekly Oregonian*, July 28, 1860; Alexander H. Stephens, *A Constitutional View of the Late War Between the States* (2 vols.; Chicago, 1868-1870), II, 274.

[55] L. L. Bradbury to Deady, August 24, 1860, Deady Papers.

Lane.[56] Intriguing as the idea may have been, however, the more
sober-minded of the politicians gave no credence to it.

In October, the Douglas State Central Committee met in Salem
and nominated Andrew J. Thayer for Congress. The Douglasites
had hoped that a bill would pass the state legislature providing for a
congressional election in November and declaring the Sheil election
of the previous June illegal. Such a bill did pass the state house of
representatives but failed in the senate. Undaunted, Bush urged the
nomination of a candidate anyway. An election in November, he
thought, would be just as legal, or illegal, as the June election had
been. If the people really wanted Sheil, he maintained, they could
re-elect him; if they did not want Sheil then he should not be forced
upon them. Thayer, a Benton County attorney, was a strenuous
advocate of popular sovereignty. Immediately after his nomination,
the *Statesman* raised his name to the masthead and formally began a
campaign on his behalf.[57] The other parties in the state took little
notice of this action. The Republicans, although they expressed a
preference for Thayer over Sheil, decided to keep out of what they
considered a Democratic party quarrel. The Breckinridge Democrats, outside of branding the Douglas strategy as part of the "wicked,
nefarious attempt to disorganize, distract, and destroy the Democratic party in the State," entirely ignored the nomination.[58]

Republicans became more and more hopeful that their ticket
would emerge victorious in the four-cornered race. Two Republican
newspapers were founded in Washington Territory to express this
confidence. The Olympia *Washington Standard* announced its determination to "do battle for the advancement of free territory, free
labor, free speech, and free men." The first issues were devoted to
the presidential election. In spite of the fact that Washington Territory had no vote in this election, the editor felt that the area had a
vital interest in its outcome. The United States Supreme Court had,
according to the paper, declared Washington a slave territory when
it ruled on the Dred Scott Case. "We have long entertained the

[56] Fite, *Presidential Campaign of 1860*, p. 223; Luthin, *The First Lincoln Cam-
paign*, pp. 200-201; Mary Scrugham, *The Peaceable Americans of 1860-1861, a
Study in Public Opinion* (Columbia University Studies in History, Economics and
Public Law, XCVI), p. 51.

[57] Salem *Oregon Statesman*, October 15, 22, 1860.

[58] Portland *Weekly Oregonian*, October 20, 1860; Corvallis *Oregon Weekly
Union*, October 27, 1860.

opinion that Washington Territory was Republican at heart," the editor continued rather naïvely. That the territorial elections disproved these assertions did not seem to deter his enthusiasm. The Northern states, he predicted, would vote for Lincoln while those of the South would support Bell. The paper was confident that "a day of brightness is about to dawn on our Territory which must dispel the dark shadows of locofocoism [rule by Democratic officeholders] under which it has been so long blighted and withered." The election of Lincoln, according to the newly founded Port Townsend *North-West,* would inaugurate "a new era, in which prosperity unparalleled shall commence with our people, justice and fitness filling our offices of trust, bribery, extortion and corruption hiding its hideous deformity, we trust, *forever.*"[59] On the eve of the election, news of Republican victories in Maine, Pennsylvania, and Indiana was received in the Pacific Northwest, presaging, Republicans thought, the national success of their party.

On election day, November 6, 1860, Winfield Scott Ebey confided to his diary:

> Who is Elected? or is any one Chosen? If the People have made a choice, which is probable, that Choice has undoubtedly fallen on Lincoln. If not then the Election goes to the House of Rep & Breckenridge has the best Show[.] I have a *faint* hope that Lincoln may be defeated—Yet I scarcely allow myself to believe Such can be the fact.

A week or so later, before the returns were known, he thought it probable that Oregon had gone for Breckinridge.[60] Ebey's hopes were dashed, however, and the Republican confidence was rewarded. Abraham Lincoln carried Oregon by the slim margin of 270 votes over Breckinridge, his nearest competitor. Douglas dropped over 1,000 votes behind Lincoln. The complete returns gave Lincoln seven counties, 5,345 votes; Breckinridge eight counties, 5,075 votes; Douglas four counties, 4,131 votes; and Bell a mere 213 votes.[61]

The election was so close that some Republicans were at first

[59] Olympia *Washington Standard,* November 17, 1860; Port Townsend *North-West,* November 1, 1860.

[60] Ebey Diary, No. 6, pp. 373 (November 6, 1860), 377 (November 15, 1860).

[61] The complete returns may be found in the Salem *Oregon Statesman,* December 3, 1860. In many cases the vote cast for the individual electors varied. All of Douglas' electors received the same total, 4,131. Lincoln's vote, however, varied from 5,329 to 5,345, Breckinridge's from 5,069 to 5,075. In computing the totals for each county and for the state, I have chosen the highest vote given any one elector.

doubtful of success. Adams commented, "It is not at all impossible that we have been defeated."[62] As soon as the returns were known, this doubt became unrestrained jubilance. Guns were fired and parades were held in even the smallest localities. Republicans in the small town of Tumwater, for instance, fired a one-hundred-gun salute, then marched to Olympia, ringing bells, blowing horns, and cheering. One Republican in the mining area of eastern Washington Territory, where news of the election was slow in arriving, wrote, "Old Abe must certainly be elected President, for the air is as clear as a bell—we have not had a cloudy day for the past week."[63] Simeon Francis, the new editor of the *Oregonian*, concluded that Baker's election as United States Senator was responsible for the Republican victory in both Oregon and California.[64] The closeness of the vote in both the Pacific Coast states, however, caused many a Republican to think twice before assessing the significance of Lincoln's victory. Lincoln himself was quoted as saying that his victory in California by a little over seven hundred votes and in Oregon by fewer than three hundred votes was "the closest political bookkeeping" he had ever known.[65]

Breckinridge Democrats, although dismayed at the slim margin of their defeat in Oregon, acquiesced in Lincoln's election. One editor thought that the Republican victory over a divided Democratic party should teach Democrats a lesson and help them to reunite their party for the future. With the election over, he hoped that "reason has regained its rule."[66] Another paper, in a fit of verbosity, declared:

> The field may be lost, but all is not lost. The granite foundation of principle will not suffer a fracture from the shock of defeat; treason may lock hands with the natural enemy, and temporarily dismay and confuse; but around our indestructible principles will we again rally, and again bare our breasts in defense. With us, annihilation is impossible, so long as there is a Union to love and a Constitution to uphold; but our enemies, like the mirage mimic of

[62] Oregon City *Oregon Argus,* November 10, 1860.
[63] Olympia *Washington Standard,* November 23, 1860; Shirley Ensign to W. N. Ayers, November 26, 1860, *ibid.,* January 5, 1861.
[64] Francis to Lincoln, November 23, 1860, Lincoln Papers.
[65] Quoted in Milton H. Shutes, "Colonel E. D. Baker," *California Historical Society Quarterly,* XVII (Dec., 1938), 316. Southerners expressed great surprise that Lincoln should have carried two such "sure" Democratic states as Oregon and California (*New Orleans Bee,* December 5, 1860, quoted in Dwight Lowell Dumond, ed. *Southern Editorials on Secession* [New York, 1931], pp. 304-306).
[66] Olympia *Pioneer and Democrat,* November 30, 1860.

castle strength, are but mock suns in the political sky, and will forever disappear from view when the light of principle blazes forth in victory.[67]

William Winlock Miller, a Breckinridge Democratic leader in Washington Territory and a close friend of Stevens, wrote, " 'Honest Abe' has routed us horse, foot, and dragoons. All us poor locofocos can now do is to grin and bear it."[68] James O'Meara, one of Oregon's defeated Breckinridge electors, was discouraged by the defeat of his party both on the Pacific Coast and in the nation but was confident that victory would return in 1862, provided the Union remained united. He was, however, annoyed at the Republican demonstrations that followed the arrival of their good news.

> The Blacks jarred my nerves and irritated my feelings on Saturday night with anvil-shooting in token (I will not disfigure the good old word "honor" by using it in such connection) of their victory. I staid within doors, ostensibly reading, (so my Wife thought) but really privately cussing the whole crowd, each shot provoking a fresh ejaculation of "God—(never mind—it wasn't "bless them.") It is some consolation to think "Lord, how *they* would have sworn if *we* had gained the day!"[69]

The Republican victory had a tragic effect upon one of the other defeated Breckinridge electors. Delazon Smith had conducted a strenuous campaign throughout Oregon, and by election day he was completely fatigued. The results of the election and the disappointment of defeat overwhelmed him, and before two weeks had elapsed he was dead.[70]

Douglas Democrats denied that the election results indicated the true feeling of Oregon's electorate. Bush lamented the defeat of his candidate; following the election he launched a bitter tirade against Buchanan as having been responsible for the "betrayal" of the Democratic party. Like the Breckinridge Democrats, he looked to victory in the future, declaring that "the men who have voted for Douglas and Johnson are the firmest nucleus that any party has ever had since the beginnings of government."[71] Had the question of popular sovereignty alone been the issue of the campaign, another Douglas editor remarked, there would have been no reason to doubt

[67] Portland *Daily Morning News,* November 9, 1860.
[68] Miller to Stevens, November 29, 1860, Stevens Papers.
[69] O'Meara to Deady, November 19, 1860, Deady Papers.
[70] One correspondent wrote that Smith's death deprived the Breckinridge Democrats of their ablest leader; without Smith they were like sheep without a shepherd (Letter from Oregon, *Sacramento Daily Union,* February 5, 1861).
[71] Salem *Oregon Statesman,* November 12, 1860.

Douglas' election. The personal prejudice against Douglas and the willful misrepresentation of Douglas' views, in addition to the introduction of other, less significant issues into the campaign by the Republicans, he thought, had turned the election against Douglas.[72] Douglas saw at least one bright spot in the election results. After the outcome was known, he commented: "We Springfield people will take the capital next year. Lincoln in the White House, Baker, and M'Dougal, and I in the Senate—we will make Washington jolly in spite of politics."[73]

Douglas Democrats in Oregon suffered an additional disappointment. Out of a total vote cast of approximately 14,500, Thayer, their candidate for Congress, received barely over 4,000. Although he ran ahead of Douglas in eleven of the nineteen counties, undoubtedly receiving some Republican or Breckinridge Democratic support, he still fell behind Douglas' total in the state. The other parties ignored the congressional election. Sheil received 131 write-in votes, 124 of them from one county, Josephine. David Logan and Joseph Lane each received fewer than ten votes. Nevertheless, the Douglas Democrats were still convinced that Thayer's election was as legal as Sheil's and prepared to contest Sheil's right to take his seat in the coming session of Congress. Thayer's vote would probably have been larger if election judges in parts of the state had not refused to accept votes for congressman on the ground that there was no legal justification for such an election at that time.[74]

The presidential vote in Oregon followed a sectional pattern. The Breckinridge counties were the southern and eastern Oregon counties. In the central portion of the state was a "Douglas belt," Marion and Polk counties. North of these two counties were the Lincoln counties. There were exceptions to this sectional pattern, but they were relatively unimportant in the final picture. In southern Oregon, for instance, Coos and Curry counties went for Douglas by a small plurality, and Umpqua County went for Lincoln by a majority. In general, the results of the election of 1860 illustrated the relative strength of the political parties in the various sections of the state. The Republican strength had always been in

[72] Portland *Oregon Weekly Times,* November 24, 1860.

[73] Quoted in John Hay, "Colonel Baker," *Harper's Magazine,* XXIV (Dec., 1861), 109. James A. McDougall was the newly elected Douglas Democratic Senator from California.

[74] Salem *Oregon Statesman,* November 19, December 3, 1860.

the north, where a larger percentage of New England migrants had settled. Many of the wealthiest landowners lived in the rural areas of the northern counties.[75] In the upper Willamette Valley and in the extreme southern portions of Oregon, the emigrants from the border states of the Mississippi Valley and the transient mining populations gave strength to the Breckinridge wing. One historian who studied urban-rural cleavages in the 1860 election has pointed out that urban areas generally voted for the moderate candidates (Douglas and Bell), while the rural areas cast their ballots for the extreme candidates (Lincoln and Breckinridge).[76] Insofar as all of Oregon was classified as a rural area this conclusion held true, since Lincoln and Breckinridge together received approximately 70 per cent of the total vote. Other considerations, however, than a cleavage between urban and rural interests were important. The towns in Oregon were generally carried by Lincoln, because town-dwellers almost invariably had New England backgrounds. The rural districts divided among all three of the major candidates. The backgrounds of the frontiersmen and the local campaigns of the political candidates on issues often quite divorced from the national issues were probably the most significant influences upon the election in the Pacific Northwest.

Oregon was one of two free states that gave Breckinridge a larger vote than Douglas. Oregon was also one of the two Lincoln states in which the Republican candidate received a plurality and not a majority of the total vote cast. Had the Democratic party been united, Oregon and California would have voted Democratic. Thus the election on the Pacific Coast differed from that in the rest of the free states. In Oregon, Douglas made a poorer showing than he did nationally. The similarity in the positions of the Republicans and the Douglas Democrats undoubtedly increased the strength of the former at the expense of the latter. Many Douglasites voted for Lincoln because the local Republican ticket had adopted Douglas' popular sovereignty. One Douglas newspaper speculated that some Douglasites had voted for Breckinridge in the mistaken belief that he also stood for "nonintervention." Some Douglas supporters in

[75] A. N. Armstrong, *Oregon: Comprising a Brief History and Full Description of the Territories of Oregon and Washington* . . . (Chicago, 1857), p. 16.
[76] Ollinger Crenshaw, "Urban and Rural Voting in the Election of 1860," Eric F. Goldman, ed. *Historiography and Urbanization: Essays in American History in Honor of W. Stull Holt* (Baltimore, 1941), pp. 57 ff.

Oregon, convinced that their leader could not be elected, voted for their preference between the other two major candidates.[77]

The vote cast for Breckinridge in Oregon did not imply an endorsement of the extreme Southern position. Like that cast for Lincoln and Douglas, the Breckinridge vote was dependent upon local considerations. The personal appeal of Joseph Lane, who was still a "hero of the people," and of Isaac I. Stevens probably swelled the Breckinridge ranks in the Pacific Northwest. To many Oregon Democrats, Breckinridge's candidacy was that of the "regular" Democratic organization; the Douglas movement was often considered the "bolting" faction. Party loyalty on the frontier was much stronger than in other areas and sometimes transcended issues and candidates. The fusion of Republicans and Douglas Democrats in the Oregon state legislature also increased Breckinridge strength at the expense of Douglas.[78] The Breckinridge vote, however, resulted from deeper motivations than these. Breckinridge's strength was found principally in the rural areas where migrants from the border states of the Mississippi Valley had settled. These settlers from an area one historian has labeled a "conservative zone" were jealous of the rights of their former neighbors in the South. While many of them opposed slavery or were indifferent toward the "peculiar institution," they nevertheless felt very keenly that the rights of Southern slaveholders in the territories should be respected. A stronger consideration was the belief that the election of Breckinridge was the only alternative to disunion. The Breckinridge vote in Oregon, unlike that in many areas in the deep South, was a Union vote. It may be compared to the vote given to Bell in the border areas of the East. In Oregon, Bell's vote was negligible; the strength that would normally have gone to Bell was given instead to Breckinridge.[79] The Breckinridge vote in Oregon further illustrates the similarity between the Pacific Northwest frontier and the border states.

In the weeks following the election, the Republican jubilation

[77] Portland *Oregon Weekly Times,* November 10, 1860; George E. Cole, *Early Oregon, Jottings of Personal Recollections of a Pioneer of 1850* ([n. p.], 1905), p. 92.

[78] Spencer to Crawford, October 5, 1860, Medorem Crawford Papers, University of Oregon Library.

[79] The old-line Whigs who supported Bell's position preferred the Breckinridge ticket to either Douglas or Lincoln (James O'Meara, "Our Pioneer Days," Scrap-Book #48, Oregon Historical Society Library).

was punctuated by ominous forebodings and words of warning. The hopes that the election would settle the differences between the North and South were soon dispelled. Democrats saw in the election a significance the Republicans, in their rejoicing, were inclined to overlook. The *Oregon Statesman,* while admitting that Lincoln had all the qualifications to make a good president, nevertheless predicted that his administration "will be the most stormy the country has ever seen, and that he will close it amidst the intense disgust of his own party, and the curses of the entire nation."[80] James O'Meara, a leader of the Breckinridge wing and a man of shrewd political insight, expressed the fears of his colleagues—"Whether he [Lincoln] shall ever be President of the Union as it is remains to be told."[81]

[80] Salem *Oregon Statesman,* November 12, 1860.
[81] O'Meara to Deady, November 19, 1860, Deady Papers.

CHAPTER SIX

```
compromise
or civil war
```

THE SIX MONTHS THAT FOL-
lowed the election of Abraham Lincoln in 1860 were a crucial period
for the United States. The fate of the nation itself hung in the
balance. The election was, from the Southern standpoint, the
culmination of a long train of abuses suffered at the hands of
Northerners. It was interpreted as a threat that struck at the very
heart of the Southern social system. Action was not long delayed.
One by one the slave states of the deep South adopted ordinances of
secession until by the first of February, 1861, seven states were out
of the Union. This action came as a profound shock to many Americans; to others, it was the logical end to which events had pointed
for many years. For the first time in its history, American democratic
government was confronted with a problem of gigantic proportions.
The life of the nation depended on whether this problem could be
solved by the democratic process. The crisis aroused the deepest
passions in the American people, both North and South. To some
Americans, however, the preservation of the Union transcended the
question of slaves in the territories. These individuals, unwilling to
stand idly by while the nation was torn asunder, worked hard to
compromise the issues.

Southern politicians had threatened secession on numerous occasions during the fifties. The threat had been used with some efficacy during the presidential campaign of 1856 when the Republican party entered national politics for the first time. For many months preceding the election of 1860, Southerners had again warned that the election of a Republican president would prove fatal to national union. This time, however, the threats had been more widely and sincerely voiced, many of them being expressed long before the national conventions met. In some instances, the threats were supported by action. Three state legislatures passed resolutions late in 1859 or early in 1860 endorsing separation from the Union if a Republican president were elected. An attempt was made to summon a convention of all the Southern states at which a united policy would be discussed.[1]

These threats and actions should have awakened the Republicans to the danger of disunion. Instead the threats were ridiculed, minimized, or ignored altogether. Since the presidency was within their grasp for the first time in their party's history, Republicans were not inclined to give serious consideration to an issue that might well lose them support. "The simple truth is," wrote the *New York Times,* "nobody is frightened because there is nothing to be frightened at. It is the most natural thing in the world that Southern men should threaten disunion, for they have something to gain by it." If Southerners could convince the nation that disunion would result from Republican victory, "they could defeat the Republicans; and that is really what they are trying to do."[2]

The failure to take serious note of the danger of secession—the "cardinal error" of the Republican campaign[3]—was reflected in the Republican press in Oregon. Early in 1860, the *Oregonian* commented, "The readers of the public newspapers of the day will not have failed to see the 'scare-crow' of dissolution of the Union hoisted upon the Democratic pole." The paper assured its readers that the dissolution of the Union would not follow Lincoln's election. "The Union is bound together and cemented by materials which no southern braggart, northern dough-face, or addle-brained, thick-skulled political *demagogue* can sunder." The "game" was successful

---

[1] Dwight L. Dumond, *The Secession Movement, 1860-1861* (New York, 1931), pp. 98-108; David M. Potter, *Lincoln and His Party in the Secession Crisis* (New Haven, 1942), pp. 3-9.

[2] *New York Times,* October 10, 1860.

[3] Allan Nevins, *The Emergence of Lincoln* (2 vols.; New York, 1950), II, 305.

in 1856; in 1860, "the cry of 'wolf!' has lost its power."[4] This attitude won the attention of Easterners who concluded that clearer and calmer views prevailed in the Far West, where the people would not "give way to senseless panic upon what they regard as the most improbable of contingencies."[5] The isolation of the Pacific Northwest from the center of political activity may have promoted the failure to appreciate the real seriousness of the sectional struggle both before and after the election of 1860.

Not all of the settlers in the Pacific Northwest were as confident of the future as the Republican press. Some Democrats were alarmed at the approaching crisis and frequently expressed fear for the safety of the Union. The Southern disunion sentiment, they thought, was "the natural and necessary result of the intolerant and persistent aggressions of Northern public sentiment." Lincoln's election, they feared, would aggravate this sentiment to such a degree that the nation would split.[6] A few discerning individuals, primarily Breckinridge Democrats, were awake to the danger that threatened the country. Following the election, James O'Meara feared that several, if not all, of the Southern states would soon be outside the Union, but he added, "can we censure them overmuch for such a step?"[7] James H. Slater, editor of Oregon's leading Breckinridge paper, concluded that the Southern threats were not merely aimed at the election of a partisan president but had a deeper foundation in the persistent hostility of the North against the South and Southern interests.[8]

Much of the opinion in the Pacific Northwest was reflected in Washington, D.C., by Joseph Lane. From the national capital, Lane, the defeated champion of Southern rights, wrote despairingly of the Union:

> Tomorrow Congress will assemble for the last time that a national Congress will ever assemble under the constitution as it now is, and it is by no means certain that such amendments can be made as will justify the South in remaining in the Union. I don't believe there is any chance for a satisfactory settlement

[4] Portland *Weekly Oregonian*, March 3, 10, 31, 1860.
[5] *New York Times*, October 25, 1860.
[6] Corvallis *Democratic Crisis*, February 9, 1859; Olympia *Pioneer and Democrat*, March 2, 1860; Salem *Oregon Statesman*, December 20, 1859; Corvallis *Oregon Weekly Union*, February 4, 1860.
[7] O'Meara to Deady, November 19, 1860, Matthew P. Deady Papers, Oregon Historical Society Library.
[8] Corvallis *Oregon Weekly Union*, December 1, 1860.

of the trouble or difficulty, consequently, look upon the Union as broken up. It is virtually broken up now. You will not regard me as an alarmist . . . for you will find that all I say will be verified.[9]

As the crisis deepened Joseph Lane and his Breckinridge Democratic supporters in Oregon came to a parting of the ways. Lane's position became increasingly more radical. By the time Congress assembled in December, 1860, he was completely identified with the Southern group and assumed the role of a defender of Southern action. He not only became reconciled to disunion but began to advocate it. To John Floyd, Buchanan's Secretary of War, Lane remarked that further resistance on the part of the South to the antislavery sentiment in the North was useless and that disunion was inevitable. He assured Floyd that in the hour of trial his services would be offered unhesitatingly to the South.[10] Lane was motivated by an almost religious devotion to principle. His views were both consistent and sincere, in spite of the opposition that was leveled against him by the more conservative Breckinridge Democrats in the Northwest.

When Congress convened, Lane placed his views on record for all the country to examine. The simple election of any man to the presidency, he declared, was not just cause for dissolution, but the principle upon which the recent election had been fought and won by the Republicans did justify secession. The question of the election, "shall the equality of the States be maintained; shall the people of every State have a right to go into the common territory with their property?" had been answered by Republicans in the negative.

It never was contemplated [Lane maintained] by those who made the Constitution that a sectional party, without an electoral ticket in nearly one half the States of the Union, upon a platform conflicting with the Constitution and with the rights of the States in one half of our country, should elect a President.

Without equality among the states the Union ought not to exist. Agreeing with President Buchanan that the national government had no power to force a state to remain in the Union, Lane unleashed his fury at those who talked of coercion:

That man who shall inaugurate civil war by undertaking to hold it together

9 Lane to Deady, December 2, 1860, Joseph Lane Papers, Oregon Historical Society Library.
10 Quoted in Elijah R. Kennedy, *The Contest for California in 1861: How Colonel E. D. Baker Saved the Pacific States to the Union* (Boston, 1912), p. 139.

by force, will be the greatest murderer that ever disgraced the form of man, and will go down to his grave covered with the curses of Heaven from his head to his heels, besides the curses of thousands of widows and orphans.[11]

The disbelief of Republican leaders in the seriousness of the crisis was reflected in part by the Democratic press in the Pacific Northwest. The Douglas Democratic *Statesman* was confident that the "substantial men of the South" opposed disunion, that the secession movement was one of "arch demagogues, and characterless and penniless outlaws." The editor blamed the Southern agitators for the election of Lincoln, but he also thought that four years of Republican rule would so humiliate them that they would regret their precipitate action at the Democratic nominating conventions. By inauguration day, the paper declared, "the secessionists of the south will have harmlessly exploded all their gas, and subsided into impotent braggarts." The paper was later forced by events to admit that the disunion movement was bolder than any that had preceded it, but still assured its readers that the South Carolina convention would probably *"fizzle."*[12]

When it became apparent that the secession movement was not going to "fizzle," the Democratic press became more rabid than the Republican in its denunciation of disunion. Although the Breckinridge wing was the dominant Democratic organization in both Oregon and Washington Territory, it did not countenance disunion as the alternative to defeat at the polls. The *Pioneer and Democrat,* strongly in favor of Breckinridge a few months earlier, now recognized "no disunionist as a fellow partisan." When the report was circulated that Lane favored the right of secession, the paper was quick to assure the country that "this doctrine is not the reflex of public opinion on this Coast, but will be heartily condemned."[13] The *Oregon Weekly Union* drew a significant distinction between resistance to Lincoln as a candidate for the presidency and as president. Although the editor had sided with the South during the campaign, he declared:

We disclaim for ourself and the democracy of Oregon, any sympathy or affiliation with the secession of any of the States; and warn them, that, if carried so far as to result in resistance to the laws of the Federal Union, it must be put

---

[11] *Cong. Globe,* 36 Cong., 2 Sess., pp. 8, 14.
[12] Salem *Oregon Statesman,* November 12, 19, December 3, 1860.
[13] Olympia *Pioneer and Democrat,* December 7, 28, 1860.

down with all the power of the government; and in this, they will find the North united as one man in support of the government, no matter who is President.

Secession, if carried to the point of armed conflict, could be defined only as "treason." The federal government, according to the editor, did not operate upon the states but directly upon the people in their individual capacity. Secession could be accomplished only if a state were declared out of the Union by her own and the concurrent act of the national government. Short of this, secession was revolution in the widest sense.[14] Other Northwest newspapers joined in the cry against the South. One Breckinridge newspaper in Washington Territory branded the secession movement as a "mere pettish gasconade" and disavowed any sympathy with those who were placing themselves in the attitude of rebels. The paper maintained that

> whilst we regret the election to the Presidency of one whose principles are aggressive of Southern rights . . . it is the patriotic duty of every good citizen to stand by that preference which the Nation has expressed conformably to the provisions of the Constitution.[15]

Some Pacific Northwest Democrats looked anxiously to the president-elect for an indication of his policy toward the threatened disunion. Firmness and decision on the part of Lincoln, they believed, would bring an end to the crisis. If, however, Lincoln should give the "renegades" any consideration, "it is a concession that a threat of revolt is the strongest power in the nation, and that is an end of the government itself." The most effective way to deal with the threatened rebellion, one Democratic editor noted, was by the "lawful employment of force and a defiant appeal to the powers granted by the constitution." A "timid, temporizing" policy would only encourage rebellion; instead of "buying up" the disunionists with promises and conciliation, the executive should employ all the powers of the government against any "overt act" of treason that should be committed.[16] The *Oregonian* seconded this view by declaring that the day for new compromises had passed.[17]

While disunion was denounced in the Democratic press, hope was expressed that Lincoln's conservative views would convince the

[14] Corvallis *Oregon Weekly Union,* November 24, December 1, 29, 1860.
[15] Port Townsend *Register,* December 5, 1860.
[16] Salem *Oregon Statesman,* November 26, December 3, January 7, 1860.
[17] Portland *Weekly Oregonian,* December 15, 1860.

South to remain in the Union. Southern fears that Lincoln's election would endanger slavery in the South were said to be unfounded. One Republican newspaper assured the South that slavery was not in danger, that Lincoln would not violate the constitutional rights of Southerners. On the contrary, he would "ever bear in mind that this country is designed for the white race."[18] Republicans blamed the Northern Democrats for the excitement that prevailed in the South. Their false charges against the Republican party in the campaign were responsible for the fears that Southern institutions were threatened. Democrats, on the other hand, declared that an "irrepressible conflict" existed within the Republican party. If the South would bide its time, the Republican party would soon fall from its own weight. Lincoln's greatest task was believed to be the reconciliation of the diverse elements in his own party. This preoccupation with party unity, it was thought, would disarm Republicanism of its dangerous features.[19] Meanwhile, the initial disbelief in Southern secession was transformed into a faith that the conservative, Unionist elements in the South would hold the Union together. Secession sentiment was limited, it was believed, to a "few hotheaded, reckless men." The conservative element, both North and South, had saved the Union on other occasions; there was an "abiding confidence" that it would be saved again. One editor expected to hear of a strong Union reaction in the South, one that would completely submerge the "fire-eaters."[20]

The first two months of the secession crisis witnessed, in the Pacific Northwest, almost universal denunciation of disunion. The lines of division that had existed among the three political parties during the election campaign were blurred. Disbelief in the sincerity of the Southern threats, expressed so often during the campaign, carried over into the weeks following the election. Although a few indi-

[18] Portland *Oregon Weekly Times,* November 24, 1860; Olympia *Washington Standard,* November 30, 1860; Portland *Weekly Oregonian,* December 1, 15, 1860.

[19] Portland *Oregon Weekly Times,* November 24, 1860; Albany *Oregon Democrat,* January 1, 1861; Isaac I. Stevens to the Editor of the Olympia *Pioneer and Democrat,* December 10, 1860, Isaac I. Stevens Papers, University of Washington Library.

[20] Port Townsend *North-West,* December 27, 1860; Olympia *Washington Standard,* December 8, 1860; Olympia *Pioneer and Democrat,* December 7, 1860; Portland *Weekly Oregonian,* December 1, 1860. Winfield Scott Ebey recorded in his diary, "Great excitement in the South[.] I think it will probably blow over" (Winfield Scott Ebey Diary, No. 6, p. 386 [December 5, 1860], University of Washington Library) .

viduals in the Pacific Northwest were awake to the danger that threatened the nation, their voices were faintly heard. The idea of secession, however, was vehemently denounced in the Pacific Northwest. Governor Whiteaker, in his September message to the state legislature of Oregon, had confidently declared:

> Though the fartherest removed from the scenes which agitate the public mind, isolated, as it were, with vast mountains and extensive deserts intervening between her borders and the older States of the Confederacy, yet Oregon is true to the Union. I doubt there being ten men within the limits of Oregon who would not prefer the integrity of the Union, with the certainty that their peculiar political views never would be adopted, than disunion with certain success in the division within which they might chance to fall. When I consider the few benefits that have resulted to Oregon from becoming a State; the almost entire neglect of her interests and rights by the general government, and then reflect that her population is made up of citizens representing every State of the Union . . . and find them all loyal, all unalterably attached to the Union, I feel like dismissing the idea of a separation as not being worthy a place in the mind of any American citizen.[21]

The Democratic press in the Pacific Northwest took the initiative in denouncing secession. Republican papers in Oregon were strangely silent on the national crisis. The *Oregonian* gave it only slight editorial notice; the *Argus* remained editorially silent, often devoting entire issues to Eastern news dispatches. All parties, however, whether partisans of Lincoln, Breckinridge, or Douglas, joined in denouncing the action of the South and in affirming loyalty to the Union.

By mid-December, the *Statesman* reported that the "disunion furor" had subsided. The collection of the revenues at the ports of entry, according to the paper, was the only issue over which a conflict could arise. As long as the federal government maintained control over the sea, revolution was improbable.[22] Reports from the Pacific Northwest's delegation in the national Congress belied this optimism. Joseph Lane, Oregon's "disunion misrepresentative" as he came to be called, continued to express his sympathy with Southern grievances and action. Although he stoutly maintained that he was not a disunionist, Lane declared, "I am for the right, and I would have it in the Union; and if it cannot be obtained there, I would go out of the Union, and have that out of the Union that I

21 State of Oregon, *Senate Journal*, 1860, p. 31.
22 Salem *Oregon Statesman*, December 17, 1860.

could not obtain in it, though I was entitled to it." A dissolution, he reiterated, was inevitable; when that event should take place he looked forward "to the day when every one of those great northwestern States shall become a portion of that southern confederacy." To those in Congress who spoke of coercing the Southern states, Lane announced that he would not march against the "gallant" state of South Carolina but, on the contrary, would meet the armies there, ready to repel them.[23] Lansing Stout, Oregon's representative in the lower house, did not follow the lead of his erstwhile political chief. "My confidence in the capacity of the people for self-government," he wrote, "will not allow me to look upon the present crisis as the end of our government, but God only knows what is in store for us." He thought an armed conflict between the two sections entirely possible. Although he was opposed to disunion, Stout favored a peaceable separation if that were the alternative to war.[24]

Isaac I. Stevens, Washington's territorial delegate, informed his constituents of developments in Congress during the crisis months. After working hard throughout the summer and autumn months in behalf of the Breckinridge ticket, he turned his energies after the election to a reconciliation of the sections. Stevens did not minimize the proportions of the crisis. It was a "deep, wide spread, earnest movement." He was optimistic, however, that "moderation and wisdom" would eventually prevail in the South and that a sense of justice toward Southern rights would soon be manifested in the North. The only hope for a reconciliation, he thought, was in the avoidance of bloodshed. "The remedy," he wrote, "is not to be sought in coercion." Stevens, however, declared that the national government must protect its property and execute the laws. He believed that nothing short of a convention of all the states could settle the crisis and entertained the possibility that such a convention might agree on separation as the best way to avoid future conflicts.[25]

As the Southern states moved closer to secession, many eyes in the nation were directed toward the youngest, most isolated area of the country. "But how will the Pacific States remain affected?" asked

[23] *Cong. Globe,* 36 Cong., 2 Sess., pp. 143-144.
[24] Stout to Deady, December 25, 1860, Deady Papers.
[25] Stevens to the Editor of the Olympia *Pioneer and Democrat,* December 10, 17, 1860, Stevens Papers. This and other letters written by Stevens to his constituents in Washington Territory have been published in Robert W. Johannsen,

one Eastern newspaper.[26] It was inevitable that the idea of an independent republic west of the Rocky Mountains should be revived at this time. This idea had its roots in the belief that the Pacific Coast was too distant from the population centers of the East to be an integral part of the United States. The isolation of the region and the belief that its interests were closely tied with the Pacific area and Far East had encouraged the notion that the Pacific Coast could not be part of the United States.[27] When the authority of the United States was extended to the Pacific Ocean following the Mexican War, this idea inspired a separatist movement with a Pacific Republic as its goal. During the fifties, the sectional differences between the North and the South served to increase the feeling that the destiny of the Pacific Coast lay outside the Union.[28] The movement centered in California, but it received some support in the Pacific Northwest. In 1855 some persons in Washington Territory favored the formation of a new republic in order "to bring nearer home to the people on the Pacific the powers of government, to secure independence, to cut off overland connection, and to make the new Republic the depot of Asiatic trade."[29] The preoccupation of the government with the sectional controversy, to the neglect of Western interests, spurred on the idea of separation. When the dissolution of the Union was threatened in 1860, the Pacific Republic movement was revived.

In July, 1860, a rumor, later proved to be without foundation, circulated in the Pacific Northwest that the entire Pacific Coast delegation in Congress had made secret plans for a Pacific Republic.[30] Some members of the delegation made public statements favoring such a move. John C. Burch, congressman from California, wrote that it would be better for the Pacific states to sever their

ed. "A Breckinridge Democrat on the Secession Crisis: Letters of Isaac I. Stevens, 1860-1861," *OHQ,* LV (Dec., 1954) , 283-310.

[26] *Boston Daily Journal,* December 28, 1860, Howard C. Perkins, ed. *Northern Editorials on Secession* (2 vols.; New York, 1942) , I, 399.

[27] This idea was expressed by many national leaders from Thomas Jefferson to Zachary Taylor. See, for example, Milo M. Quaife, ed. *The Diary of James K. Polk During His Presidency, 1845 to 1849* (4 vols.; Chicago, 1910) , IV, 293-294, 375-376; Applegate to Lisbon Applegate, June 16, 1845; Applegate to Deady, November 6, 1864, Jesse Applegate Papers, Oregon Historical Society Library.

[28] Joseph Ellison, "Designs for a Pacific Republic, 1843-1862," *OHQ,* XXXI (December, 1930) , 319-342.

[29] Olympia *Pioneer and Democrat,* April 14, 1855.

[30] Salem *Oregon Statesman,* July 24, 1860.

connection with a people who seemed bent on self-destruction, to seek refuge from the "blighting effects of dis-union and civil war, by retiring and establishing a prosperous, happy and successful Republic on the Pacific slope."[31] The idea was seriously discussed in the East. "The gold of California," it was said, "is even a greater Potentate than Cotton, which is proclaimed King."[32] A supporter of the Pacific Republic movement argued that in such a separation all the advantages would be on the side of the Pacific states since there was no natural commercial connection with the Atlantic Coast. If it remained in the Union, the area might be heavily taxed to support a war in which it had no vital stake. Moreover, neither the North nor the South had shown a desire to construct a Pacific railroad.[33]

In spite of the discussion regarding the advantages of a Pacific Republic, sentiment in the Pacific states was overwhelmingly against such a scheme. One California newspaper declared that the people on the Pacific Coast, even though isolated, were devotedly attached to the Union.[34] Oregon's new Senator, James W. Nesmith, emphasized this feeling when he wrote from San Francisco late in December, 1860, "There is no public sentiment here in favor of disunion." He blamed the movement on the Knights of the Golden Circle, a secret Southern society that was trying to foment disunion feeling in California.[35] Similar condemnations came from the Pacific Northwest. The movement for a Pacific Republic was denounced as "useless, idle treasonable nonsense." One Democratic paper declared, "Our duty is plain—the path is straight—go with the North and West, or the confederacy formed by them."[36]

[31] John C. Burch to Charles H. Street, November 22, 1860, Salem *Oregon Statesman*, January 14, 1861; San Francisco *Evening Bulletin*, January 16, 1861.

[32] Albany (N.Y.) *Atlas and Argus*, November 22, 1860, Perkins, ed. *Northern Editorials on Secession*, I, 387. See also the *New Albany* (Ind.) *Daily Ledger*, November 21, 1860; Milwaukee (Wis.) *Daily People's Press*, November 30, 1860; and *Daily Chicago Times*, December 10, 1860, in Perkins, ed., *Northern Editorials on Secession*, I, 385, 389, 572.

[33] Gen. Volney E. Howard to E. D. Baker, January 25, 1861, San Francisco *Herald*, January 25, 1861.

[34] *Sacramento Daily Union*, December 13, 1860.

[35] Nesmith to Bush, December 31, 1860, James W. Nesmith Papers, Oregon Historical Society Library. Senator Latham of California assured Congress that the Pacific states would remain loyal to the Union (*Cong. Globe*, 36 Cong., 2 Sess., p. 27).

[36] Olympia *Pioneer and Democrat*, January 4, 18, 1861; Olympia *Washington Standard*, January 12, 1861.

The political leaders of the Pacific Coast urged their constituents to be peacemakers between the warring sections. During the election campaign a California Douglas Democrat expressed the idea that the Pacific states should not ally with either the North or the South but rather urged them to assume the position of a mediator.[37] Similar appeals were made to the Pacific Northwest. Isaac Stevens felt that the distance which separated the Northwest both from the area of political activity in the East and from the issues which were precipitating the conflict would make the region a balance wheel between the warring sections. He wrote:

> The action of the people in the Pacific States and Territories will be watched here with the deepest interest. It is felt that the great west is entitled to a potential voice in counsels affecting the integrity and future of the confederacy, and the hope is cherished that the position you occupy as neutrals—it may be as an arbiter—in the irritating contest between north and south, will enable you to exercise a beneficial influence upon both sections; on one hand checking aggression, and on the other restraining rashness, and so helping to extricate the Union from a danger which no rational man can contemplate without a shudder.[38]

This feeling of detachment from the sectional struggle was expressed by others in the region. Lansing Stout wrote, "Our people in Oregon are now reaping the reward for their former privations and hardships, for they are out side of immediate danger and cannot easily be involved in the struggle." A Washington Territory newspaper commented:

> We distinctly withhold any expression of sympathy for them [the North] on the slavery question, because that question here is not one of vital nor practical interest. Avoiding its complications—for our political condition has long since been settled by latitude and climate—there is no need for discussing it among us, nor for our involving ourselves in the terrible and angry excitement of the States.[39]

At the same time, however, the people in the Pacific Northwest expressed a vital interest in the national crisis; they denounced disunion and looked for positive governmental action against the Southern secessionists.

[37] James W. Denver to Jonathan Logan, William T. Barbour, *et al.*, August 1, 1860, *Sacramento Daily Union*, August 4, 1860.
[38] [Stevens] to the Editor, November 28, 1860, Olympia *Pioneer and Democrat*, January 11, 1861.
[39] Stout to Deady, December 25, 1860, Deady Papers; Olympia *Pioneer and Democrat*, January 4, 18, 1861; Portland *Oregon Advertiser*, January 19, 1861.

In the second week of January, 1861, Pacific Northwest newspapers solemnly announced to their readers that disunion was a reality. On December 20, 1860, the South Carolina convention had passed a unanimous ordinance severing relations with the United States. Four days later, the convention issued a "Declaration of the Immediate Causes" which had impelled South Carolina to leave the Union. Commissioners were appointed to treat with the federal government concerning the transfer of federal property to the state government, and to represent South Carolina elsewhere in the South. South Carolina's secession was followed closely by the secession of the remaining Gulf, or cotton, states. By February, 1861, seven Southern states had left the Union. Delegates from the seceded states met at Montgomery, Alabama, to organize an independent Southern government.

The secession of the cotton states forced the people in the Pacific Northwest to re-evaluate the crisis. Discussions turned from concern with Southern threats and warnings to the reality of disunion. The people began to consider practical means by which a settlement between the warring sections could be achieved. Discussions centered about three choices facing the American nation: compromise, coercion, or peaceable separation. "The times are indeed ominous," wrote one Washington Territory settler; "God only knows what is to be the result."[40]

The first reactions to secession were many and varied. The Republicans, convinced now that Southerners had been sincere, first inclined to the view that a peaceable separation of the two sections was the best solution. The *Oregonian* questioned the desirability of a Union that could be held together only by force; coercion as a means of preserving the Union was rejected as inexpedient. The editor quoted with approval the statement of Horace Greeley, "If they are determined to go, let them go in peace." Should all the Southern slave states leave the Union, this Republican paper suggested that an amicable adjustment between the two sections was the only "available" plan.[41] The *Argus* still remained silent on the crisis, but its editor privately expressed the belief that a "friendly

[40] Ebey Diary, No. 6, p. 400 (January 13, 1861).
[41] Portland *Weekly Oregonian*, January 12, 19, 1861. For Greeley's attitude, see Thomas N. Bonner, "Horace Greeley and the Secession Movement, 1860-1861," *Mississippi Valley Historical Review*, XXXVIII (December, 1951) 425-444.

separation" of the two sections was preferable to any other mode of settlement.[42] In Washington Territory, one Republican wrote:

> If slavery has become too strong for the Union and if freedom or the Union must fall, then by all that is sacred "let the Union slide!" We will have population and territory left amply sufficient to demonstrate the feasibility of free institution . . . and if our scattered fragments do not again reunite, we will have two happy and prosperous republics on which the hopes of the patriot may depend for all coming time.[43]

The Douglas Democratic press continued to advocate a firm policy toward the seceders. The question of secession, "the paramount question of our existence as a nation," demanded an immediate solution. Congress, it was hoped, would devise some means for the preservation of the Union, but there was no faith in any more compromises. A war for the maintenance of the Union, it was thought, was not the greatest evil which could befall the country. Worse than that would be "the war of discordant, independent States which would surely follow the proposed quiet disunion." Both Buchanan and Lincoln were denounced for their "pusillanimous" policies. "If the Government has not power to enforce its laws, the constitution is not worth the paper it is written upon."[44] One Washington Territory newspaper, a supporter of Breckinridge in the campaign, lashed out at South Carolina's secession in no uncertain terms: "The pretensions of South Carolina . . . to a distinct National recognition, are absurd and untenable, and the duty, it seems to us, of the Federal Executive is to compel her position *in statu quo*."[45]

The third choice, compromise, was strongly urged by the Breckinridge Democrats. Like many of the compromise proposals in the East, however, "compromise" signified the complete surrender of the Republican position, actually no compromise at all. The only "avenue of retreat," according to one former Breckinridge organ, lay in a Northern acquiescence to the Southern demands, "indemnity for the past and security for the future." Guarantees, "sufficient to cover all possible future contingencies touching the slavery question," must be made to the South in the form of constitutional

42 Adams to David Craig, [n. d.], David W. Craig Papers, Oregon Historical Society Library.

43 "Consistency" to the Editor, January 24, 1861, Olympia *Washington Standard*, February 9, 1861.

44 Salem *Oregon Statesman*, January 14, 1861.

45 Port Townsend *Register*, January 30, 1861.

amendments. Unless this were done, the paper declared, the year 1861 would be the last of the Union and the first of anarchy among the states. Peaceable secession would be ruinous to both sections. Compromise was the only way out, and the only effective compromise was the "backing down" of the Republican party.[46]

The search for a remedy for the nation's disunion ills began in earnest in early December, 1860, when the second session of the Thirty-sixth Congress met. The months following South Carolina's secession witnessed a deluge of schemes and plans, both in Congress and in the public journals, designed to restore harmony between the sections. On the Pacific Northwest frontier, as in the border states to the East, sentiment favoring the settlement of the sectional difficulties by compromise grew stronger. This was partially explained by the fact that the Pacific Northwest was, in reality, a "border" region. Settled by pioneers from all sections of the country, harboring an aversion to the Negro race, either slave or free, and a devotion to the Union, the area was similar to the border region of the Ohio and Mississippi valleys. The feeling of detachment from the sectional struggle in the Pacific Northwest reinforced the desire for compromise. Oregon's Senator Baker characterized the feeling of his constituents: "I come from the midst of a people not directly concerned in this controversy; a population about half northern, half southern. We have intermarried together. Our interests, our fears, our hopes, our recollections, are mingled north and south."[47]

The conservatism of the Pacific Northwest frontier had been demonstrated early in the sectional crisis. The support of compromise was further indication that these frontiersmen desired to avoid extremes and to seek a middle road through the difficulties. However, while compromise was urged in the Pacific Northwest, little thought was given to practical compromise solutions. Thus, there was an air of unreality to much of the compromise talk. Slight consideration was given to satisfying the deep-seated grievances that existed between the North and the South. If either section rejected compromise, it was denounced in the Pacific Northwest for hindering a speedy reconciliation. This attitude resulted partly from a lack of understanding of the difficulty involved in settling the secession

[46] Corvallis *Oregon Weekly Union*, January 12, 1861; Portland *Oregon Advertiser*, January 19, 1861; *Portland Daily Advertiser*, January 21, 1861.
[47] *Cong. Globe*, 36 Cong., 2 Sess., p. 1316.

crisis; few people in the United States in 1861, however, understood the bases for hostility.

Not everyone in the Pacific Northwest supported compromise as the best solution. Many persons, believing that the time for compromise had passed, still felt that coercion was not the answer. They were also guilty of misunderstanding. The belief that secession was a bluff still persisted. Many thought that the government could continue to execute the laws of the United States within the limits of the seceded states with little or no opposition. The enforcement of the laws, they pointed out, was not coercion. If a conflict resulted it would be brief, limited probably to a blockade of Southern seaports. Drawing a fine distinction between coercion and the execution of the law, this group opposed coercion as strongly as compromise.

The early months of 1861 demonstrated the depths of confusion to which Americans plunged when confronted with a national crisis of serious proportions. Having first regarded the threatened disunion with confident complacency, they were thrown completely off guard when disunion became a reality. They grabbed at every straw of hope, amplified rumors to alarming proportions, and expressed themselves in the vaguest of terms. People changed their minds overnight with little apparent justification. Newspaper editors supported one policy one day and, on the next, would probably be found urging the opposite. This situation was bad enough in the East; on the frontier it was perhaps worse. The haphazard transmission of news to the Pacific Coast and the resulting time lag often multiplied the confusion.[48] The Southern secession threats were universally denounced by Pacific Northwest frontiersmen between November and January. All parties expressed their devotion to the Union in unequivocal terms. When the news of South Carolina's secession arrived, this unanimity broke down. Out of the welter of voices that followed the event emerged all shades of opinion. As the crisis continued, and as the national government continued to waver in its policy, sentiment in the Pacific Northwest was stabilized, although it never again achieved its earlier unanimity.

"The true doctrine," it was suggested in one newspaper,

---

[48] News, usually in the form of Eastern newspapers, traveled from Missouri to California by the pony express. From San Francisco it was brought to the Pacific Northwest by ocean steamer.

is now to reconcile existing differences, and to allay the terrible revolution through which our country is passing; any measures of that kind, no matter where it comes, whether from Bell, Breckenridge, Douglas or Seward, should be carefully and patriotically considered.—The question should not be, "who presented this?" but "what is it?"[49]

The issue of union or disunion, it was hoped, would unite the conservative men of all parties. One Republican newspaper strongly urged that "all just and appropriate compromises or concessions" be made in order to avert both disunion and coercion. The power of the sword, the editor maintained, might end all popular evils but would cure none. Two alternatives faced the United States: compromise or anarchy and despotism. Everyone, both North and South, should seek the perpetuation of the Union by compromise. "The time has arrived," the editor urged, "when concessions *must* be made to hold this fabric together." However, if the South refused to accept compromise, as events seemed to indicate, then the paper favored any remedy, "even to cauterization," that would produce harmony and unison.[50] A Breckinridge paper in the Willamette Valley advocated serious consideration of compromise proposals if for no other reason than to encourage the Union men in the South. As time passed, the need for compromise became greater.

> It is now a well ascertained fact, that there must be made large concessions by the North; not in party platforms, not in legislative enactments, or even congressional enactments; not merely for the present, but concessions which must become the fundamental law of the land, absolute and unalterable.[51]

The chief justice of Washington Territory, a Buchanan Democrat, was confident that "conciliation, harmony and concession, may yet save our beloved country from the perils which are impending over her." He urged everyone to cultivate a spirit of conciliation, "to restore that spirit of harmony, brotherly affection and public confidence."[52]

While compromise was advocated and discussed, little attention was given to the practical necessity of satisfying both the sections. Most of the discussion was rather nebulous. When it came to making concrete compromise suggestions, there was disagreement. One of the most publicized of the compromise plans, and the one which

---

49 Olympia *Pioneer and Democrat*, February 22, 1861.
50 Olympia *Washington Standard*, February 16, March 23, 1861.
51 Corvallis *Oregon Weekly Union*, March 2, 1861.
52 Olympia *Pioneer and Democrat*, March 15, 1861.

probably came closest to success, was presented to Congress by John J. Crittenden, veteran Senator from Kentucky. His compromise proposals received some support in the Pacific Northwest. One paper optimistically asserted that all of Washington Territory favored the compromise.

> We feel safely justified in pledging the warm support of the people of Washington Territory for Crittenden's compromise resolutions, so far as our expression of opinion is concerned. Although we have no voice in national affairs, yet we are allowed the privilege of expressing our warm and earnest devotion to the Union, and its preservation by a just and honorable compromise.

The Crittenden proposals were described as both "fair and just."[53] James W. Nesmith believed that the Crittenden Compromise, if adopted, would keep the border states in the Union; he had already written off the cotton states.[54] In Congress, Joseph Lane supported the Crittenden Compromise as the "most important measure that has been introduced into this Senate." He thought the compromise, if approved, would "delay the movements which are now going on, that are to result ultimately in the entire dissolution of the Union." The states that had left the Union should be invited to return "upon terms that will afford security to them." Lane's colleague in the Senate, Edward Dickinson Baker, opposed the Crittenden Compromise because he believed something better could be accomplished and because he thought the Crittenden proposals would not be acceptable to all the states.[55]

The Republican press in the Pacific Northwest either ignored the Crittenden Compromise proposals or took a strong stand against them. The *Oregonian* registered strong disapproval. In a rather unusual bit of invective, the editor branded the compromise as

> a sop thrown to Cerberus; a concession to Union-haters; blackmail to secession fillibusters; a retrogressive step; a cowardly giving up of cherished and true principles, and a victory over Union-loving men. It is not asked by Southern Union men for their own sakes, but to pacify a parcel of mobocrats.

Furthermore, the Crittenden Compromise contained nothing that would allay the excitement.[56] The other Republican organs in the Pacific Northwest maintained an unbroken silence with regard to the Crittenden proposals.

53 *Ibid.*, February 22, March 8, 22, 1861.
54 Nesmith to Harvey Gordon, March 18, 1861, Nesmith Papers.
55 *Cong. Globe,* 36 Cong., 2 Sess., pp. 382-383, 1314.
56 Portland *Weekly Oregonian,* March 2, February 9, 1861.

A compromise plan suggested by Stephen A. Douglas shortly after Congress convened received passing notice in the Pacific Northwest. Based on popular sovereignty, the plan provided that the question of slavery in any new territory should be determined by its status under the prevailing law of the area at the time of its acquisition. When the population reached fifty thousand, the territory could become a state with or without slavery, as its inhabitants decided. Nationally, the plan was almost completely overshadowed by the Crittenden Compromise. In the Pacific Northwest, the Portland *Advertiser,* a Douglas Democratic paper, thought that Douglas' plan was the most satisfactory for a settlement of the national troubles. The Douglas proposal was denounced in a rather perfunctory fashion by the *Oregonian.*[57]

Several newspapers in the Pacific Northwest attempted to define the terms of a compromise they thought would serve as a satisfactory basis for a settlement. The terms that were offered demonstrate the unrealistic nature of most of the compromise discussion. Many of the proposals were actually no compromises at all. To some of the more extreme Democrats in the Pacific Northwest, for instance, "compromise" meant the utter abandonment of the Republican position and acquiescence in all the Southern demands.[58] The Republican press dodged the fundamental issue. The *Washington Standard,* probably the most consistent backer of compromise among the Republican organs, urged the adoption of a "fair" compromise, but one which would not conflict with the cardinal principles of the Republican party. The paper called for the repeal of all the personal liberty laws in the North and the prompt rendition of fugitive slaves. In addition, it was willing to grant "rigid constitutional protection" to slavery in the slaveholding states, and what was called a "modification of abstract principles," whatever that might mean. The basic issue between the two sections, the status of slave property in the territories, was not mentioned. The *Oregonian,* although not enthusiastic about compromise as a means of settling the difficulties, did outline a series of steps that would be acceptable as a settlement:

[57] *Portland Daily Advertiser,* January 29, 1861; Portland *Weekly Oregonian,* February 9, 1861.

[58] Corvallis *Oregon Weekly Union,* January 12, 1861; Portland *Oregon Advertiser,* January 19, 1861; *Portland Daily Advertiser,* January 21, 1861.

We are in favor of giving the most ample guarantees to the Southern States against domestic insurrection; have no objection to the reenactment of the Missouri Compromise . . . will do almost anything to satisfy the Union-loving men of the South; will demand and expect freedom of speech . . . all over the Union; and will demand the rigid enforcement of every law on the Federal statute-books.[59]

The most widely discussed plan in the Pacific Northwest for ending the sectional difficulties was the proposal to "reconstruct" the national government. Supported primarily by Democratic elements, it was based on the belief that the government provided by the Constitution had failed and no longer answered its purpose. The Constitution was understood and interpreted differently in the different sections of the country; the best solution was the drafting of a new Constitution that would eliminate the ambiguity. Joseph Lane expressed this belief when he submitted several compromise resolutions to Congress early in December, 1860. "The present system of government," he declared, "is not adequate to the exigencies of the times, to the changes of opinions and circumstances." Lane compared the situation to that existing in 1787, when the Articles of Confederation were thought to be inadequate. His resolutions called for a new constitutional convention at which delegates from all the states would discuss the "changes which the present times require."[60]

An active supporter of "reconstruction" was Lane's colleague from north of the Columbia River, Isaac I. Stevens. Stevens maintained that delegates from all the states must meet again in convention, "as did our fathers in 1787." The responsibility for a settlement of the sectional differences must, he thought, be taken out of the hands of Congress, whose members had been elected "in the heat and excitement of the recent canvass."

The road through these discords and troubles has not been marked out in our constitutional chart. They were never, in their present magnitude, foreseen by our fathers. Old saws will not do. Logic and Rhetoric are of no avail. We have to deal with stern facts and the rapid movement of great events. . . . Then let us meet in Convention as soon as possible. Let the whole matter be referred to the fountain of power.

Stevens did not elaborate on how the government might be "reconstructed." He did not overlook, however, the possibility that

[59] Olympia *Washington Standard*, February 16, March 23, April 13, 1861; Portland *Daily Oregonian*, March 1, 1861; Port Townsend *North-West*, March 7, 1861.
[60] *Cong. Globe*, 36 Cong., 2 Sess., p. 112.

such a convention might result in a peaceable separation of the two sections. "If it cannot cement or re-establish the present government," he wrote, "it may possibly arrange the terms of peace and good will between its several parts." Although he did not sympathize with the course adopted by the Southern states, which he described as "mad, headlong and unjustifiable," Stevens placed the blame for disunion on the Republican party. Writing to his constituents in Washington Territory, Stevens viewed the crisis more realistically than did many of the statesmen in the national capital. Arguments over the validity of Southern complaints, he wrote, dodged the issue. "The South *do* feel agrieved. They *believe,* their rights, their homes, their peace is in danger. They are madly moving in the blind path of revolution. . . . These are the stubborn facts, which statesmen have to deal with."

> It must be constantly borne in mind, that we have to deal with a revolution, where event succeeds event with the rapidity of a dream, where the restorer or palliative of the day becomes obsolete on the morrow, and where the most patient and wise forecasts can discern but dimly the shadow of coming events.

A "reconstruction" of the government by a convention of all the states seemed to Stevens the safest and sanest way to meet the crisis. He was confident that such a convention would find it easier to unite than to separate. The advantages were all on the side of Union. "If Union seems to be accompanied with occasional discord, separation will threaten perpetual war. If in Union, there is not always harmony, in separation there will never be peace."[61]

A "reconstruction" of the Union was also urged by the two Pacific Coast members of the Select Committee of Thirty-three on the Disturbed Condition of the Country. This committee was appointed by the House of Representatives to receive, consider, and finally to report upon the many suggestions for compromise. Headed by Thomas Corwin of Ohio, the committee included one representative from each state. Corwin presented the report of the committee on January 14, 1861; there were, however, seven minority reports. A minority report written by Lansing Stout and John C. Burch, the two Pacific Coast members of the committee, urged the adoption of a plan for

---

[61] Stevens to the Editor of the Olympia *Pioneer and Democrat,* December 10, 17, 24, 1860; January 3, 10, 21, 1861, Stevens Papers. See also Johannsen, ed. "A Breckinridge Democrat on the Secession Crisis: Letters of Isaac I. Stevens, 1860-1861," pp. 283-310.

"reconstruction." Much of the ill feeling between the North and the South, they maintained, had originated in Congress; consequently it was desirable that the responsibility for solving the problems facing the nation should be taken out of the hands of Congress. They recommended that a constitutional convention, fresh from the people, amend the Constitution in such a way "as will more adequately respond to the wants, and afford more sufficient guarantees to the diversified and growing interests of the government and of the people composing the same." This recommendation, they wrote, represented the wishes of the people on the Pacific Coast, who were devoted to the Union and desired that every effort be made to secure its perpetuation. Finally, they summarized the attitude of the Pacific Northwest frontier to the secession crisis:

> While our people have neither been a party to or sufferers from this agitation, so far as their local interests are at this time involved, yet they are equally as anxious and as deeply interested in the settlement of the present difficulties as the people of any other section of this great confederacy.[62]

The idea of "reconstruction" was supported in the Pacific Northwest by some elements of the Democratic party. In mid-January, the *Pioneer and Democrat* urged that a convention of all the states be summoned to settle the sectional differences, that representatives direct from the people be called together, instead of allowing the "insane red republican" views of such politicians as Senators Benjamin F. Wade and Alfred Iverson to hold sway. This view was supported by the *Oregon Weekly Union,* which declared that "legislative compromises will not reach the issue," and by the *Oregon Sentinel,* whose editor urged that Oregon's Senators and Representatives resign so that new men "fresh from the people" could be elected.[63] To other Democrats, "reconstruction" implied prior disunion. One paper declared:

> If the Government shall be unable to withstand the assaults of revolution, there is we confess neither hope of a united confederacy afterward, or any

[62] Minority Report of John C. Burch and Lansing Stout, *Report of the Select Committee of Thirty-three on the Disturbed Condition of the Country, Reports of Committees of the House of Representatives,* 36 Cong., 2 Sess., No. 31.

[63] Olympia *Pioneer and Democrat,* January 25, 1861; Corvallis *Oregon Weekly Union,* January 26, 1861; Salem *Oregon Statesman,* March 4, 1861. One Breckinridge Democrat in Oregon concluded that the American experiment was a failure if domestic feuds were unavoidable. Obviously, some stronger form of government must be sought (J. H. Reed to Deady, January 31, 1861, Deady Papers).

permanent good government, until the issues that now distract the parties, and the two sections of the country shall have become extinct through the success or defeat of those inaugurating revolution.

The *Oregon Statesman* considered "reconstruction" a concession to the disunionists, a recognition of the "success of the revolution already inaugurated." The Constitution had not failed; to maintain that it had was to uphold the validity of the Southern demands. The editor recognized a new danger implicit in a revision of the Constitution and placed his finger on a dilemma that plagued many Northerners throughout the war:

> The effect of the trouble in the South has been to impress every one with the necessity of a strong federal government. If the constitution is to be amended or if any compromises are entered into to serve as precedents for the future, we apprehend the rights of the States as sovereignties within a certain sphere will be greatly curtailed. . . . If any change is now made, it will be to weaken the States and strengthen the Union. We are opposed to any infraction of the rights of the States, about as much as to secession itself. A consolidated empire would be nearly as great, possibly a greater curse to the people than a dismembered Union.[64]

Republicans gave the plan for "reconstruction" slight notice. The South, they thought, would never agree to a "reconstruction" that did not recognize its demands; the North would be equally reluctant to accept a "reconstruction" that did not embody its position.[65]

Support for a "reconstruction" of the national government was widespread at one stage of the secession crisis. Many Southern leaders endorsed the idea even though their states were out of the Union. Alexander H. Stephens declared that many Georgians voted for secession under the impression that their demands would be more readily accepted if the state were out of the Union. The idea was also popular in the border states, where it was felt that secession was "impermanent," and many conservative Republicans supported it.[66]

Although the majority of Northerners favored an adjustment of the sectional controversy, the Republican leaders in Congress were

[64] *Portland Daily Advertiser*, February 12, 1861; Salem *Oregon Statesman*, February 18, March 11, April 29, 1861.

[65] Portland *Weekly Oregonian*, March 23, 1861; Holbrook to Craig, March 30, 1861, Amory Holbrook Papers, Oregon Historical Society Library.

[66] Potter, *Lincoln and His Party in the Secession Crisis*, pp. 219-248; Henry Clyde Hubbart, *The Older Middle West, 1840-1880* (New York, 1936), pp. 161-165.

reluctant to consider the possibilities of compromise. A compromise, many of them reasoned, would not only weaken their position in national politics but also would undermine the very basis of their party. Responsibility for the fact that no effective compromise was ever offered the South has been ascribed to the Republicans in Congress.[67] Nevertheless, there were many in Congress who labored up to the last minute on behalf of compromise and conciliation.

The last hope of the compromisers was the Washington Peace Conference which assembled on February 4, 1861. Sponsored by the Virginia state legislature, the conference included delegates from twenty-one states, although the Pacific Coast was not represented. Isaac Stevens was confident that the labors of the conference would be successful. "Virginia," he wrote, "will indeed have most gloriously succeeded in her mission, and we shall see her with her sister border Slave States using their best exertions to bring back the wanderers to the fold."[68] Late in February, the conference reported a compromise closely resembling the one previously proposed by Crittenden. The few remaining days of the congressional session were spent in several vain attempts to bring the new compromise to a vote. These efforts, like all earlier ones, were opposed and blocked by Republican votes.[69]

Not all Republicans in Congress opposed compromise. Edward Dickinson Baker, Oregon's Republican Senator, strongly urged the acceptance of compromise during the latter days of the session. His position drew him into debates with other Republicans, notably Lyman Trumbull of Illinois. Although Baker had earlier voted against the Crittenden Compromise, he supported the proposal of the Washington Peace Conference. Baker exclaimed, to the hearty applause of the galleries:

> If in my judgment, conceding so much, yielding so much, compromising so much, abandoning so much, would restore to this great country peace, to our

[67] Kenneth M. Stampp, *And the War Came: The North and the Secession Crisis, 1860-1861* (Baton Rouge, 1950), p. 141.

[68] Stevens to the Editor of the Olympia *Pioneer and Democrat*, February 11, 1861, Stevens Papers.

[69] The only exception was the so-called Corwin amendment, providing for the protection of slavery in the states where it then existed. This amendment barely received the required two-thirds majority in both houses of Congress, despite the overwhelming Republican opposition. In Oregon it was considered "liberal in spirit and kind and courteous in terms" (Salem *Oregon Statesman*, April 15, 1861).

Government union, and bring us back to where we were, I would do it now, to-morrow, a thousand times, and forever, though the act would sink me into oblivion a thousand fathoms deep.

He favored submitting the compromise plan to the people; he doubted the right of the Republican party, a minority party, to settle the difficulties for the whole country: "I do not believe that it is possible for one third of the people to coerce the opinion of two thirds." Baker accused the Republicans of shutting their eyes to the actual condition of the country:

We talk of ourselves as the Union party. It is very easy to be for the Union when it costs us nothing. It costs no man anything to say that the Union is a great institution, to sing peans in its praise, to shout hallelujahs to its glory. This is easily done; but when we have got to give up something of pride of opinion, if you like, of past conviction for the Union, "there's the rub."

When his fellow Republicans accused him of disloyalty to the Chicago platform, Baker countered, "I cannot for my life see, if Congress had the constitutional power to prohibit, why it had not the same constitutional right to establish."[70] Republicans in the Senate remained adamant in their refusal to consider any of the compromise schemes.

Baker's colleague, Joseph Lane, had no kind words for the Peace Conference proposal. It was, to him, a "cheat, a deception, a humbug."[71] He had long since given up hope that the sectional difficulties could be settled by compromise. Although he gave some support to the idea of "reconstruction" and repeatedly expressed his devotion to the Union, nothing short of a complete Northern, or Republican, surrender would have satisfied Lane. In January, after six Southern states had seceded, Lane predicted that all the slave states would soon be out of the Union and organized into a confederacy that would "command the respect and confidence of all the nations of Europe." The withdrawal of the Southern states had become an imperative duty.[72] In the debates in Congress during the secession winter, Lane became one of the extreme proponents of the Southern

[70] *Cong. Globe,* 36 Cong., 2 Sess., pp. 1314, 1381-1386. Following his speech Baker received the warm congratulations of Stephen A. Douglas.

[71] *Ibid.,* p. 1318.

[72] Lane to Deady, January 27, 1861, Lane Papers. See also Lane's letter to the Breckinridge and Lane club of New York City, November 20, 1860, Albany *Oregon Democrat,* January 1, 1861; and the letter to his cousin in Georgia, December 14, 1860, quoted in the Columbus (Ga.) *Times* and reprinted in the Salem *Oregon Statesman,* March 11, 1861.

position. With the consideration of the Washington Peace Conference proposal, Lane became even more obsessed with the Southern position. At the same time, his remarks were his valedictory, for his Senatorial term was drawing to a close. On the floor of the Senate, he reviewed the history of the sectional crisis and reiterated the Southern demand for "equal rights" in the territories. The Davis resolutions, which he had supported a year earlier, were the only principles upon which a reunion could be based. He warned the Southerners:

> We should never compromise principle nor sacrifice the eternal philosophy of justice. . . . beware of "compromising" away the vital rights, privileges, and immunities of one portion of the country to appease the graceless, unrelenting, and hostile fanaticism of another portion.

He predicted again that all the slave states would soon join in a "great, homogeneous, and glorious southern confederacy." To those who proposed coercion, he announced that the South could never be conquered by tyrannical interference. In one final gesture, Lane urged the recognition of the independence of the Confederate States, as an ally and as a friendly nation.[73] Lane's opinions remained unchanged throughout the war.[74]

In the Pacific Northwest, the Peace Conference was not seriously considered as a means by which sectional tensions could be eased. While it was hoped that some measures might be adopted that would bring peace to the nation, there was a general feeling that the attempt would prove a failure. By the time news of the conference arrived in the region, compromise feeling had begun to wane. The fruitless wranglings in Congress and the determined course of the Southern states indicated to many on the frontier that the conflict between the North and the South might indeed prove irrepressible. "The people," one editor reflected, "have entrusted the management of national affairs to other hands and must look for the present to other counsels, for safety."[75]

While compromise was discussed in the Pacific Northwest during the early months of 1861, the question of governmental policy toward the seceded states became a serious one. President Buchanan, in his

---

[73] *Cong. Globe,* 36 Cong. 2 Sess., pp. 1342-1348.
[74] Joseph Lane, The Autobiography of Joseph Lane, MS in the Bancroft Library (microfilm in the University of Washington Library), pp. 145-146.
[75] Portland *Weekly Oregonian,* March 2, 1861; Salem *Oregon Statesman,* March 25, 1861.

message to Congress in December, had formulated a policy in abstract terms. A state, he maintained, had no constitutional right to secede from the Union, but the national government had no power to force a state to remain in the Union. As long as the Southern states remained in the Union, there was no necessity to go beyond this abstraction. As soon as secession became a reality, however, a policy of action was demanded. Buchanan's answer was the ill-fated expedition of the "Star of the West." Following this episode, he determined to leave the whole ticklish question to his successor. Isaac Stevens urged Buchanan to withdraw his confidence in the Southern members of his cabinet and to take a positive stand in defense of the government, but the president continued to vacillate.[76] For approximately three months the United States government was without a definite policy toward the seceded states.

What the attitude of the incoming executive would be toward the seceded South was as much a matter of speculation in the Pacific Northwest as in the rest of the nation. From the beginning some elements on the Pacific Northwest frontier felt that the national troubles should be solved within the existing framework of government. They opposed compromise as a solution because it involved little more than the complete surrender of one or the other position. At the same time, coercion was discountenanced. The difficulty, they thought, would have a way of working itself out—a policy reminiscent of Republican party attitudes during this period.

A distinction was drawn between the execution of the laws in the Southern states and coercion. Both Republican and Democratic newspapers made this distinction. One Breckinridge editor favored the enforcement of the laws, "tempered with prudence," in the South, but opposed a policy of coercion. "Executing the Federal law against the individual citizens of a State is one thing, and the coercion of a State is quite another."[77] The *Oregonian* pointed out that, if the laws of the United States should be resisted, the individuals responsible, not the state, would be answerable to the government; the idea of shedding blood was "revolting to all."[78] The government had no power to coerce a state back into the Union or to force a

---

[76] Hazard Stevens, *The Life of Isaac Ingalls Stevens* (2 vols.; Boston, 1900), II, 311-312.

[77] Corvallis *Oregon Weekly Union,* February 2, 1861.

[78] Portland *Weekly Oregonian,* February 9, March 16, April 20, 1861.

state to be represented in Congress, but it did have the authority and the duty to enforce the laws of the United States in all the states. Even in this, however, "nothing like harshness or precipitancy ought to be indulged in towards even such a State as South Carolina, where treason is a chronic distemper."[79] The application of the term "coercion" to the mere maintenance of law was a trick of the disunionists. One editor argued that coercion, that is, making war on a state, was not only unconstitutional but impossible. No one would propose such a course.[80] Republicans agreed. By enforcing the laws, the federal government was not making war upon a state but rather upon the individuals who were in revolt. No Republican "has ever talked about coercion." One Republican, however, hinted that the enforcement of federal law in the South might necessitate the employment of force. "The peace spirit of the North is to *maintain* the laws, if need be, at the point of the sword."[81]

Behind the belief that the federal government could enforce the laws of the United States in the seceded areas and still avoid a collision with the forces of secession was a failure to grasp the real import of the Southern position. Some Republicans still refused to believe that secession was anything more than a temporary phenomenon. One former resident of Washington Territory, writing from the national capital, even denied that secession had occurred. The ratification of the Constitution was forever, he argued, and the government created by that document was indissoluble and everlasting. The secession ordinances passed by the Southern states were meaningless.[82] Byron J. Pengra, editor of one of Oregon's Republican newspapers, also wrote from Washington, D.C., that disunion was temporary and that it would not be necessary for Lincoln to use force against the seceding states. By inauguration day, secession would have had "its run."[83]

A lull in the secession movement encouraged this feeling in the Pacific Northwest. Following the initial flurry of secession in January and early February, a period of calm ensued. The Washington Peace

[79] Oregon City *Oregon Argus,* February 9, 1861.
[80] Salem *Oregon Statesman,* March 4, 1861.
[81] "Kitsap" to the Editor, March 1, 1861, Olympia *Washington Standard,* March 9, 1861; Oregon City *Oregon Argus,* March 2, 1861.
[82] Letter from "L.," December 23, 1860, Olympia *Washington Standard,* February 23, 1861.
[83] B. J. Pengra to Adams, January 18, 1861, Oregon City *Oregon Argus,* March 30, 1861; Portland *Daily Oregonian,* February 4, 1861.

Conference met, and both Virginia and Tennessee rejected secession. In the Pacific Northwest, it was reported that "the tumult"
had been quelled, "the great secession flame has burned out, or is
apparently doing so, for want of fuel." "Nothing has yet been accomplished but a paper revolution," one newspaper observed. "From
all the indications of the present, it seems more probable that the
Southern Empire brought forth at Montgomery will amount to
nothing; that it is an abortive dead-born nuisance, which will be
buried out of sight by its own authors within a few months at the
utmost." The secession movement was a "mere stage trick"; the
conservative, Unionist element in the South would soon rise and
strangle what was left of the rebellion.[84] Others thought that a
show of determination by the national government would result in
the collapse of the entire Southern movement. The Republican
press, particularly, argued that a few months' blockade of Southern
ports and the collection of the revenue by the government would
demonstrate to Southerners the "folly" of their attempts to leave
the Union. With its ports closed and its postal facilities withdrawn,
the South would soon submit.[85]

The national policy of the Republican party was in part based
upon such a belief. Republican leaders, Lincoln included, had a
strong faith in the Southern Unionist element and felt certain that
the trend of secession would soon be reversed. Republicans adopted
a policy of "watchful waiting," opposing all suggestions of compromise. This policy encouraged one Breckinridge newspaper in Oregon to believe that a reunion would soon be effected,[86] but generally
there was great dissatisfaction in the Pacific Northwest with the "do-
nothing" policy. Lincoln's apparent lack of interest in active measures to save the Union particularly galled the Democrats in the
Northwest. His inaugural address was considered little more than
a "studied effort" to show the nation that the new president had
no plans to meet the emergency.

> True, he indicates that he will administer the government according to the
> Constitution [one newspaper declared], but, inasmuch as the difference and
> trouble grows out of different and adverse interpretations of that instrument,

[84] Salem *Oregon Statesman*, February 18, 25, March 11, 18, 1861.
[85] Portland *Weekly Oregonian*, April 13, 1861; Portland *Daily Oregonian*, February 14, 1861; Oregon City *Oregon Argus*, March 2, 1861.
[86] Albany *Oregon Democrat*, April 9, 1861.

this declaration is not only not satisfactory, but calculated in the very nature of the controversy to intensify the strife and discord.[87]

In the opinion of James W. Nesmith, Lincoln was obviously not the man for the crisis. From the East, Nesmith wrote:

It is already demonstrated that an inherant weakness pervades our government which in the end will be its ruin. In other times of trial that weakness has in some degree been compensated by the strength of the executive head, but that very quality so much needed has not of late been sought for in Presidential candidates. The people have become infatuated with the notion that some damned old fool who drank hard cider, skinned coons, ran a flat boat, cut cordwood or made rails was the very man to be placed in the last position where those qualifications were required.[88]

One paper summed up the public attitude: "Everything is drifting towards some almost unknown and unseen danger, and everybody seems to be stupefied into inaction, without making an effort to evade it, calmly waiting the final crash."[89]

As the possibility for a peaceful restoration of the Union diminished, Pacific Northwesterners drifted into more extreme positions. Stevens became discouraged as the states of the lower South continued to withdraw from the Union and as all attempts at reconciliation failed in Congress. "The public mind," he wrote, "cannot possibly seize and seasonably adjust itself to the times. Our public men, many of them, cannot or will not." The destiny of the nation had been placed in the hands of Congress, where "men must give up pride of opinion to prevent the shedding of fratricidal blood."[90] In Washington Territory, the Republican *Washington Standard* suggested coercion for the first time. *"The Union must be preserved,"* the editor maintained, "and if necessary, at the point of the bayonet." In the same issue a report that a Northern lady had been tarred and feathered in Alabama provided an opportunity for an outburst of invective:

Talk of compromise with these fiends! Much as we desire peace with the Southern States, we say, if the perpetrators of the above fiendish outrage are a fair representation of the whole, No compromise but extermination, no peace till the stain be washed from our national fame with their blood.[91]

[87] Corvallis *Oregon Weekly Union,* April 20, 1861.
[88] Nesmith to Gordon, March 18, 1861; Nesmith to Deady, April 8, 1861; Nesmith Papers.
[89] Corvallis *Oregon Weekly Union,* March 16, 1861.
[90] Stevens to the Editor of the Olympia *Pioneer and Democrat,* January 10, 1861, Stevens Papers.
[91] Olympia *Washington Standard,* March 30, 1861.

The *Oregonian* was discouraged. Although hope was still held out for a Unionist reaction in the South, the tone of the paper became more and more pessimistic:

> We do not know that the South will not come back. We hope the people there will become satisfied of the foul game that has been played upon them, and this fact, with the difficulties of their position, it is possible, may induce them to return to the Union they have abandoned. We hope it may be so.— We have fears, however, almost amounting to certainty, that this hope will not be realized.[92]

The following week the editor reviewed the situation and attempted to answer the question, "What is to be done?" The government of the United States had been overthrown in the seceded states except for two small beleaguered forts. With the formation of a Southern republic, all compromise between the two sections seemed impossible; Lincoln could not recognize the independence of the South, and Davis could not surrender the independence of the South. The Southerners must have calculated the cost of their action, the editor thought, which now appeared to be war. Lincoln had no alternative but to enforce the laws in the South until either the one or the other section should be defeated. "We are of those who do not believe that this government can be broken up without war," the editor declared.[93]

Some Democrats turned briefly to a "let-them-go-in-peace" attitude. Although the *Pioneer and Democrat* consistently maintained that the South acted wrongly in not giving Lincoln a chance and that the only hope for a reconciliation lay in "compromise and reconstruction," it nevertheless favored "peace at all events, if it be had honorably,—even if by acknowledging the Confederated States —not as a matter of principle—but one of policy and necessity." The patience of this frontier editor had grown thin. Early in March he expressed annoyance at the preoccupation of Congress with the national crisis at the expense of legislation for the territories.

> If we could only get rid of the slavery question we could have our quota of legislation. The discussion of it has kept us back ten years. The Pacific coast all this time have been standing respectfully outside the doors of Congress, hat in hand, waiting for them to get done with their "irrepressible conflict."[94]

[92] Portland *Weekly Oregonian,* April 20, 1861.
[93] *Ibid.,* April 27, 1861.
[94] Olympia *Pioneer and Democrat,* March 8, April 5, 26, 1861.

One other Breckinridge paper expressed itself in vague and inde-finite terms: "For our own part we want to see the Union as it was, and Oregon faithful to it, as she has ever been."[95]

With the change of administration on March 4, the Thirty-sixth Congress officially came to an end. For a few days following, the Thirty-seventh Congress met in special session. James W. Nesmith journeyed to the national capital early in the winter and was a close observer of events during the secession crisis. One of Nesmith's con-stituents urged him to do all he could to bring about a reasonable settlement between the sections, declaring, "a Senator *about to be* is more than equal in moral force to one at the end of his term."[96] Early in February, Nesmith wrote, "The South is out of the Union for good, and I do not think that there will be any effort made to coerce them, or reduce them to submission." He expected no benefi-cial results from the many efforts that were being made to compro-mise the difficulties, but he later looked to compromise as the best way to resolve the differences. He opposed both coercion and peace-able separation. His disgust with Lincoln's inaction grew. "Whilst Lincoln and his cabinet seem undetermined," Nesmith wrote, "the Republic is falling to pieces, and Jeff Davis a man of great executive mind, and experience is rapidly consolidating his strength, and establishing his Southern confederacy upon a principle but little short of a Military despotism, and in which it will finally result."[97] On the floor of the Senate, Nesmith opposed coercion:

> I know that there are a great many people who are anxious to go down South and cultivate that feeling of fraternal friendship and brotherly love upon which this Union is predicated, with the bayonet. . . . I do not believe I can make a man love me any better by thrusting a bayonet into his stomach.[98]

Nevertheless, he observed the rapid approach of armed conflict. When the government decided to reinforce the besieged forts in the South, Nesmith predicted a "general resort to arms" as only a matter of time. In mid-March, he wrote to his constituents:

> *My opinion is* that this Union, (once called glorious!) is now dissolved, as Delazon would have said *"beyond a paradventure,"* The cotton states have

[95] Jacksonville *Oregon Sentinel,* February 23, 1861.
[96] Deady to Nesmith, February 28, 1861, Deady Papers.
[97] Nesmith to Gordon, February 6, 1861; Nesmith to Gordon, March 18, 1861, Nesmith Papers.
[98] *Cong. Globe,* 37 Cong., Special Session, p. 1516.

"gone out to stand," and I do not believe that there will be any re-construction with the free states. The Commissioners from the "confederated states," will shortly present their *"Credentials"* to Abraham, and he will have to construe his inaugiral by acts! It is useless to talk about *"peaceable separation."*

It is time that we may *Separate* in peace, but with our extended common frontier, and the thousand complications growing out of the seperation, how long can peace be maintained? In any event *War* with all of its stern realities will be upon us in a few days, and all of our 4th of July orations upon the subject, of the perpetuity of our glorious Union, and the capacity of our free institutions for indefinate expansion, will be laughed at as chimmeras of the brain.

I do not believe that the "border Slave states" can be kept with the North, Madness rules the hour, and people who were once only fools, have become d——d Fools!

Regarding separation as inevitable, it becomes us of the Pacific to determine *what we shall do.* Upon this subject I have never had but one opinion, and that is *stick to the Union or what ever may be left of it.* Our interests are identified with the Great North West. There will still be a Powerful Government left in the free states, and we must stick by it.[99]

The Pacific Northwest followed Nesmith's advice but not until after the idea of a Pacific Republic had been further discussed and debated. The actual secession of the Southern states gave encouragement to the proponents of a Pacific Republic. "If the Union should go into more than two pieces," wrote one settler in the Pacific Northwest, "then it [the Pacific Republic] would most likely become a fact, and rather a small one."[100] During the early months of 1861, rumors circulated in Washington Territory that groups of men stood ready to assume control of the government machinery should the Union fall to pieces. One Republican newspaper reported:

It has long been understood that a secret, sworn society of armed men, numbering several thousands, existed on the shores of the Pacific, whose sole aim was to possess the arms, treasure and fortifications of the Federal Government, levy taxes *a la* South Carolina, and subjugate, by force and arms, such of the people as had the temerity to demur to their attempt at coercive control.

Earlier the same paper had reported that certain citizens of the territory had already received their commissions in the new government but that the "precise time of their entering upon the discharge of their self-imposed duties" remained uncertain.[101] These alarms

[99] Nesmith to Deady, April 8, 1861, Nesmith Papers; Nesmith to Gordon, March 9, 1861, Oliver Cromwell Applegate Papers, University of Oregon Library.
[100] Deady to Nesmith, February 28, 1861, Deady Papers.
[101] Port Townsend *North-West,* March 7, February 28, 1861.

proved unfounded. Sentiment in the region was strong against breaking away from the Union. The *Argus* stated that "no one in Oregon thinks of such a thing, unless it is some brainless squirt of Democracy who is not able to pay his board bill."[102] The Breckinridge press denounced the idea as simply a phantom designed to give trouble to "imaginative politicians" and to bedevil the fussy and fidgety Republicans "who are ever ready to be frightened at their own shadows." "The people of Oregon entertain no such disloyal schemes as a Pacific Republic, or even a Union with the Southern Confederacy—however much they may sympathise with the South and oppose the principles of coercion."[103]

Washington Territory declared for the Union in unequivocal terms. The territorial legislature debated through the winter a series of resolutions "expressive of our attachment to the national Union, and pledging Washington for the parent government." Toward the end of the session, which was described by a participant as one of "marked excitement," the resolutions were passed with but one dissenting vote.[104] Later a mass meeting was summoned at the capitol in Olympia for all who loved the Union and were opposed to a Pacific Republic. "A large and enthusiastic" crowd gathered, elected a president and seventeen vice-presidents, six secretaries, and a committee on resolutions, including men drawn from all parties. Four resolutions were approved by the meeting, deploring the efforts to break up the Union, repudiating the attempts to establish a Pacific confederacy, proposing an amicable settlement of all grievances between the North and the South, and declaring the attachment of Washington Territory to the Union. It was hoped that these "evidences of our loyalty may not be without their weight, as they plainly show that we appreciate with warm gratitude, the care of our government."[105] No such demonstrations were held in Oregon. A small Union meeting was held at Astoria early in April at which a former Breckinridge Democrat urged the formation of a Union party and exhorted all present to support the Union. Reso-

[102] Oregon City *Oregon Argus*, February 2, 1861.
[103] Corvallis *Oregon Weekly Union*, April 27, 1861.
[104] Augustus Ripley Burbank Diary, Library of Congress (microfilm in the University of Washington Library), p. 198 (February 7, 1861); Territory of Washington *House Journal*, 1860-1861 (Olympia, 1861), p. 387; Territory of Washington *Council Journal*, 1860-1861 (Olympia, 1861), pp. 310-311.
[105] Olympia *Washington Standard*, March 2, 16, 1861; Olympia *Pioneer and Democrat*, March 15, 1861.

lutions were passed expressing confidence in Lincoln and demanding the enforcement of the laws and the retention of United States property in the South. The leadership of a former Breckinridge Democrat at this meeting caused many Republicans to view it with suspicion, which, of course, defeated its purpose.[106]

All hopes for a peaceful restoration of the Union and for the avoidance of an armed collision between the North and the South were dashed by the Confederate batteries in Charleston harbor. In the early morning hours of April 12, 1861, after fruitless negotiations with the small garrison, Southern guns began the bombardment of Fort Sumter. News of the attack reached the Pacific Northwest on April 29, when the steamer "Cortes" arrived in Portland from San Francisco. The reaction was electric. The settlers on this far frontier, like people throughout the North, responded to the headlines with an unquestioned devotion to the Union. The fine distinction between coercion and the enforcement of the laws was forgotten. All agreed that the government must suppress the rebellion. One newspaper reflected the attitude of these pioneers: "Call it 'coercion' or aught else they please, the laws must be executed either by the consent of the governed or by force." If blood must be spilled, "be it so."[107]

For almost four months, particularly since the news of South Carolina's secession had reached the area, the people in the Pacific Northwest had watched Eastern developments. Although they felt detached from the sectional struggle so far as the issues involved were concerned, they nevertheless showed a deep interest in and anxiety about the national difficulties. From the very first they expressed and felt a devotion to the Union; their efforts were bent toward the preservation of the Union by the best means they knew, compromise and cautious moderation. In contrast to the divisions that had existed during the campaign of 1860, all political groups joined in a common crusade to save the Union. The former Breckinridge party was one of the most vocal in support of the Union, further indication that the Breckinridge vote in the Pacific Northwest had been a Union vote. Naturally disappointed at their defeat, the members

[106] Portland *Weekly Oregonian*, April 20, 1861.
[107] Olympia *Washington Standard*, May 4, 1861.

of this group did not countenance disunion. In sympathy with the Southern grievances, they yet did not tolerate resistance to the national government as the alternative to defeat. The Douglas Democrats, no less vocal in favor of the Union, still remembered the actions of the Southern delegates in the Democratic nominating conventions a year previous. They were inclined to consider the Southern position with more bitterness, and at times seemed to be motivated by feelings of revenge against the disaffected Southern states. Republicans exhibited a good deal more caution in their reactions to the events of the secession crisis. One eye was always trained on the party leaders and on the national party policy. All parties, however, agreed fundamentally that the sectional difficulties should find resolution in the tradition of compromise. Even Republicans in the Pacific Northwest strongly favored the settlement of the crisis through compromise and mutual concession despite the fact that their national organization remained steadfast against such a policy throughout the crisis period.

With the sentiment in favor of compromise in the Pacific Northwest went an aversion toward coercion. None of the groups ventured to suggest coercion, but on the contrary all made repeated efforts to disavow such a policy. This led to a rather fine distinction between coercion and the enforcement of federal law in the South, a distinction Lincoln himself later made in his inaugural address. Not until all hope for a peaceful settlement was gone did Pacific Northwesterners reluctantly reach the conclusion that coercion, or civil war, was the only alternative.

Underlying the reactions in the Pacific Northwest to the secession crisis was a basic misunderstanding of the seriousness of the sectional struggle, as well as a human unwillingness to face the stern alternatives. There was a constant tendency to indulge in "wishful thinking," first to minimize the proportions of the secession threat, finally to anticipate a reversal of the trend toward disunion and a reunion of the sections on the initiative of the Southerners themselves. Compromise received wide support, but little thought was given to the practical terms of a compromise that would satisfy all the parties. The detachment of the region from the centers of activity in the East and the haphazard means of communication between the Pacific Coast and the East may have been partially responsible for this lack of understanding. However, this lack becomes more intelligible when one considers that most of the people in the North (and South) at this time harbored the same misunderstanding.

In its attitude toward the secession crisis, the Pacific Northwest assumed the character of a "border region." Its feeling of detachment from the sectional struggle, its refusal to admit either slave or free Negroes, its wholehearted devotion to the Union, its support of compromise and aversion toward coercion, its failure to grasp the real seriousness of the crisis, its general inclination toward a conservative and moderate policy, and its abhorrence of all that smacked of radicalism—all these were characteristics of both the Pacific Northwest and the "border region" of the Ohio and Mississippi valleys. The similarity between this far Northwest frontier and the border states to the East was further manifested in the months that followed the bombardment of Fort Sumter.

CHAPTER SEVEN

> *the union, conserv-
> atism, and peace*

THE BOMBARDMENT OF FORT
Sumter inaugurated a new phase in the attitude of the Pacific Northwest toward the sectional conflict. Ideas and opinions changed, and
party lines shifted to meet the new facts. On May 3, 1861, Winfield
Scott Ebey, a Douglas Democrat in Washington Territory, wrote in
his diary:

> Great Excitement prevails throughout the Country and the probabilities are
> that we are on the Eve of a General Civil war the results of which is hard
> to foretell[.] Should Mr Lincoln pursue an agressive Policy there is little
> hope for any thing but war & blood shed—I pray that he may be [guided] by
> wisdom from on high for the help of man is surely well nigh hopeless—Should
> *war* be the policy of the Govt the slave States will make Common Cause.[1]

Reaction in the Pacific Northwest to the fall of Fort Sumter was
immediate. All but a few individuals recognized it as the beginning
of a bloody contest between the sections. The hope that a compromise could be reached or that a brief show of force by the North
would be sufficient to awe the South into reconciliation fled with the
arrival of the news that the South had fired the first shot. There was
an almost universal rush to the side of the Union and, with some-

---

[1] Winfield Scott Ebey Diary, No. 6, p. 437 (May 3, 1861), University of Washington Library.

what less enthusiasm, to the administration which was pledged to maintain the Union.

The *Oregonian* warned its readers that the contest would determine "whether the sun of freedom shall set in blood." The editor accused Buchanan and Lane of "treachery." "Mr. Lincoln," he wrote, "is the representative of the supreme executive power, and all opposition to him, with a view to paralyze the government, works as much injury to the nation as if assistance were given direct to the Disunionists."[2] The *Washington Standard* abandoned its support of compromise and came out squarely for the restoration of the Union and the enforcement of the laws, by spilling blood if necessary.[3]

The *Statesman* recalled with bitterness that barely a year had elapsed between the disruption of the Democratic party in Charleston and the final disruption of the Union. There was a close relationship, the editor believed, between the two events. The paper took a strong Union position: "We must confide in no man who does not boldly and unconditionally take the part of the government on every issue affecting the great question of its perpetuity." In a somewhat less emphatic tone, the editor lamented that "a first class power of the earth is approaching toward the condition of Mexico, and the other Spanish republics of the South."[4] The *Pioneer and Democrat* made a full swing from sympathy with the Southern position to unconditional support of the Union and the government. A supporter of Breckinridge and a consistent advocate of compromise, the paper had approved peaceable separation and recognition of the Confederate States just before the bombardment of Sumter. With the news from Charleston harbor, the newspaper emphatically declared, "Now that war has been formerly [*sic*] inaugurated by the Confederate States, there remains but one course for the patriot: to stand by the Government."[5]

The citizenry received the news of Fort Sumter's surrender with a great deal of excitement and indignation. Many persons expressed their devotion to the Union in large and enthusiastic Union meetings. This enthusiasm spread to all parts of the region. A large Union meeting held in Portland soon after the news had arrived

2 Portland *Weekly Oregonian*, May 4, 1861.
3 Olympia *Washington Standard*, May 4, 1861.
4 Salem *Oregon Statesman*, May 6, 1861.
5 Olympia *Pioneer and Democrat*, May 10, 17, 1861.

reported, "The Union feeling is prevalent; it overrides all politics; it cannot be resisted." Several days later a similar gathering was held in Salem, where two hundred and twenty-five persons signed a roster declaring their support of the Union and then whistled "Yankee Doodle" in unison. The Reverend Gustavus Hines delivered a rousing speech in which he declared: "Had I a brother even—who, forgetting his duty as a citizen, should dare to raise his hand against that flag,—however dear might be the relations between us, I would not hesitate one instant to turn the gun of the Union against him." A group meeting in Albany resolved to "act with no party, vote for no man not fully and unequivocally committed to the eternal Union of the United States."[6]

Bigger and better Union meetings followed. At Oregon City a flag was raised to the accompaniment of patriotic speeches and music by the town's German brass band. Union resolutions were passed at a meeting in Milwaukie, and thirty-four guns, one for each state, were fired at Amity, after which a group of ladies presented the town with a newly made flag. Meetings followed at Belpassi, a town in Marion County; at Dayton, where it was reported, "partyism has completely winked out here, and all go as one for the Union"; and at Lebanon. At Dallas, a crowd of between fifteen hundred and three thousand persons gathered to listen to the Monmouth brass band and speeches from an array of local notables; over one thousand persons gathered at Silverton; and, at Albany, three brass bands paraded through the flag-filled town to an area where the participants enjoyed a picnic while listening to patriotic declarations for the Union.[7] One of the largest gatherings met at Corvallis, where five thousand persons from Benton, Polk, and Yamhill counties were in attendance. The meeting had been advertised in the press for weeks.[8]

Local politicians made the circuit, delivering patriotic speeches at Union meetings throughout the region and at the same time promoting their own political stock. Joseph W. Drew, a Douglas Democrat and an aspirant for the governorship, wrote:

[6] Portland *Weekly Oregonian,* May 11, 18, 1861; Salem *Oregon Statesman,* May 13, 1861.
[7] Portland *Weekly Oregonian,* May 18, 25, June 1, 1861; Salem *Oregon Statesman,* May 27, 1861; Oregon City *Oregon Argus,* June 15, 1861.
[8] Salem *Oregon Statesman,* June 17, 1861; Oregon City *Oregon Argus,* June 29, 1861; George Abernethy to Nesmith, July 6, 1861, George Abernethy Papers, Oregon Historical Society Library.

The abolitionists are pleased when I pitch into secession and secessionists and talk in favor of sustaining the administration and enforcing the federal laws and expound the constitution according to Hamilton and Webster, while the secessionists shout and clap, when I denounce abolitionists and disorganizers in the north, who in times past have refused to aid in the execution of federal laws and have trampled on the constitution, as interpreted by our Supreme Court, denouncing said Court—our highest judicial tribunal, as a proslavery institution to be reorganized and reconstructed at the earliest moment, even by revolution, if it can not otherwise be done speedily.[9]

Union feeling was expressed in other ways. Union meetings often resulted in the formation of Union clubs. In Salem, such a club was organized by a group of Douglas Democrats, and resolutions were passed repudiating the idea of a Pacific Republic and declaring that "neutrality is cowardice, if not premeditated disloyalty." Republicans looked askance at this organization, but on the whole party feeling was held to a minimum. In Oregon City, the regular election for city officers was fought on the issue of union or "disunion," and there was general rejoicing when the union ticket was triumphant.[10] In Washington County, Joe Meek, retired mountain man, wrote, "I am a Duglas man and Courtney and I keep the stars and Stripes flying 80 feet over my hous all the time . . . and go Decidley for the union[.] If the union is lost every thing is lost."[11] At Yoncalla, in southern Oregon, school children cut the word "disunion" out of their spelling books.[12]

Many Democrats were converted to full support of the Republican administration. Democrats participated freely in the Union meetings and in some cases inspired them. One Breckinridge Democrat declared he had voted for Breckinridge as the "regular" Democratic candidate and because he thought his election would benefit the country. Now he pledged his unwavering support to the Republican administration in the prosecution of the war.[13] One of the most complete conversions was that of Matthew P. Deady. He turned his

[9] Drew to Deady, July 11, 1861, Matthew P. Deady Papers, Oregon Historical Society Library. See also Addison C. Gibbs, Notes on Oregon History (microfilm in the University of Washington Library), p. 18.

[10] Salem *Oregon Statesman*, May 20, 1861; Portland *Weekly Oregonian*, May 11, 18, 1861.

[11] Joseph L. Meek to Olive Meek, June 12, 1861, quoted in Harvey Elmer Tobie, *No Man Like Joe* (Portland, 1949), pp. 251-252.

[12] Harriet Applegate to Oliver [Applegate], September 3, 1861, Oliver Cromwell Applegate Papers, University of Oregon Library.

[13] "A Breckinridge Voter" to the Editor, [n. d.], Portland *Weekly Oregonian*, August 3, 1861.

back on the Jeffersonian principles he had supported earlier and became an avowed Federalist. A proslavery advocate in the years before the election of 1860 and a partisan of Breckinridge during that election, Deady wrote in May, 1861, that he had got over the "seductive Jeffersonian humbugs . . . about, every man being his own government, rotation in office, and 'eternal vigilance (which means eternal *sedition*) is the price of liberty.' "

> Jefferson [Deady continued] overthrew the Federal govt as well as the Federal party with his resolutions of /98, and to day we are reaping the consequences. He has been the model for every disturber of the public peace ever since, and his resolutions and declarations of Independence contain enough of revolution nullification secession and anarchy, to set the four corners of the world by the ears.

Of the Democratic party, Deady wrote, "[It] has only been a piece of party machinery kept running by power of former prestige and force of habit since Polk's administration." He still believed, however, that the Southern people had "been driven into rebellion by the licensed and unrestrained pens and togunes [tongues] of abolition demagogues of the north, who in a well ordered government would have found their way to the penitentiary as fast as they turned up."[14] Others followed Deady's lead. Benjamin Simpson, another former proslavery agitator, became a stanch Unionist; William Tichenor, former member of the "Salem Clique," pledged his support to the administration in its struggle against rebellion and promised to lay aside all political prejudices for the duration.[15]

Some Democrats still hoped that the sectional difficulties could be settled peaceably. Winfield Scott Ebey looked forward to the meeting of Congress in July. "By that time," he wrote, "the Public Mind will have calmed a good Deal[.] I think the Northern States will see the utter folly & madness of attempting to reduce the South to Submission & the matter will be settled peaceably." The *Oregonian*, however, echoed the dominant sentiment in the region when it declared that "there will be no compromise until the rebels lay down their arms."[16]

14 Deady to Nesmith, May 16, 1861; Deady to William Meek, February 17, 1861; Deady to Applegate, November 12, 1861, Deady Papers.

15 William Tichenor to Deady, November 14, 1861, Deady Papers. See also Augustus R. Burbank to James Lodge, May 7, 1861, Olympia *Pioneer and Democrat*, May 10, 1861.

16 Ebey Diary, No. 6, p. 438 (May 4, 1861) ; Burbank to Lodge, May 7, 1861,

The expression of Union feeling in the Pacific Northwest encouraged the conviction that party lines should be—indeed, had been—obliterated by the national emergency. The political issues that divided the parties were narrowed down "to the shortest span—*for, or against the Union!*" One Washington Territory newspaper believed that party platforms were more productive of evil than of good, that party spirit was antagonistic to popular welfare. Some felt that the Democratic party had been destroyed by the election of 1860 and the secession crisis. Deady wrote: "A radical difference of opinion among its leaders north and south, gradually extended itself to the rank and file of both Sections, until almost any serious controversy about rival leaders, was sufficient to permanently separate them."[17] Douglas Democrats blamed the emergency on the Breckinridge wing: "Their leaders have succeeded in their revenge upon Douglas who stood in their way for the attainment of which they have bro't misery and ruin upon a Continent." The Douglas party, they admitted, had died with the crisis, but it had "died struggling for its country." One Douglas Democrat analyzed the situation:

> The republican party was founded in error and never should have been born. The democratic party lived too long, it survived its virtue. For my part I acknowledge allegiance only to my Country[.] And I feel that a man who clings to party tenaciously in times such as these; in doing so, sins against God and his country.[18]

Republicans were bitter in their hostility toward the Democratic party:

> The late Democratic party—for it is now defunct beyond the posibility of a resurrection—is responsible for all the ill that has befallen the country. Every drop of human blood shed during the present internecion will call for vengeance upon the heads of Democratic party leaders.[19]

The foundation for the reorganization of political groupings during the early months of the Civil War was laid in the weeks following the bombardment of Sumter. But, while the Union meetings in the Pacific Northwest represented a wide support of the

Olympia *Pioneer and Democrat*, May 10, 1861; Portland *Weekly Oregonian*, July 27, 1861.

[17] Elisha L. Applegate to Nesmith, October 29, 1861, James W. Nesmith Papers, Oregon Historical Society Library; Olympia *Overland Press*, August 12, 1861; Deady to Joseph Watt, January 20, 1862, Deady Papers.

[18] James M. Pyle to Deady, June 30, 1861, Deady Papers.

[19] Port Townsend *North-West*, July 4, 1861.

Republican administration, they did not reflect unanimity of opinion in this region. The lines dividing the political parties were too deeply imbedded in the minds of many Pacific Northwest frontiersmen to be obliterated even by a crisis of such major proportions. The struggle between party and patriotism began as soon as hostilities commenced.

Most of the settlers enthusiastically supported the government and the administration, but there was a sizable minority, notably former Breckinridge Democrats, who refused to support a Republican president in a war against Southern people and institutions. The convictions of some led them to join the Confederate army. Most, however, favored a peaceful restoration of the Union; their opposition to the war was reflected in a policy of "neutrality" for the Pacific Northwest. The *Oregon Weekly Union* became the spokesman for this group. During the secession crisis, the paper had been an unwavering advocate of compromise. Since the Republicans had played a significant role in the defeat of compromise, the paper held them responsible for the war that resulted. Laying the groundwork for the opposition to the Lincoln administration that became characteristic of Oregon's "Copperhead" press, the *Oregon Weekly Union* declared:

> Compromise is past. No hope can now be entertained of a peaceful solution of our national questions, short of an unconditional acknowledgement of the independence of the Southern Confederacy, and its alternative is war, with all its horrors and calamities, aggravated by that hatred which only rankles in the bosom of men who have once been friends. Yes, war! And that, too, waged for the success of an impracticable and visionary idea. Ruined credit, desolated fields, a wasted heritage, sacked and ruined cities, dismantled forts, an annihilated commerce, a dissevered country, and a total loss of that respect abroad which has ever been the shield of our citizens in foreign climes, are the results most likely to flow from this fratricidal strife.[20]

Others argued the right of secession and accused the Northern states of first nullifying the federal laws.[21] They held the Union meetings in contempt, considering them as the efforts of a "few Abolition Negro thieves who howl loud for the *Union* & *Stars* & *Stripes* and adgitate the people a little by their Efforts to assemble *Union Clubs* and Union meetings." In June, 1861, Anson G. Henry, alarmed, wrote, "There is a much stronger secession feeling in Oregon than is

[20] Corvallis *Oregon Weekly Union*, May 4, 1861.
[21] Steilacoom *Puget Sound Herald*, July 11, 1861.

generally believed."[22] In some areas, Southern sympathizers did not dare open their mouths; in the central and southern parts of Oregon, however, they became quite bold in expressing their opposition to the war.[23]

Two weeks after the news of Fort Sumter's bombardment arrived in the Pacific Northwest, one of Oregon's early pioneers reported the existence in the state of "traitors," persons who withheld sympathy from the national government during the crisis. Another early settler, after traveling extensively throughout Oregon, claimed that there were disunionists active among the population. His definition of a disunionist was one who thought the South had been imposed upon.[24] Many settlers in the Pacific Northwest denounced as disloyal to the government those who expressed a feeling of sympathy for the South, exclusive of their regard for the Union. To others, simple opposition to the Republican party in national and local politics was the hallmark of treason.[25] As the war continued, the frontier population gave credence to Stephen A. Douglas' assertion that there were no neutrals in the struggle for the Union. The problem of where to draw the line between loyalty and disloyalty persisted throughout the Civil War. As a result reports of disunionists or secessionists in Oregon were often misleading and did not necessarily mean that Oregonians were supporting the Confederacy or actually disloyal to the Union. There were, however, many isolated incidents throughout the Pacific Northwest to inspire such reports.

Rumors circulated almost immediately that the Knights of the Golden Circle had established lodges in The Dalles, Albany, and Corvallis and were plotting the overthrow of the United States

[22] Thomas Pyle to Deady, May 18, 1861, Deady Papers; Henry to Lincoln, June 21, 1861, quoted in Elijah R. Kennedy, *The Contest for California in 1861: How Colonel E. D. Baker Saved the Pacific States to the Union* (Boston, 1912), p. 223.

[23] David Logan to Mrs. Milton Hay, September 16, 1861, Harry E. Pratt, ed. "22 Letters of David Logan, Pioneer Oregon Lawyer," *OHQ*, XLIV (Sept., 1943), 282; Charles Stevens to [Brother and Sister], May 19, 1861, E. Ruth Rockwood, ed. "Letters of Charles Stevens," *OHQ*, XXXVIII (1936), 330; Joseph L. Meek to Olive Meek, June 12, 1861, quoted in Tobie, *No Man Like Joe*, pp. 251-252.

[24] J. Quinn Thornton to the Editor, May 13, 1861, Oregon City *Oregon Argus*, May 25, 1861; Jesse Applegate to the Editor, [n. d.], Portland *Weekly Oregonian*, October 19, 1861.

[25] In September, 1861, Elwood Evans, one of the early organizers of the Republican party in Washington Territory, listed several former Democratic officeholders as "avowed secessionists" (Evans to William H. Wallace, September 1, 1861, William H. Wallace Papers, University of Washington Library). Their crime, however, seems to have been no more serious than opposition to Evans and to the Republican party.

government.[26] At Long Tom precinct in Lane County, an area in which persons of Southern birth and background predominated, the Confederate flag was raised and waved undisturbed for some time. Nearby in the small town of Monroe, a church meeting was broken up when the minister urged the audience to sustain the government. A camp meeting of the Southern Methodist Church ended in a riot when the minister refused to display the American flag and made several "harsh remarks" about it.[27] In the mining district of eastern Washington Territory, a government official was reported to have drunk a toast to Jefferson Davis as a greater man than George Washington. On Sauvie's Island, near Portland, a group of men declared that "no d——d Abolitionist should raise the American flag on that island."[28] These incidents were multiplied many times.[29] Of and by themselves they were not of great significance, but, when taken in conjunction with the growing attitude of opposition by many former Breckinridge newspapers to the prosecution of the war, they became more serious in the eyes of the loyal settlers.

Opposition to the prosecution of the war was expressed as soon as the policy of the Lincoln administration became known, and the groundwork for the later "Copperhead" movement was laid. The *Oregon Weekly Union,* a leading spokesman of the opposition, urged an attitude of calmness on the part of the people, and defined its position:

> The call of President Lincoln for 75,000 soldiers—if it means anything—is a declaration of war upon the South, and means that his policy is to compell an unconditional submission. . . . It is not strange that the war policy of the Administration should find opposers, North as well as South, among those who have never justified secession or entertained a sentiment other than of loyalty to the government of the Union.

The best way to subdue revolutions, the paper declared, was to seek out the causes and the grievances, then remove them.[30] The *Oregon*

[26] Portland *Weekly Oregonian,* May 11, 1851; Corvallis *Oregon Weekly Union,* June 1, 1861. Slater, editor of the *Union,* vehemently denied the existence of lodges of the Knights of the Golden Circle in Oregon.

[27] Jesse Applegate to the Editor, [n. d.], Portland *Weekly Oregonian,* October 19, 1861; Elisha L. Applegate to the Family, August 24, 1861, Oliver Cromwell Applegate Papers; Portland *Weekly Oregonian,* June 8, August 31, 1861; Robert Horace Down, *A History of the Silverton Country* (Portland, 1926) , p. 176.

[28] Olympia *Overland Press,* August 26, 1861; Olympia *Washington Standard,* December 7, 1861.

[29] See Robert Treat Platt, "Oregon and Its Share in the Civil War," *OHQ,* IV (June, 1903) , 89-109.

[30] Corvallis *Oregon Weekly Union,* May 11, 1861.

Democrat lamented that the determination of the government to put down the rebellion by force had dashed the last hopes for peace and prosperity: "The first blow has been struck—reason and justice have been completely dethroned, and folly and madness seem to have assumed uncontrolable sway." The *Oregon Sentinel,* published at Jacksonville, favored the peaceful recognition of the Confederate States, not because it was any the less devoted to the Union but because it could not "discover any possible practicable benefit or wise end to result from the contest pending between the North and the South." On the problem of loyalty during this emergency, the *Sentinel* observed:

> In such a war, one may be called disloyal by some, or a traitor by the fanatical few, if he declines to approve the rash policy of the Administration, yet we think the judgment of later days and cooler movements will be that he simply had an abhorrence of shedding the blood of his countrymen in a cause out of which no ultimate benefit could spring, but through which an endless crop of dragon's teeth must assuredly be sown, never to be rooted from the land until devastation, utter ruin, and hopeless wretchedness should be the common lot of all.[31]

As time went on, the opposition press drifted into a more extreme position. The *Oregon Weekly Union* expressed fear for the preservation of civil liberties in the United States. Any government which must be sustained by the bayonet would become a military despotism; civil liberty would inevitably be supplanted by military power. The violence of war, the editor warned, would sweep away all traces of constitutional freedom. The "sectional pestilence" which dragged the country into civil war had its origins, it was claimed, in the churches of New England, the "hot beds of abolitionism." The Portland *Advertiser,* a Douglas paper during the election campaign, declared that the North would "exhaust the wealth and energies of the country to spread desolation and sorrow throughout the land—and in the name of freedom . . . maintain a reign of terror."[32]

To counteract the numerous Union meetings sweeping the Pacific Northwest, the Breckinridge Democrats held a "Democratic Union Mass Convention" at Albany on June 5. Resolutions were passed opposing the use of coercion and denouncing the Pacific Republic.

[31] Albany *Oregon Democrat,* May 7, 1861; Jacksonville *Oregon Sentinel,* May 18, 1861.

[32] Corvallis *Oregon Weekly Union,* May 18, 25, July 15, 1861; Portland *Advertiser,* May 2, 1861, quoted in Portland *Weekly Oregonian,* May 4, 1861.

Unity, the delegates declared, could never be secured by war but must be sought through a spirit of conciliation and compromise. To this end, the meeting endorsed the Crittenden Compromise as a satisfactory basis for sectional adjustment, in spite of the fact that this compromise had already proved unsatisfactory. Benjamin Stark delivered an address in which he maintained that the Democratic party alone could save the Union. "Public opinion," commented one editor, "ought to compel the administration and the coming Congress to call a National Convention, instead of voting war supplies."[33]

During the summer months of 1861, as news of military preparations and armed clashes in the East arrived on the Pacific Coast, some newspapers took stock of the situation and attempted to find answers to the question of why this catastrophe had descended on the land. In an editorial entitled "The True Cause of Secession," one of the older Republican papers in Washington Territory declared:

> It is *not* the agitation of the slavery question which has brought the present trouble upon the country, but simply the loss of power consequent upon the increase of free over slave States. Had there been *no* agitation of this question, the result would have been the same, precisely.

The same result would have followed, the paper suggested, if Douglas or Breckinridge had been elected president.[34] Later one editor attempted to answer the question, "What are we fighting for?" The war was not one for or against a sectional president or for slavery or abolition. Rather it was a war between the forces of democracy and those of aristocracy, to be fought "for the privilege of another Century's trial of a purely Democratic form of Government." If the abolition of slavery should result from the war, "it is because the labor-owning oligarchists have, like the dog in the fable, dropped their pieces of flesh to grasp the shadow of 'rights of minorities to govern.' "[35] In one of its last issues, the *Pioneer and Democrat* declared that the political questions that had caused the disunion were not the issues that were now at stake. "The question now is not one of slavery in the Territories, but a struggle to maintain the existence of the government itself as an escape from anarchy and despotism."

[33] Corvallis *Oregon Weekly Union,* June 8, July 1, 1861; Albany *Oregon Democrat,* November 12, 1861.
[34] Steilacoom *Puget Sound Herald,* August 15, 1861.
[35] Port Townsend *North-West,* October 26, November 2, 1861.

The editor added, "There would seem no solution at present but by the sword."[36]

South of the Columbia River, the Republican *Argus* maintained that the central idea of the "American revolution of 1861," like that of 1776, was liberty.

> The abyss of moral degradation into which the slave power has plunged the nation, has created a *moral necessity for a revolution.* Whether that revolution will work a radical cure of the disease by removing the cause, or not, is the question. . . . Of one thing all may rest assured, that slavery as a great political power in the Union will be known no more forever. Its doom is to be chained, if not destroyed.[37]

The Douglas Democratic *Statesman,* while supporting the government against the rebellion, anticipated a change in the character of the national government as a result of the rebellion, one which would "prove a lasting calamity to all concerned." A new set of precedents would emerge from the war, guiding both Congress and the president "we know not whither." "Terminate as it may," the editor wrote, "we have henceforth a new government. It cannot prove more beneficent in most respects than the old regime, and in many others it may prove much worse."[38]

In the Pacific Northwest, the belief that the conflict would be brief ended with the bombardment of Fort Sumter and the opening of hostilities. There was a growing realization that the war between the sections might drag on at great expense of lives and money. Amory Holbrook, writing from the East, expressed no doubt as to the final triumph of the North but believed that it would be achieved only after a terrible sacrifice of lives on both sides. "The South is not to be conquered in a month, or a year; and perhaps not for several. Their leaders are accomplished soldiers, who are fighting not merely for reputation, but for life, for if overcome, they know they must be tried & convicted as traitors."[39] As the two sides girded themselves for their first significant encounter on the battlefield at Bull Run, the *Argus* also dismissed the idea that the war would be a short one. "We may conclude," wrote the editor, "to suffer all the

[36] Olympia *Pioneer and Democrat,* May 17, 1861.

[37] Oregon City *Oregon Argus,* July 6, 1861.

[38] Salem *Oregon Statesman,* May 27, 1861.

[39] Holbrook to Craig, May 10, 1861, Amory Holbrook Papers, Oregon Historical Society Library.

attitude was strongly urged by the Breckinridge wing of the Democratic party, and because of the strength and influence of this group in local politics it achieved wide circulation in the region. The advocacy of a policy of detachment or neutrality was one of the bases of the Northwest's "Copperhead" opposition and became a matter for serious concern to the "Unionist" element.

The sentiment in favor of a neutral policy in the Pacific Northwest stemmed from two characteristics of the region itself, in turn traceable to the frontier status of the area: its isolation from the eastern part of the United States; and the heterogeneous origins of its population, including people from both the North and the South. The conservatism of many of the settlers reinforced the feeling in favor of detachment, causing many of them to cling to the belief that compromise might yet save the country from a bloody civil war. One editor commented that it would be the height of folly for the people of Oregon to become involved in a quarrel that was not legitimately theirs, one for which they felt no responsibility. Since Oregon had been settled by people from all the states, "it is peculiarly fit that we shall refrain from interfering with the affairs now distracting the States east of the Rocky Mountains." This feeling was not motivated by a desire for complete aloofness, for the editor added, "Let us by wise counsels, and good examples, aid as far as we can in securing a return of our Nation's unity, peace and prosperity."[49] Other Oregon newspapers, notably the Portland *Advertiser,* the Jacksonville *Sentinel,* and the Corvallis *Oregon Weekly Union,* echoed these sentiments. The last urged that Oregon must assume the role of peacemaker.

> Three thousand miles of mountain and desert, of plain and river, separates us from the scene of angry contest. Our very isolation ought to render our position that of a spectator, rather than a party to the war of sections. While our brethren in the Atlantic States are inflamed and maddened by prejudice and passion we ought to be rendered cool by the fearful spectacle of their passions. And being kept cool by our position, we ought to act the part of mediator between the contending sections.[50]

The editor suggested once again that a national convention be called to settle the sectional difficulties in a peaceful way before it was too late.

[49] Albany *Oregon Democrat,* May 7, 1861.
[50] Corvallis *Oregon Weekly Union,* July 1, 1861.

The attitude in favor of neutrality was translated into official action by John Whiteaker, Oregon's governor. A lifelong Democrat, sincere in his convictions, Whiteaker refused to give up his Democracy in the interests of the Union and the war. Born in southern Indiana and living successively in Illinois, Missouri, and, after trying his luck in the California mines, in Oregon, he had combined the two principal frontier professions, agriculture and politics. Entering territorial politics by way of membership in the local legislature, Whiteaker was elected Oregon's first state governor in 1858. Strongly proslavery, he took the side of Breckinridge in the election of 1860. When hostilities broke out between the sections, Whiteaker refused to support the administration. In his own words: "In 1861 a revolution broke out and all of the officers of the Oregon state government except myself and Judge P. P. Prim changed their politics to Lincoln. We did not do so, and in consequence the abuse of the press and the people was very bitter,"[51] Although his steadfastness made him many enemies, there were others who respected Whiteaker as a man of thorough integrity. Matthew P. Deady, a political opponent, wrote, " 'Old Whit' is a good specimen of a sturdy, frontier farmer man, formed of a cross between Illinois and Missouri, with a remote dash of something farther Down East. Although wrong in the head in politics, he is honest and right in the heart."[52]

On May 28, 1861, a little over a month after the fall of Fort Sumter, Governor Whiteaker issued a manifesto from his home at Pleasant Hill in Lane County, expressing his opinions regarding the national political situation and the policy he intended to follow. He saw no reason why "we should be precipitated into civil discord." On the contrary, he hoped that "the good sense and discretion of the people would in a great measure exempt Oregon from many of the evils growing out of the troubles now threatening the perpetuity of our once united country." Whiteaker thought that public assemblages for the purpose of expressing patriotic sentiments were praise-

[51] Quotation from Whiteaker's diary, Portland *Oregon Daily Journal*, July 17, 1922.

[52] Deady to the San Francisco *Bulletin*, October 13, 1862, Letters of Matthew P. Deady to the San Francisco *Bulletin*, 1862-1866, Scrap-Book #112, Oregon Historical Society Library; Deady to Nesmith, September 4, 1867, Deady Papers. For the details of Whiteaker's life and career, see Robert W. Johannsen, "John Whiteaker, Governor of Oregon, 1858-1862," *Reed College Bulletin*, XXVI (January, 1948), 63-87.

worthy but charged that the Union meetings then sweeping the state had been organized merely to manufacture a partisan sentiment. Those who opposed the war and who advocated a policy of reconciliation and compromise, he thought, should not be branded as traitors or disunionists; they were as patriotic as the strongest Union man.

Concerning the course which the Southern states had adopted, Whiteaker maintained that

> the right of a State to secede from the Union is neither expressed nor implied in the Constitution, and . . . secession is only another name for revolution. All admit the right of revolution for a good cause; yet, though I think the South has had some provocation, I do not think she has had sufficient cause for acting as she has done. I have no doubt, however, that the seceded States think they have good cause, and feel justified before God and man in their present undertaking.

He expressed the fullest confidence in the loyalty of every state officer and promised that "if treason should show its hydra head within our borders it will receive the punishment provided by law." A Pacific Republic, he thought, would be a calamity to the Pacific Coast; he hoped that no one in Oregon would seriously entertain such an idea. As for the war then commencing, Whiteaker warned, "Beware of making a war for the ultimate or immediate extinction of slavery," and added a word of caution, "that in freeing the negro you do not enslave the white man." The North would never conquer the Southern revolutionists. A standing army would be required to keep the seceded states in the Union and would inevitably lead to an untold amount of bitterness between the two sections. Oregon's geographical position, he thought, should exempt it from any demands for troops, but he intimated that, if such demands were made, Lincoln would get no troops from Oregon to carry on his "wicked and unnatural war upon the South." Instead of pursuing a policy of coercion, the North should convince the South of its error "by expressions of friendship and a willingness to grant her citizens their just and equal rights in the Union." As an evidence of sincerity, Whiteaker proposed that the Crittenden proposals be adopted as constitutional amendments. In closing, he voiced his determination to stick by his convictions:

> I have no earthly hope which can survive the fall of this Government, and no dread of abuse shall deter me from raising my voice in what I believe to

be its support. I would rather be right, and live and die in obscurity, than be wrong, and President of the United States.[53]

Whiteaker's "Address to the People of Oregon" brought a storm of opposition on his head. Leading the field in the denunciation of Whiteaker was the *Statesman*. "Jeff. Davis," wrote Asahel Bush, "will learn with melancholy satisfaction [that] . . . Gov. Whiteaker, of little far-off Oregon, still holds fast to the faith once delivered, and bears testimony to the honesty and purity of purpose 'before God and man' of the traitors in their present undertaking." Accusing Whiteaker of being a conspirator against the government, Bush noted that with his proclamation all hopes for both the governor and his party at the next election died. A movement to organize a petition calling for Whiteaker's resignation was initiated, but it apparently met with little success.[54] The Republican papers generally ignored the manifesto. The *Argus* merely "noticed" the address, and added, "He is the biggest ass in the State. . . . Whiteaker is at heart as rotten a traitor as Jeff. Davis." The *Oregonian* made sarcastic mention of the address but refused to print it.[55] A Union meeting in Lane County, shortly after Whiteaker's manifesto was published, resolved that "indifference is impossible to the patriot, and neutrality is cowardice, if not premeditated disloyalty."[56]

On the other hand, the *Democratic Herald,* published at Eugene, declared that Governor Whiteaker's position was impregnable. The Union could only be preserved by making concessions and compromise. "Civil War, with its horrors too numerous and loathsome to mention, can never repair the breach in the affections of the American people."[57]

Whiteaker's statement was a declaration of neutrality for the state of Oregon. Although Oregon had not been included in Lincoln's first proclamation for troops in April, 1861, Whiteaker's policy regarding recruiting in Oregon indicated his determination to follow a policy of neutrality.[58] As a statement of principles, Whiteaker's ad-

[53] Whiteaker's manifesto was originally published in the Corvallis *Oregon Weekly Union*, June 8, 1861.

[54] Salem *Oregon Statesman,* June 10, July 15, 1861.

[55] Oregon City *Oregon Argus,* June 8, 1861; Portland *Weekly Oregonian,* June 8, 1861.

[56] Salem *Oregon Statesman,* June 24, 1861.

[57] Eugene *Democratic Herald,* quoted in Portland *Weekly Oregonian,* June 22, 1861.

[58] For Whiteaker's later recruiting policy, see Johannsen, "John Whiteaker,

dress stood as a "Copperhead creed." Although the charges of treason and conspiracy continued, there was nothing in Whiteaker's actions to warrant such accusations. Oregon's "Copperheads" were no less loyal to the Union than were those who gave active support to the Lincoln administration. To both groups, the ends were the same— the preservation of the Union and the reconciliation of the sections; they differed only concerning the means to these ends.

No such feelings of neutrality characterized the official attitude of Washington Territory. Although Lincoln's call for troops had no application to the territories, Acting Governor Henry M. McGill, a Buchanan appointee and a strong supporter of the Union, ordered the territorial militia to be organized and held in readiness for possible military duty in the East. The proclamation did not receive a very hearty response, but only a few "sympathizers" in McGill's own party criticized the move.[59]

With the adjournment of Congress in March, the Pacific Northwest's two principal actors on the national stage, Joseph Lane and Isaac I. Stevens, left the national capital for their homes. Lane arrived in Portland on the same steamer that brought the news of Fort Sumter's bombardment. His reception was far from cordial. Rumors circulated throughout the Northwest that Lane would attempt to take Oregon out of the Union. Just before embarking for the Pacific Coast, he was supposed to have announced: "I am out of politics; but I shall continue to stand by the right. I will urge the democrats of Oregon to adopt the Constitution of the Confederate States as their platform."[60] Many people, including some in his own party, were convinced that Lane would bring the Pacific Republic to fruition if given half the chance. Nesmith wrote as early as February that Lane was returning to Oregon for the purpose of inaugurating the Pacific Republic.[61] His unequivocal position in Congress in favor of the right of secession and his justification of the

Governor of Oregon, 1858-1862," pp. 82-83. Whiteaker's attempts to maintain Oregon's neutrality were compared at the time to those of Governor Magoffin of Kentucky (Salem *Oregon Statesman*, October 14, 1861).

[59] *The War of the Rebellion: A Compilation of the Official Records of the Union and Confederate Armies* (128 vols.; Washington, D.C., 1880-1901), Series I, Vol. L, Pt. I, p. 489; Olympia *Washington Standard*, August 24, 1861; Clinton A. Snowden, *History of Washington, the Rise and Progress of an American State* (4 vols.; New York, 1909), IV, 104.

[60] Portland *Weekly Oregonian*, April 27, 1861.

[61] Nesmith to Harvey Gordon, February 26, 1861, Nesmith Papers.

course of the Southern states were widely publicized in the Pacific Northwest. In addition, his son, John Lane, had left West Point, where he was a cadet, and had entered the Confederate army.

Lane was received in Portland with a coolness that bordered on downright hostility. Plans for a public reception at the steamer landing had been dropped by his son-in-law when friends strongly advised against it.[62] Rumors that Lane was planning to address the citizens of Portland greatly agitated the population. The *Oregonian* graciously urged the people to listen to him, if he chose to make a speech. "As long as Gen. Lane is guilty of no overt act here in Oregon, let him speak." Lane, however, had no such intentions. In the public barroom of one of the hotels, he was overheard saying that Lincoln was responsible "for all the consequences that shall result from the attack on the Fort" since, all the while he was detaining the Southern commissioners with promises of evacuation, he was actually making plans to reinforce it.[63] Outside of this impromptu expression, Lane made no attempt to speak to the populace. Even his old colleagues in the Democratic party spurned him. Matthew P. Deady, once an ally but now an enemy, was an exception, taking a certain pride in befriending Lane. Describing Lane's arrival, Deady wrote to Senator Nesmith, "A few old women tried to get up a panic that he was going to *secesh* us, but it did not take."[64]

Lane's journey up the Willamette Valley to his home in Umpqua County was received with only slightly less hostility. In Dallas, where he spent a night, Lane was hanged in effigy—not in good taste, according to the *Oregonian,* but "tolerably expressive." In Corvallis his reception was more cordial. The home of his son, Nathaniel, and of many of his old friends, the town scheduled a public reception at the courthouse. There Lane delivered a brief address in which he reaffirmed his devotion to the Union but maintained that only the Democratic party could save it from disaster.[65] After his arrival on his farm at Winchester, Lane settled down to a quiet life, rarely leaving his home for the next twenty years.

[62] "Nuevo" to the Editor, May 3, 1861, Salem *Oregon Statesman,* May 6, 1861; Oregon City *Oregon Argus,* May 4, 1861.

[63] Portland *Weekly Oregonian,* May 4, 11, 1861.

[64] Deady to Nesmith, May 16, 1861, Deady Papers.

[65] Portland *Weekly Oregonian,* May 11, 1861; Corvallis *Oregon Weekly Union,* May 11, 1861; Portland *Weekly Oregonian,* May 18, 1861; Sister M. Margaret Jean Kelly, *The Career of Joseph Lane, Frontier Politician* (Washington, D.C., 1942), p. 186.

The Union, Conservatism, and Peace
211

Stevens returned to Olympia late in April, looking "grave and care-worn, for he had taken deeply to heart the troubles between the north and the south."[66] Soon afterward, he delivered an address in which he not only denied the right of secession but also declared that the election of a Republican president was not sufficient cause for seceding, although he held the Republican party responsible for disunion. The only salvation, he said, was through a united Democratic party. He urged every citizen to stand by the government and maintain it against aggression.[67] Stevens, however, soon learned that he was under the odium of disunion. As early as January, the anti-Stevens members of the territorial legislature had pushed through a resolution censuring the delegate for his participation in the national election.[68] Many persons questioned his loyalty and emphasized his leadership in the Breckinridge organization, in the course of which he had become intimately associated with many secession leaders. The *Oregonian* saw little difference between Stevens and Lane.

> Both of these men co-operated the past year, with the disunionists. They did all they could to shield them from the resentment of the people. They both came to the Pacific coast to gull the people by pretended devotion to the Union. They both preach that the re-uniting of the democratic party is the only hope of "re-construction."[69]

The year 1861 was an important election year for Washington Territory. Stevens' term as delegate had expired with the adjournment of Congress in March, and he returned to the territory confident of re-election. National events, however, intervened. Washington Territory's Republicans looked forward to success in the delegate election. The national success of the Republican party brought increased confidence to the territorial Republicans. Stevens' activities on behalf of the Breckinridge campaign, it was thought, would "kill him dead" in the territory. The Douglas, or anti-Stevens, Democrats also made plans for the forthcoming election.[70] Demo-

[66] Hubert H. Bancroft, *History of Washington, Idaho and Montana, 1845-1889* (San Francisco, 1890), p. 206; Olympia *Pioneer and Democrat*, May 3, 1861; William H. Tappan, "Reminiscences of Early Days in Washington," *Washington Historian*, I (Sept., 1899), 22.
[67] Olympia *Pioneer and Democrat*, May 10, 1861.
[68] Territory of Washington, *House Journal*, 1860-1861, pp. 337-338. The resolution passed by the close vote of 15 to 14.
[69] Portland *Weekly Oregonian*, May 18, 1861.
[70] Alexander Abernethy to Elwood Evans, July 2, July 19, 1860, Elwood Evans Papers, 1843-1894, Yale University Library (microfilm in the University of Wash-

cratic leaders were undaunted in the face of national defeat. Before the election of Lincoln was known, William Winlock Miller, superintendent of Indian affairs under Buchanan and a leading administration Democrat in the territory, cautioned Stevens that "we must keep up the Organization of the Democratic party and fight on and fight always."[71] A few days later, Miller sent Stevens a few "honest words" regarding the future of the party in the territory. Lamenting the party's loss in the national election, Miller was confident that the Democracy could retain political possession of Washington Territory.

> A few faint-hearted Democrats, it is true [he wrote], will follow off after the victorious camp, but these will be more than counterbalanced by the Democratic increase in the interior of the Territory. This winter we shall do all we can to harmonize the party and I think we shall succeed.

Stevens was assured that he could be nominated and re-elected "in spite of all opposition from the Republicans or from enemies in our own ranks."[72] In January, 1861, the Democratic Central Committee issued an appeal for unity in one last attempt to bring the two factions of the party together. The committee urged territorial Democrats to ignore "issues that have no practical importance in this Territory" and to look only to "those paramount principles that in the past have elevated our common country."[73]

The Democratic nominating convention was beset with difficulties from the very first. By the ruling out of proxies, control of the meeting was seized by the anti-Stevens or Douglas wing. A majority over the Breckinridge Democrats was maintained, however, only by expelling one delegate, ruling out another proxy delegate, and shifting four votes from a Stevens county to one of the new counties created out of the mining region which as yet existed only on paper.[74] Following the organization of the convention, Stevens withdrew his name as a candidate, partly in an attempt to restore harmony to the party and partly because he had determined to offer his services to the Union army.[75] With the attack on Fort Sumter he gave up his

ington Library) ; Butler P. Anderson to Bush, March 1, 6, 1860, Asahel Bush Papers, Oregon State Library (photostats in the University of Oregon Library) .

[71] William W. Miller to Stevens, November 18, 1860, Isaac I. Stevens Papers, University of Washington Library.

[72] Miller to Stevens, November 20, 29, December 6, 1860, Stevens Papers.

[73] Olympia *Pioneer and Democrat,* January 25, 1861.

[74] Portland *Daily Oregonian,* May 17, 1861.

[75] Stevens to Simon Cameron, Hazard Stevens, *The Life of Isaac Ingalls Stevens*

former conviction that the nation could be saved by compromise and made the full swing to a policy of coercion. In offering his services to the secretary of war, he favored "conquering a peace"—"this secession movement must be put down with an iron hand." Discouraged by the failure of compromise, he wrote:

> The policy of conciliation to which I adhered as long as it presented the least hope has not only been exhausted, but it has been contemptuously rejected by the South. The war ought to be prosecuted with the utmost vigor.[76]

After bitter debates between the two factions of the party, the convention nominated Selucius Garfielde, a former administration Democrat. Resolutions reaffirming the principle of popular sovereignty and approving any amendments to the Constitution which would "clarify" the status of slavery were passed. The convention further declared that "the constitutional right of secession is a contradiction in terms," and that Washington Territory stood "for the Union, the whole Union." A minority report from the resolutions committee opposed armed aggression against the South.[77] The administration, or Breckinridge, wing of the party was in a quandary, deprived of both a leader and an organization. The *Pioneer and Democrat,* which had always urged united action and support of the party's "regular" nominees, disowned Garfielde from the very beginning. Protesting against the manner in which the Democratic convention had been conducted, the paper declared that "no Democrat is bound to support the nominee."[78] One week later, this oldest newspaper in the territory, long the official organ of the Democratic party, passed out of existence. An opposition paper, commenting on the demise, stated that "unless an Editor can consistently and honestly support the nominee of his party, it is manifestly proper for him to suspend the paper."[79] The Port Townsend *Register* was

(2 vols.; Boston, 1900), II, 316; Stevens to Henry M. McGill, June 17, 1861, Stevens Papers.

[76] Stevens to Nesmith, May 22, 1861; Stevens to Brigadier General Joseph G. Totten, June 19, 1861, Stevens Papers; Stevens to Nesmith, May 22, 1861, Stevens Papers. Stevens' offer of his services at first met with a cold response, probably because of his past politics and his friendship with many of the Southern leaders. He was finally given command of a New York regiment. After participation in campaigns in northern Virginia and along the South Carolina coast, Stevens, a major general and division commander, was killed while leading his troops in the Second Battle of Bull Run.

[77] Olympia *Pioneer and Democrat,* May 24, 1861.

[78] *Ibid.*

[79] Port Townsend *North-West,* June 13, 1861.

"astounded" at Garfielde's nomination. Garfielde, the editor charged,
"had no claims for consideration from a Democratic Convention . . .
[and] would accept cheerfully a nomination from the Republican
party if he thought he could obtain it." The members of the convention, the paper continued, "whose motto was, 'rule or ruin,' were
. . . actuated . . . to defeat a particular nomination, namely, Mr.
Stephens."[80]

Members of the Breckinridge wing of the party were not content
to sit back in idle amazement at the sudden loss of their organization. After the convention disbanded they presented as their candidate Edward Lander, former chief justice of the territory and an old
anti-Stevens man who had resisted the transition to Douglas Democracy.[81] One contemporary charged that Lander was an "avowed
secessionist," and his support was said to have been drawn from
those "who were so strong in their pro-slavery affinities that they
would not be brought to sustain the cause of the Union under any
circumstances."[82] A Republican paper defined Lander's position
more precisely as that of "a candidate of the more numerous or *ultra*
secession wing of the modern democracy."[83] His candidacy was announced on a meaningless platform of "Our Country, The Union,
The Constitution, Peace," embellished with such ambiguous phrases
as "Revolution, by Force of Arms, is Civil War," and "The Sovereignty of the Nation is Supreme. Its dignity must be vindicated."
Lander's platform was, according to the Port Townsend *Register,*
"as broad as the country and as comprehensive." Lander was "the
advocate of Peace, while maintaining the integrity of the Union, and
the soverignity and the Dignity of the Nation."[84] Although
Lander's support came from the Breckinridge element, his ticket
was reminiscent of the Bell-Everett ticket during the presidential
campaign of 1860. His position was summed up by an opposition
paper as being "for the Union," but against "all practical and
efficient means to sustain it."[85]

The Republicans in Washington Territory, united and encour-

[80] Port Townsend *Register,* June 5, July 10, 1861.
[81] Olympia *Pioneer and Democrat,* May 24, 1861.
[82] Elwood Evans to William H. Wallace, September 1, 1861, Wallace Papers;
Harvey K. Hines, *An Illustrated History of the State of Washington* (Chicago,
1893), p. 160.
[83] Port Townsend *North-West,* June 13, 1861.
[84] Port Townsend *Register,* May 29, June 26, 1861.
[85] Portland *Daily Oregonian,* June 12, 1861.

aged by the trend of national politics and by the troubles within the Democratic party, nominated a candidate with considerable unanimity. The leading Republican newspaper in the territory favored "a man who, whilst firm, [is] strictly conservative, and who is unwavering in his devotion to the Union."[86] Some Republicans thought that the chances between a Douglas Democrat and a Republican were about even. The election of either was apparently acceptable, indicating that the tendency of these two groups to co-operate politically was strong north as well as south of the Columbia River.[87] With a minimum of debate, they nominated William H. Wallace, a perennial candidate for the delegateship, who had just been appointed territorial governor by President Lincoln. The platform of resolutions adopted by the Republican convention was surprisingly brief and simply worded. The sentiments expressed in Lincoln's inaugural address were "cordially" endorsed, and confidence was expressed in his administration. The preservation of the Union was declared to be the "first of all patriotic duties."[88]

National issues predominated in the campaign that followed. Lander took a strong Union position, declaring that all political principles and issues had been absorbed by the larger issue of union or disunion. However, he opposed the policy of coercion that was being inaugurated by the national administration. The country was in no danger, he maintained; the sober second thought of the American people would save it. Wallace, on the other hand, declared that "the Union must and shall be preserved, and the laws enforced, though the land should run rivers of blood." Garfielde took a position somewhere in between. While it was necessary to maintain the Union by force of arms if necessary, it was also essential that a spirit of peace should prevail. He urged the members of his party

> to at the same time show that they are not republicans but democrats; that though they have arms in their hands, it is not for the purpose of infringing upon State rights or of abolishing slavery, but to employ them in enforcing the laws as they now exist . . . to assure our brethren of the South that we will, in the shape of any reasonable compromise, secure them from any violation of their rights, and assure them that their fears on that score are groundless.[89]

[86] Olympia *Washington Standard*, April 20, 1861.
[87] Abernethy to Evans, March 7, 1861, Evans Papers.
[88] Olympia *Washington Standard*, May 25, 1861.
[89] "Washington Democrat" to the Editor, [n. d.], Salem *Oregon Statesman*, June 24, 1861.

North as well as south of the Columbia, the ends of all the political groups were the same; they differed only in the means.

Six weeks before the election, a supporter of Garfielde discouragingly recorded: "The Stevens men will all vote for Lander. If so Col. W. is Sure of his Election."[90] The election followed the pattern set by the national presidential election. Wallace, although receiving a minority of the total vote cast, was elected by 309 votes over Garfielde, his nearest competitor.[91]

The election for delegate in Washington Territory in 1861 was the last echo of the campaign of 1860 in the Pacific Northwest. Although the issues of the local election shifted from those of the national election, the lines of division in Washington Territory followed the national pattern. The intervention of the secession of the Southern states and the bombardment of Fort Sumter between the two elections made any discussions of popular sovereignty or slavery in the territories anachronistic. The fundamental issue of the election was the vital one of union by coercion or union by peaceful means. The Lander ticket, and certain elements of the Garfielde ticket, presaged the Pacific Northwest "Copperhead" position.

The months following the arrival of the news of Fort Sumter's fall witnessed the beginnings of political realignment in the Pacific Northwest. The Douglas wing of the Democratic party moved closer to the Republican position in favor of a vigorous prosecution of the war against the seceded states. The coalition that began in the summer elections of 1860 continued through the following year. The Breckinridge wing of the party provided the foundations for "Copperheadism" in the Pacific Northwest. While expressing a strong support of the Union, this element nevertheless opposed the use of coercion. Opposition to the Republican administration became more and more severe. Many clung to the hope that compromise might yet succeed and supported a policy of "neutrality" for the Pacific Northwest. On the level of official action this attitude was expressed by Governor Whiteaker of Oregon.

The cause of Union-Republicanism in the Pacific Northwest suffered three setbacks in the months that followed the initial crisis in

[90] Ebey Diary, No. 6, p. 447 (May 31, 1861).
[91] The total vote was Wallace, 1,585; Garfielde, 1,276; and Lander, 747, Election Returns, 1861, Washington Territory, Washington State Archives (microfilm in the University of Washington Library).

1861. During the summer, Congress seated George K. Sheil, Oregon's pro-Southern representative, after weeks of investigation. Andrew J. Thayer, the Douglas Democratic contestant for the seat, made an unsuccessful appeal to the patriotic sympathies of the Northern congressmen. The seating of a pro-Southern Democratic congressman by a Congress controlled by Northern Republicans has been interpreted as an effort to conciliate the border and Pacific Coast states.[92] The indignation of the Republicans and Douglas Democrats in Oregon was somewhat tempered by the realization that Sheil's election had been regular and legal.

In October, 1861, Edward Dickinson Baker, Oregon's Republican Senator and one of the mainstays of the Union cause on the Pacific Coast, was killed in action at the battle of Ball's Bluff on the Potomac River.[93] Baker had decided early in the crisis to participate militarily in the war against the South. Receiving an appointment as colonel, he raised a regiment of volunteer troops in the East. His death was a hard blow to Republicans in Oregon, who regarded Baker as their most "reliable medium of communication" with the Lincoln administration.[94] Republicans, however, sustained an even harder blow when Governor Whiteaker appointed Benjamin Stark to occupy Baker's Senate seat until the next meeting of the state legislature.[95] Stark, like Whiteaker, was a Union man, but he remained in the Democratic party, opposing at every opportunity the coercive policies of the national administration. His sympathies had been with the South throughout the sectional crisis. Republicans and Douglas Democrats in Oregon made a concerted, though unsuccessful, attempt to have Stark barred from the Senate.[96]

Washington Territory seemed safely Republican for the duration with the election of a Republican delegate and with Lincoln-appointed Republican officeholders arriving in the territory. The Democratic majority in the territory, however, was not diminished.

---

[92] *Cong. Globe,* 37 Cong., 1 Sess., pp. 352-357; Lester Burrell Shippee, "An Echo of the Campaign of Sixty," *OHQ,* XII, 351-360.

[93] Oregon City *Oregon Argus,* November 2, 1861.

[94] Anson G. Henry to Lincoln, November 11, 1861, Anson G. Henry Papers, Illinois State Historical Society Library (typescript copies in the Oregon Historical Society Library).

[95] Portland *Weekly Oregonian,* November 9, 1861.

[96] Oregon City *Oregon Argus,* November 30, 1861; Elisha L. Applegate to Nesmith, October 29, 1861, Nesmith Papers; Portland *Weekly Oregonian,* May 17, 1862.

Although most members of the party favored a vigorous prosecution of the war, a small minority remained firm in its opposition to the Republican administration. These Democrats were sufficiently strong in the territorial legislature of 1861-62 to defeat a series of Union resolutions. According to one Republican newspaper, "so far as a declaration on the part of the Legislative Assembly can effect it, this Territory has deliberately seceded from the Union."[97] The Republican party, however, was preoccupied with the territorial patronage that was suddenly opened up to them. These early months were marked by internal quarrels and dissension over the offices and officeholders which tended to strengthen the Democratic party.[98] By 1863 a reunited Democratic organization overturned the local Republican leadership and elected George E. Cole to the delegateship.

These Democratic gains were more than offset by the successes of the Union party in Oregon. The reorganization of the political parties that began in the months following the fall of Fort Sumter was completed early in 1862. In anticipation of the first statewide election since the opening of hostilities, the Republicans and Douglas Democrats carried their original legislative coalition one step further and organized the Union party. In the election of 1862, the Union ticket achieved an overwhelming victory. The Democratic candidates carried only one county in the state, and that by a small margin.[99] The new Union governor, Addison C. Gibbs, a former Douglas Democrat, embarked on a policy of close cooperation with the national administration. In the early fall of 1862, the state legislature elected another Douglas Democrat, Benjamin F. Harding, to fill the Senate seat left vacant by Baker's death. The strength of the Democrats in the new Union organization may be measured by the fact that Oregon throughout the remainder of the war was represented in Congress by two Douglas Democratic Senators and had a Douglas Democratic governor. The "Copperhead" opposition continued to denounce the prosecution of the war and the infringement of civil liberties by the Lincoln administration.

Frontier nationalism and conservatism were characteristic of the feeling in the Pacific Northwest during the months of the crisis and persisted throughout the war. Asahel Bush wrote in 1857, four years

[97] Olympia *Washington Standard*, February 8, 1862.

[98] Alexander Abernethy to Elwood Evans, March 9, 1862, Evans Papers.

[99] Oregon City *Oregon Argus*, June 28, 1862.

before the secession crisis, "the people of Oregon are eminently National in their sentiments and attachments . . . she will be a conservative National State, and in every emergency will stand by the Union and the constitution."[100] This prophecy of conservatism revealed the course frontier politics in the Northwest was to take in future years.

While the Northwest frontiersmen were busy building a social, economic, and political structure of their own on the far shores of the Pacific, they nevertheless were not too occupied to glance now and again at the political upheaval in the East. The settlers were indeed, as one editor put it, spectators to the war of sections.[101] Yet they expressed a strong interest in the national political difficulties. One pioneer wrote:

> Politicians . . . urge that this Territory is far remote from contending sectional interests, that we are in a latitude unprofitable to slave labor, that therefore it is of but little interest to us whether the Federal Government protects slavery in the territories, or excludes it. Whether it be of consequence or not, *there is a principle involved.*[102]

It was with this principle that Northwesterners were chiefly concerned.

When the crisis erupted into war, the settlers of the Pacific Northwest stood by the Union. Their contribution to the war effort was perhaps negligible insofar as men and arms were concerned, but the Republican and Union victories in the elections of 1860 and 1862 illustrated their support of the administration. Throughout these difficult years the conservatism of the frontier kept them safely within the folds of the Union, and it guided their footsteps long after the last shot had been fired.

[100] Salem *Oregon Statesman,* March 31, 1857.
[101] Corvallis *Oregon Weekly Union,* June 1, 1861.
[102] Letter to the Editor, Olympia *Washington Standard,* February 9, 1861. Italics mine.

bibliography

MANUSCRIPT SOURCES

Private Collections and Diaries:

George Abernethy Papers, Oregon Historical Society Library, Portland.
Jesse Applegate Papers, Oregon Historical Society Library.
Oliver Cromwell Applegate Papers, University of Oregon Library, Eugene.
George H. Atkinson Papers, Henry E. Huntington Library (microfilm in the University of Washington Library, Seattle).
Asahel Bush Papers, Oregon State Library (photostats in the University of Oregon Library).
Augustus Ripley Burbank Diary, 1849-1880, Library of Congress (microfilm in the University of Washington Library).
David W. Craig Papers, Oregon Historical Society Library.
Medorem Crawford Papers, University of Oregon Library.
Henry Cummins Papers, University of Oregon Library.
George L. Curry Papers, Oregon Historical Society Library.
Matthew P. Deady Papers, Oregon Historical Society Library.
Benjamin F. Dowell Papers, University of Oregon Library.
Benjamin F. Dowell Papers, Bancroft Library, University of California, Berkeley (microfilm in the University of Washington Library).
Winfield Scott Ebey Diary, Nos. 5-6, University of Washington Library.
Elwood Evans Papers, Winlock Miller Collection, Yale University Library, New Haven (microfilm in the University of Washington Library).
Addison C. Gibbs Papers, Oregon Historical Society Library.
Anson G. Henry Papers, 1862-1865, Illinois State Historical Library (typescript copies in Oregon Historical Society Library).

Amory Holbrook Papers, Oregon Historical Society Library.
Bion F. Kendall Papers, University of Washington Library.
Bion F. Kendall Papers, Oregon Historical Society Library.
Joseph Lane Papers, Oregon Historical Society Library.
Abraham Lincoln Papers, Robert Todd Lincoln Collection, Library of Congress (microfilm in the University of Washington Library).
James W. Nesmith Papers, Oregon Historical Society Library.
Benjamin Stark Papers, Oregon Historical Society Library.
Isaac I. Stevens Papers, University of Washington Library.
Isaac I. Stevens Papers, Winlock Miller Collection, Yale University Library (microfilm in the University of Washington Library).
William H. Wallace Papers, University of Washington Library.
John Whiteaker Papers, University of Oregon Library.
George H. Williams Papers, Oregon Historical Society Library.

Statements, Bancroft Library, University of California, Berkeley:

Applegate, Jesse. Views of Oregon History (microfilm in the University of Washington Library).
Burnett, Peter H. Recollections of the Past. 2 vols.
Deady, Matthew P. History and Progress of Oregon after 1845 (microfilm in the University of Washington Library).
Gibbs, Addison C. Notes on the History of Oregon (microfilm in the University of Washington Library).
Barnes, G. A. Oregon and California in 1849 (microfilm in the University of Washington Library).
Grover, LaFayette. Notable Things in a Public Life in Oregon (microfilm in the University of Washington Library).
Lane, Joseph. Autobiography (microfilm in the University of Washington Library).
Nesmith, James W. Reminiscences (microfilm in the University of Washington Library).
Strong, William. History of Oregon (microfilm in the University of Washington Library).

Official Manuscripts:

Election Returns, Washington Territory, 1855–1863, Washington State Archives (microfilm in the University of Washington Library).
Letters and Documents Relating to the Offices of Governor and Secretary of Washington Territory, 1860–1864, University of Washington Library.
Oregon Provisional and Territorial Government Papers, Oregon State Archives (microfilm in the Oregon Historical Society Library).
Proceedings, Oregon Senatorial Election, Oct. 1860, Oregon Historical Society Library.
Summary of Census Returns of the Territory of Oregon for the Year 1849, Oregon Historical Society Library.
U.S. Department of Interior, Interior Department Territorial Papers, National Archives (microfilm in the University of Washington Library).
U.S. Department of State, Territorial Papers, Washington Series, National Archives (microfilm in the University of Washington Library).

U.S. House of Representatives, Territorial Papers of the United States, "House file," Oregon and Washington Territories, National Archives (microfilm in the University of Washington Library).

U.S. Senate, Territorial Papers of the United States Senate, Oregon and Washington Territories, National Archives (microfilm in the University of Washington Library).

NEWSPAPERS

Oregon:

Albany *Oregon Democrat.*
Corvallis *Democratic Crisis.*
Corvallis *Occidental Messenger.*
Corvallis *Oregon Weekly Union.*
Eugene *The People's Press.*
Jacksonville *Oregon Sentinel.*
Oregon City *Oregon Argus.*
Oregon City *Oregon Spectator.*
Portland *Daily Advertiser.*
Portland *Daily Morning News.*
Portland *Daily Oregonian.*
Portland *Daily Portland Times.*
Portland *Oregon Advertiser.*
Portland *Oregon Weekly Times.*
Portland *Weekly Oregonian.*
Salem *Oregon Statesman.*
The Dalles *Weekly Mountaineer.*

Washington Territory:

Olympia *Overland Press.*
Olympia *Pioneer and Democrat.*
Olympia *Washington Standard.*
Port Townsend *North-West.*
Port Townsend *Register.*
Steilacoom *Puget Sound Herald.*
Steilacoom *Washington Republican.*

California:

Sacramento Daily Union.
San Francisco *Daily Alta California.*
San Francisco *Daily Evening Bulletin.*
San Francisco Herald.

New York:

New York Times.
New York Tribune.

PUBLISHED PRIMARY SOURCES

[Applegate, Jesse.] "Umpqua Agriculture, 1851," *OHQ,* XXXII (June, 1931), 135–144.

Beale, Howard K., ed. *The Diary of Edward Bates, 1859–1866, Annual Report of the American Historical Association,* 1930, IV. Washington: Government Printing Office, 1933.

[Bright, Jesse D.] "Some Letters of Jesse D. Bright to William H. English (1842–1863)," *Indiana Magazine of History,* XXX (Dec., 1934), 370–392.

[Burnett, Peter H.] "Documentary," *OHQ,* XXIV (March, 1923), 105–108.

Carey, Charles H., ed. *The Oregon Constitution and Proceedings and Debates of the Constitutional Convention of 1857.* Salem: State Printing Dept., 1926.

Catterall, Helen Honor, ed. *Judicial Cases Concerning American Slavery and the Negro.* 5 vols. Washington: Carnegie Institute, 1926–37.

Cole, Cornelius. *Memoirs of Cornelius Cole.* New York: McLaughlin Bros., 1908.

Cole, George E. *Early Oregon, Jottings of Personal Recollections of a Pioneer of 1850.* N. p.: Privately printed, 1905.

Culmer, Frederic A., ed. "Emigrant Missourians in Mexico and Oregon," *Missouri Historical Review,* XXV (Jan., 1931), 285–288.

[Deady, Matthew P.] Letters of Matthew P. Deady to the San Francisco *Bulletin,* 1862–1866. Scrap-Book #112, Oregon Historical Society.

[Dickinson, Daniel S.] *Speech of Hon. Daniel S. Dickinson of New York, Delivered at the Cooper Institute, New York, July 18, 1860.* Breckinridge and Lane Campaign Documents, No. 6. Washington: National Democratic Executive Committee, 1860.

Dickinson, John R., ed. *Speeches, Correspondence, etc., of the Late Daniel S. Dickinson, of New York.* 2 vols. New York: G. P. Putnam & Son, 1867.

Dumond, Dwight Lowell, ed. *Southern Editorials on Secession.* New York: The Century Co., 1931.

Greeley, Horace, and John F. Cleveland, eds. *A Political Text-Book for 1860: Comprising a Brief View of Presidential Nominations and Elections: Including All the National Platforms Ever Yet Adopted: Also, a History of the Struggle Respecting Slavery in the Territories. . . .* New York: The Tribune Association, 1860.

Halstead, Murat. *Caucuses of 1860; a History of the National Political Conventions of the Current Presidential Campaign: Being a Complete Record of the Business of All the Conventions. . . .* Columbus, Ohio: Follett, Foster & Co., 1860.

Henderson, Sarah Fisher, Nellie Edith Latourette, and Kenneth Scott Latourette, eds. "Correspondence of the Reverend Ezra Fisher, Pioneer Missionary of the American Baptist Home Mission Society in Indiana, Illinois, Iowa and Oregon," *OHQ,* XVI (1915), 65–104, 277–310, 379–413; XVII (1916), 55–76, 149–176, 267–339, 431–480; XIX (1918), 134–163, 234–261, 351–372; XX (1919), 95–137.

Johannsen, Robert W., ed. "John Burkhart and Oregon Territory, 1849," *OHQ,* LIII (Sept., 1952), 196–203.

———, ed. "A Breckinridge Democrat on the Secession Crisis: Letters of Isaac I. Stevens, 1860–1861," *OHQ,* LV (Dec., 1954), 283–310.

Jones, Dorsey D., ed. "Two Letters by a Pioneer from Arkansas," *OHQ,* XLV (Sept., 1944), 228–237.

[Lincoln, Abraham.] "Letters," *OHQ,* VIII (March, 1907), 76–77.

Bibliography 225

Lockley, Fred. "Some Documentary Records of Slavery in Oregon," *OHQ*, XVII (June, 1916), 107–115.

McBride, John R. "Annual Address," *Transactions of the Oregon Pioneer Association*, 1897, pp. 31–55.

Moore, John Bassett, ed. *The Works of James Buchanan, Comprising His Speeches, State Papers, and Private Correspondence.* 12 vols. Philadelphia: J. B. Lippincott Co., 1910.

Nesmith, James W. "The Occasional Address," *Transactions of the Oregon Pioneer Association*, 1875, pp. 42–62.

Nicolay, John G., and John Hay, eds. *Complete Works of Abraham Lincoln.* 12 vols. New York: Francis D. Tandy Co., 1905.

Oliphant, J. Orin, ed. "Thomas S. Kendall's Letter on Oregon Agriculture, 1852," *Agricultural History*, IX (Oct., 1935), 187–197.

O'Meara, James. "The Pioneer Days [newspaper clipping dated Nov. 30, 1890]," Scrap-Book #48, Oregon Historical Society.

Pease, Theodore Calvin, and James G. Randall, eds. *The Diary of Orville Hickman Browning.* 2 vols. Springfield: Illinois State Historical Library, 1925.

Perkins, Howard Cecil, ed. *Northern Editorials on Secession.* 2 vols. New York: D. Appleton-Century Co., 1942.

Pratt, Harry E., ed. "22 Letters of David Logan, Pioneer Oregon Lawyer," *OHQ*, XLIV (Sept., 1943), 253–285.

Quaife, Milo Milton, ed. *The Diary of James K. Polk During His Presidency, 1845 to 1849.* 4 vols. Chicago: A. C. McClurg & Co., 1910.

Robinson, Edgar Eugene, ed. "The Day Journal of Milton S. Latham, January 1 to May 6, 1860," *California Historical Society Quarterly*, XI (March, 1932), 3–28.

Rockwood, E. Ruth, ed. "Letters of Charles Stevens," *OHQ*, XXXVII (1936), 137–159, 241–261, 334–353; XXXVIII (1937), 63–91, 164–192, 328–354.

[Stevens, Isaac I.] *Address to the Democracy and the People of the United States.* Washington: National Democratic Executive Committee, 1860.

[———.] *Minority Report of Mr. Stevens, Delegate from Oregon, Showing the Grounds upon which the Regular Southern Delegation were entitled to Seats in the Convention at the Front Street Theatre, Baltimore.* Breckinridge and Lane Campaign Documents, No. 2. Washington: National Democratic Executive Committee, 1860.

Tappan, William H. "Reminiscences of Early Days in Washington," *Washington Historian*, I (Sept., 1899), 19–22.

Todd, Ronald, ed. "Letters of Gov. Isaac I. Stevens, 1857–1858," *PNQ*, XXXI (Oct., 1940), 403–459.

[Williams, George H.] "The 'Free-State Letter' of Judge George H. Williams," *OHQ*, IX (Sept., 1908), 254–273.

Winton, Harry N. M., ed. "The Death of Colonel Isaac N. Ebey, 1857," *PNQ*, XXXIII (July, 1942), 325–347.

DOCUMENTS

Andrews, C. C., ed. *Official Opinions of the Attorneys General of the United States. . . .* Vol. VII: Containing the Opinions of Hon. Caleb Cushing, of Massachusetts. . . . Washington: Robert Farnham, 1856.

Biographical Directory of the American Congress, 1774-1949. Washington: Government Printing Office, 1950.

Congressional Globe, 29, 30, 36, 37 Congresses, 1845–1849, 1859–1863.

Grover, LaFayette, ed. *The Oregon Archives, Including the Journals, Governors' Messages and Public Papers of Oregon.* Salem: Asahel Bush, 1853.

House Executive Document, 29 Congress, 1 Session, I, No. 2 (#480).

Journal of the Committee of Thirty-three, Report of the Select Committee of Thirty-three on the Disturbed Condition of the Country, Reports of Committees of the House of Representatives, 36 Congress, 2 Session, I, No. 31 (#1104).

Journal of the Council of the Territory of Oregon, 1849–1858. Title and imprint vary.

Journal of the Council of the Territory of Washington, 1854–1861. Title and imprint vary.

Journal of the House of Representatives of the Territory of Oregon, 1849–1858. Title and imprint vary.

Journal of the House of Representatives of the Territory of Washington, 1854–1861. Title and imprint vary.

Journal of the Proceedings of the House of the Legislative Assembly of Oregon, 1860. Salem: Asahel Bush, 1860.

Journal of the Proceedings of the Senate of Oregon, 1860. Salem: Asahel Bush, 1860.

Senate Executive Document, 28 Congress, 2 Session, I, No. 1 (#431).

U.S. Bureau of the Census. *Agriculture of the United States in 1860.* Washington: Government Printing Office, 1864.

U.S. Bureau of the Census. *Historical Statistics of the United States, 1789–1945.* Washington: Government Printing Office, 1949.

U.S. Bureau of the Census. *Population of the United States in 1860.* Washington: Government Printing Office, 1864.

War of the Rebellion: . . . Official Records of the Union and Confederate Armies. 128 vols. Washington, 1880–1901.

UNPUBLISHED THESES

Klement, Frank L. Middle Western Copperheadism: Jeffersonian Democracy in Revolt. Ph.D. dissertation, University of Wisconsin, 1945.

McNeil, Floyd Avery. Lincoln's Attorney General: Edward Bates. Ph.D. dissertation, State University of Iowa, 1930.

Moody, William Penn. The Civil War and Reconstruction in California Politics. Ph.D. dissertation, University of California, Los Angeles, 1950.

Poulton, Helen Jean. The Attitude of Oregon toward Slavery and Secession, 1843–1865. M.A. thesis, University of Oregon, 1946.

Walls, Florence. The Letters of Asahel Bush to Matthew P. Deady, 1851–1863. B.A. thesis, Reed College, 1941.

BOOKS

Armstrong, A. N. *Oregon: Comprising a Brief History and Full Description of the Territories of Oregon and Washington. . . .* Chicago: Charles Scott & Co., 1857.

Auchampaugh, Philip G. *James Buchanan and His Cabinet on the Eve of Secession.* Privately printed, 1926.

Bancroft, Hubert Howe. *History of Oregon.* 2 vols. San Francisco: The History Co., 1888.

———. *History of Washington, Idaho and Montana, 1845–1889.* San Francisco: The History Co., 1890.

Brown, Ralph H. *Historical Geography of the United States.* New York: Harcourt Brace, 1948.

Carey, Charles H. *A General History of Oregon, Prior to 1861.* 2 vols. Portland: Metropolitan Press, 1935–36.

Coman, Edwin T., Jr., and Helen M. Gibbs. *Time, Tide and Timber, a Century of Pope & Talbot.* Stanford: Stanford University Press, 1949.

Crenshaw, Ollinger. *The Slave States in the Presidential Election of 1860.* Baltimore: The Johns Hopkins Press, 1945.

Down, Robert Horace. *A History of the Silverton Country.* Portland: The Berncliff Press, 1926.

Dumond, Dwight L. *The Secession Movement, 1860–1861.* New York: Macmillan Co., 1931.

Ellison, Joseph. *California and the Nation, 1850–1867: A Study of the Relations of a Frontier Community with the Federal Government.* Berkeley: University of California Press, 1927.

Evans, Elwood. *History of the Pacific Northwest: Oregon and Washington.* 2 vols. Portland: North Pacific History Co., 1889.

Fite, Emerson D. *The Presidential Campaign of 1860.* New York: Macmillan, 1911.

Gilbert, James H. *Trade and Currency in Early Oregon, a Study in the Commercial and Monetary History of the Pacific Northwest.* (Columbia University Studies in History, Economics and Public Law, XXVI.) New York: Columbia University Press, 1907.

Going, Charles Buxton. *David Wilmot, Free Soiler.* New York: D. Appleton & Co., 1924.

Gray, Wood. *The Hidden Civil War: The Story of the Copperheads.* New York: Viking Press, 1942.

Harris, Norman Dwight. *The History of Negro Servitude in Illinois and the Slavery Agitation in That State, 1719–1864.* Chicago: A. C. McClurg, 1904.

Hesseltine, William B. *Lincoln and the War Governors.* New York: Alfred A. Knopf, 1948.

Hines, Harvey Kimball. *An Illustrated History of the State of Washington.* Chicago: Lewis Publishing Co., 1893.

Hubbart, Henry Clyde. *The Older Middle West, 1840–1880, Its Social, Economic and Political Life and Sectional Tendencies Before, During and After the Civil War.* New York: D. Appleton-Century Co., 1936.

Jacobs, Melvin Clay. *Winning Oregon: A Study of an Expansionist Movement.* Caldwell, Ida.: Caxton Printers, 1938.

Kelly, Sister M. Margaret Jean. *The Career of Joseph Lane, Frontier Politician.* Washington, D.C.: Catholic University Press, 1942.

Kennedy, Elijah R. *The Contest for California in 1861, How Colonel E. D. Baker Saved the Pacific States to the Union.* Boston: Houghton Mifflin, 1912.

Lowery, Lawrence Tyndale. *Northern Opinion of Approaching Secession, October, 1859–November, 1860.* (Smith College Studies in History, III.) Northampton, Mass.: Smith College, 1918.

Luthin, Reinhard H. *The First Lincoln Campaign.* Cambridge, Mass.: Harvard University Press, 1944.

Milton, George Fort. *The Eve of Conflict, Stephen A. Douglas and the Needless War.* Boston: Houghton Mifflin, 1934.

Nevins, Allan. *The Ordeal of the Union.* 2 vols. New York: Charles Scribner's Sons, 1947.

——. *The Emergence of Lincoln.* 2 vols. New York: Charles Scribner's Sons, 1950.

Nichols, Roy Franklin. *The Disruption of American Democracy.* New York: Macmillan Co., 1948.

Potter, David M. *Lincoln and His Party in the Secession Crisis.* New Haven: Yale University Press, 1942.

Quaife, Milo M. *The Doctrine of Non-intervention with Slavery in the Territories.* Chicago: M. C. Chamberlin Co., 1910.

Randall, James G. *Lincoln the President: Springfield to Gettysburg.* 2 vols. New York: Dodd Mead & Co., 1946.

——. *The Civil War and Reconstruction.* Boston: D. C. Heath & Co., 1937.

Russel, Robert R. *Improvement of Communication with the Pacific Coast as an Issue in American Politics, 1783–1864.* Cedar Rapids, Iowa: Torch Press, 1948.

Scott, Harvey W. *History of the Oregon Country.* 6 vols. Cambridge, Mass.: Riverside Press, 1924.

Scrugham, Mary. *The Peaceable Americans of 1860–1861: A Study in Public Opinion.* (Columbia University Studies in History, Economics and Public Law, XCVI.) New York: Columbia University Press, 1921.

Simms, Henry H. *A Decade of Sectional Controversy, 1851–1861.* Chapel Hill: University of North Carolina Press, 1942.

Smith, Edward C. *The Borderland in the Civil War.* New York: Macmillan Co., 1927.

Snowden, Clinton A. *History of Washington, the Rise and Progress of an American State.* 4 vols. New York: Century History Co., 1909.

Stampp, Kenneth M. *And the War Came: The North and the Secession Crisis, 1860–1861.* Baton Rouge: Louisiana State University Press, 1950.

Stephens, Alexander H. *Constitutional View of the Late War Between the States, Its Causes, Character, Conduct and Results.* 2 vols. Philadelphia: National Publishing Co., 1868.

Stevens, Hazard. *The Life of Isaac Ingalls Stevens.* 2 vols. Boston: Houghton Mifflin & Co., 1900.

Thornton, J. Quinn. *Oregon and California in 1848.* 2 vols. New York: Harper & Brothers, 1849.

Turnbull, George S. *History of Oregon Newspapers.* Portland: Binfords & Mort, 1939.

"Western," pseud. *Biography of Joseph Lane.* Washington, D.C.: Congressional Globe Office, 1852.

Wiltse, Charles M. *John C. Calhoun, Sectionalist, 1840–1850.* Indianapolis: Bobbs-Merrill Co., 1951.

Woodward, Walter Carleton. *The Rise and Early History of Political Parties in Oregon, 1843–1868.* Portland: J. K. Gill Co., 1913.

ARTICLES

Auchampaugh, Philip G. "James Buchanan and Some Far Western Leaders, 1860–1861," *Pacific Historical Review,* XII (June, 1943), 169–180.

——. "The Buchanan-Douglas Feud," *Journal of the Illinois State Historical Society*, XXV (April–July, 1932), 5–48.

Bonner, Thomas N. "Horace Greeley and the Secession Movement, 1860–1861," *Mississippi Valley Historical Review*, XXXVIII (Dec., 1951), 425–444.

Bradley, Marie M. "Political Beginnings in Oregon—The Period of the Provisional Government, 1839–1849," *Oregon Historical Quarterly*, IX (March, 1908), 42–72.

Carey, Charles H. "The Creation of Oregon as a State," *Oregon Historical Quarterly*, XXVI (Dec., 1925), 281–308; XXVII (March, 1926), 1–40.

Chatelain, Verne E. "The Federal Land Policy and Minnesota Politics, 1854–1860," *Minnesota History*, XXII (Sept., 1941), 227–248.

Crenshaw, Ollinger. "Urban and Rural Voting in the Election of 1860," in Eric F. Goldman, ed. *Historiography and Urbanization: Essays in American History in Honor of W. Stull Holt* (Baltimore: Johns Hopkins Press, 1941), pp. 43–66.

Davenport, T. W. "The Slavery Question in Oregon," *Oregon Historical Quarterly*, IX (Sept., 1908), 189–253.

Dickerson, Oliver M. "Stephen A. Douglas and the Split in the Democratic Party," *Proceedings of the Mississippi Valley Historical Association, 1913–1914*, VII, 196–211.

Dickson, Edward A. "Lincoln and Baker: The Story of a Great Friendship," *Historical Society of Southern California Quarterly*, XXXIV (Sept., 1952), 229–242.

Douglas, Jesse. "Origins of the Population of Oregon in 1850," *Pacific Northwest Quarterly*, XLI (April, 1950), 95–108.

Duniway, Clyde A. "Slavery in California after 1848." *Annual Report of the American Historical Association, 1905*, I, 241–248.

"Echo of the Dred Scott Decision," *Washington Historical Quarterly*, I (Oct., 1906), 71.

Ellison, Joseph. "Designs for a Pacific Republic, 1843–1862," *Oregon Historical Quarterly*, XXXI (Dec., 1930), 319–342.

Fenton, William D. "Edward Dickinson Baker," *Oregon Historical Quarterly*, IX (March, 1908), 1–23.

Gilbert, Benjamin F. "The Confederate Minority in California," *California Historical Society Quarterly*, XX (June, 1941), 154–170.

Hay, John. "Colonel Baker," *Harper's Magazine*, XXIV (Dec., 1861), 103–110.

Hill, D. G. "The Negro as a Political and Social Issue in the Oregon Country," *Journal of Negro History*, XXXIII (April, 1948), 130–145.

Howay, F. W. "The Negro Immigration into Vancouver Island in 1858," *British Columbia Historical Quarterly*, III (April, 1939), 101–114.

Hubbart, Henry C. "Revisionist Interpretations of Stephen A. Douglas and Popular Sovereignty," *Social Studies*, XXV (March, 1934), 103–107.

Hull, Dorothy. "The Movement in Oregon for the Establishment of a Pacific Coast Republic," *Oregon Historical Quarterly*, XVII (Sept., 1916), 177–200.

Johannsen, Robert W. "John Whiteaker, Governor of Oregon, 1858–1862," *Reed College Bulletin*, XXVI (Jan., 1948), 63–87.

——. "National Issues and Local Politics in Washington Territory, 1857–1861," *Pacific Northwest Quarterly*, XLII (Jan., 1951), 3–31.

——. "The Secession Crisis and the Frontier: Washington Territory, 1860–1861," *Mississippi Valley Historical Review*, XXXIX (Dec., 1952), 415–440.

———. "The Kansas-Nebraska Act and the Pacific Northwest Frontier," *Pacific Historical Review*, XXII (May, 1953), 129–141.

Johansen, Dorothy O. "A Tentative Appraisal of Territorial Government in Oregon," *Pacific Historical Review*, XVIII (Nov., 1949), 485–499.

———. "Oregon's Role in American History: An Old Theme Recast," *Pacific Northwest Quarterly*, XL (April, 1949), 85–92.

Johnson, Allen. "The Nationalizing Influence of Party," *Yale Review*, XV (Nov., 1906), 283–292.

Knuth, Priscilla. "Oregon Know Nothing Pamphlet Illustrates Early Politics," *Oregon Historical Quarterly*, LIV (March, 1953), 40–53.

Lazenby, Marie. "Down-Easters Out West," *Reed College Bulletin*, XXV (April, 1947), 1–33.

Lockley, Fred. "The Case of Robin Holmes *vs.* Nathaniel Ford," *Oregon Historical Quarterly*, XXIII (June, 1922), 111–137.

Lokken, Roy N. "The Martial Law Controversy in Washington Territory, 1856," *Pacific Northwest Quarterly*, XLIII (April, 1952), 91–119.

Luthin, Reinhard H. "Organizing the Republican Party in the 'Border-Slave' Regions," *Missouri Historical Review*, XXXVIII (Jan., 1944), 138–161.

———. "The Democratic Split During Buchanan's Administration," *Pennsylvania History*, XI (Jan., 1944), 13–35.

Lynch, William O. "The Westward Flow of Southern Colonists Before 1861," *Journal of Southern History*, IX (Aug., 1943), 303–328.

McArthur, Mrs. Harriet K. "Biographical Sketch of Hon. J. W. Nesmith," *Transactions of the Oregon Pioneer Association, 1886,* pp. 28–36.

McBride, John R. "The Oregon Constitutional Convention, 1857," *Proceedings of the Oregon Historical Society, 1902,* pp. 20–35.

Matheny, James H. "A Modern Knight Errant—Edward Dickinson Baker," *Journal of the Illinois State Historical Society*, IX (April, 1916), 23–42.

Minto, John. "Antecedents of the Oregon Pioneers and the Light These Throw on Their Motives," *Oregon Historical Quarterly*, V (March, 1904), 38–63.

Mooney, Chase C. "The Literature of Slavery: A Re-Evaluation," *Indiana Magazine of History*, XLVII (Sept., 1951), 251–260.

"Negro Pioneers: Their Page in Oregon History," *Oregon Native Son*, I (Jan., 1900), 432–434.

Odgers, Charlotte. "Jesse Applegate, Study of a Pioneer Politician," *Reed College Bulletin*, XXIII (Jan., 1945), 7–20.

Owen, Homer L. "Nesmith: Pioneer Judge, Legislator, Farmer, Soldier, Senator and Congressman," *Reed College Bulletin*, XXVIII (June, 1950), 139–176.

Platt, Robert Treat. "Oregon and Its Share in the Civil War," *Oregon Historical Quarterly*, IV (June, 1903), 89–109.

Potter, David M. "Horace Greeley and Peaceable Secession," *Journal of Southern History*, VII (May, 1941), 145–159.

Pratt, Harry E. "Dr. Anson G. Henry, Lincoln's Physician and Friend," *Lincoln Herald*, XLV (Oct., 1943), 3–17; (Dec., 1943), 31–40.

Prucha, F. Paul. "Minnesota's Attitude toward the Southern Case for Secession," *Minnesota History*, XXIV (Dec., 1943), 307–317.

Raleigh, Eldorah M. "General Joseph E. Lane," *Indiana History Bulletin*, IV (Dec., 1926, suppl.), 71–82.

Ramsdell, Charles W. "The Natural Limits of Slavery Expansion," *Mississippi Valley Historical Review*, XVI (Sept., 1929), 151–171.

Reid, Robie L. "How One Slave Became Free," *British Columbia Historical Quarterly*, VI (Oct., 1942), 251–256.

Robertson, James Rood. "The Social Evolution of Oregon," *Oregon Historical Quarterly*, III (March, 1902), 1–37.

Savage, W. Sherman. "The Negro in the History of the Pacific Northwest," *Journal of Negro History*, XIII (July, 1928), 255–264.

Schafer, Joseph. "Jesse Applegate: Pioneer, Statesman and Philosopher," *Washington Historical Quarterly*, I (July, 1907), 217–233.

Scott, Leslie M. "Oregon's Nomination of Lincoln," *Oregon Historical Quarterly*, XVII (Sept., 1916), 201–214.

Shippee, Lester Burrell. "An Echo of the Campaign of Sixty," *Oregon Historical Quarterly*, XII (Dec., 1911), 351–360.

Shutes, Milton H. "Colonel E. D. Baker," *California Historical Society Quarterly*, XVII (Dec., 1938), 303–324.

Simms, Henry H. "The Controversy Over the Admission of the State of Oregon," *Mississippi Valley Historical Review*, XXXII (Dec., 1945), 355–374.

"Slavery in the Pacific Northwest," *Oregon Native Son*, II (Nov., 1900), 314.

Snigg, John P. "Edward Dickinson Baker—Lincoln's Forgotten Friend," *Lincoln Herald*, LIII (Summer, 1951), 33–37.

Stenberg, Richard R. "An Unnoted Factor in the Buchanan-Douglas Feud," *Journal of the Illinois Historical Society*, XXV (Jan., 1933), 271–284.

Teiser, Sidney. "A Pioneer Judge of Oregon—Matthew P. Deady," *Oregon Historical Quarterly*, XLIV (March, 1943), 61–81.

Venable, Austin L. "The Conflict Between the Douglas and Yancey Forces in the Charleston Convention," *Journal of Southern History*, VIII (May, 1942), 226–241.

Wertenbaker, Thomas J. "The Molding of the Middle West," *American Historical Review*, LIII (Jan., 1948), 223–234.

Wickersham, James. "Life, Character, and Public Service of Elwood Evans, Pioneer, Lawyer, Governor and Historian," *Washington Historian*, I (Jan., 1900), 53–64.

Williams, George H. "Political History of Oregon from 1853 to 1865," *Oregon Historical Quarterly*, II (March, 1901), 1–35.

Zorn, Roman J. "Minnesota Public Opinion and the Secession Controversy, December, 1860–April, 1861," *Mississippi Valley Historical Review*, XXXVI (Dec., 1949), 435–456.

index